LIFE WITH

Lindsay
& Crouse

Portrait by Hirschfeld   (Reproduced by permission of the artist)

Cornelia Otis Skinner

○ ○

LIFE WITH
Lindsay
& Crouse

Illustrated with Photographs

Houghton Mifflin Company Boston

1976

Library of Congress Cataloging in Publication Data

Skinner, Cornelia Otis, date
Life with Lindsay & Crouse.
Includes index.
1. Lindsay, Howard, 1889–1968 — Biography.
2. Crouse, Russel, 1893–1966 — Biography. I. Title.
PS3523.I575Z86   790.2'092'2 [B]   76-22571
ISBN 0-395-24511-7
Printed in the United States of America

V 10 9 8 7 6 5 4 3 2 1

WITH LOVE AND GRATITUDE TO

Anna Crouse
and
Dorothy Lindsay

FOREWORD

BY BROOKS ATKINSON

Although Howard Lindsay and Russel Crouse wrote some fabulously successful comedies, they believed that writers of comedy were not taken seriously. Writers of tragedy, they thought, were more respected. I once asked Mr. Lindsay and Mr. Crouse and also S. N. Behrman, one of their colleagues, to discuss this subject at luncheon at the Players. I hoped to wring out of them some ideas I could pour into my newspaper column.

Since all of them had many friends there, the Players was probably the worst place in which to discuss a philosophical idea. Mr. Lindsay was president of the Players, many of whom could not resist the temptation of acquiring prestige by greeting him enthusiastically. But the conversation did provide some relevant ideas. Comedies are more intricate than tragedies from the technical point of view and therefore more difficult to write. Mr. Lindsay quoted Garrick in support of his point of view. "Comedy is a very serious thing," said Garrick; acting comedy, he continued, is the supreme

○ ○

achievement on the stage. Mr. Lindsay also remarked that
Sidney Howard's *The Silver Cord* was an epoch-making play
that was never properly appreciated because it was written as
comedy. Mr. Behrman quoted W. H. Auden: "There is more
criticism of life in comedy than in serious drama." I was
tempted to point out that comedy is difficult to write because
it goes contrary to the nature of life; life is tragic. But that
did not sound like a suitable subject to wrestle with over
luncheon at the Players.

Mr. Lindsay and Mr. Crouse wrote *Life with Father* and *Life
with Mother* (which was lamentably unappreciated), *State of
the Union* (which the Pulitzer Prize judges appreciated hand-
somely) and they rewrote the Cole Porter musical show *Anything Goes,* which delighted everyone for many months. *Life
with Father* had the longest run — nearly eight years — of
any straight American play. They also produced another
comedy classic that had a long run, Joseph Kesselring's *Arsenic and Old Lace.* They did not write the original text but the
performance had the crack-brained exuberance of the
Lindsay-Crouse style. It was also Lindsay and Crouse who
wrote the book for *The Sound of Music,* which is still performed every evening somewhere in the world.

I knew and respected both of them for many years. (Once I
was surprised to meet Mr. Lindsay at the preliminary meeting of the New York City grand jurors; he became one of the
foremen after the individual juries were organized.) Both of
them represented the best in the theatre. After reading this
book I am particularly grateful to Cornelia Otis Skinner for
pointing out something crucial to understanding them. They
were both men of high principle. They were generous and
outgoing. They were original and funny on their own plane
of civilized good taste. Although they were anything but
prudish, they did not pander to or shock their audiences.

I have just looked up an unsigned review of the 1927

○ ○

Tommy, written by Howard Lindsay and Bertram Robinson. "Their play," said the anonymous reviewer in the New York *Times,* "while hardly significant, is a fairly workmanlike job in its particular field and should meet with the approval of those who like their theatre up to the standards of Ivory Soap ideals of purity." The reviewer was obviously contemptuous of clean comedy.

It had never occurred to me that Lindsay and Crouse were clean playwrights. No one ever complained of the good taste of *Life with Father* or *State of the Union.* Both plays were distinguished by ingenuity of craftsmanship, spontaneity of humor and respect for the audience. The suspicion of cleanliness does not apply.

Since Mr. Lindsay and Mr. Crouse were working in a world they found congenial they loved the vitality and variety of theatre people and the excitement and insanity of the theatre's business methods. Miss Skinner also reminds us that in and out of the theatre they were thoroughbreds.

ILLUSTRATIONS

(following page 114)

○ ○

PART I

○ ○

Howard Lindsay

Atlantic City during the 1890's was not a very different place from what it is now. To be sure, the hotels, far from being the skyscraper monsters of later days, were big frame buildings, spacious and doubtless highly inflammable, with wide porches for the comfort of the sedentary residents taking it easy in wicker chairs or swinging settees, rugs tucked over their laps, breathing deeply of what they believed to be "health-giving ozone." But in between these leisurely caravansaries were the same catchpenny shops, the rifle ranges, the Japanese Ping-Pong counters, the auction rooms where wily Near Eastern rug and "art" vendors unloaded their horrendous merchandise on gullible vacationers, the booths of fortunetellers, phrenologists, handwriting experts and comic photographers, who would take your picture as though you were walking along the sea clad only in a barrel, and, of course, every hundred yards or so were those glass-enclosed stalls where before the very eyes of passersby is created that jaw-adhering candy known as "saltwater taffy."

○ ○

The itinerant public either strolled or was propelled in wheelchairs along the Boardwalk, Atlantic City's main attraction. The local Chamber of Commerce proudly claimed that it had no equivalent in the world, being forty feet wide, four miles long and having cost the city $240,000 in those less costly times. From the Boardwalk on the ocean side jutted out the great amusement piers . . . the Steeplechase, where one could ride squealing on the roller coaster or take a more sedate observation of sea and land from a slow-moving gondola of the ferris wheel . . . Young's, with its auditorium where theatrical troupes like the Wilbur Opera Company matched their voices against the roar of the incoming tide smashing its waves on the piles directly below. Out at the end of another pier was the Life Saving Station, an impressive "Gothic" structure with a lookout tower from which "a constant watch is kept for vessels in distress" — a reassuring bit of information.

The words are from an enlightening pamphlet called *Heston's Handbook of Atlantic City, Illustrated.* It contains a panegyric of the Boardwalk: "The life, the light and the color that one sees on this promenade are indescribable. It is an endless dress parade, a grand review . . . The animation, the overflowing good nature, the laughter and contagious hilarity of this restless throng are irresistible." In short, life on the Boardwalk would seem "to have rivaled in charm and color the milling crowds in Venice's Piazza San Marco."

Such was the picturesque atmosphere of Atlantic City in those unhurried times. In 1894, scuttling in and out of the early morning strollers, could be seen an energetic five-year-old newsboy hawking his papers in a remarkably powerful voice, proclaiming:

> The Daily Union one cent
> To help my mother pay the rent!

○ ○

He was a smart-looking little boy, with clear grayish-blue eyes and an engaging smile, and usually he sold his heavy load of newspapers in record time. When they were gone, he resorted to a further device for helping his mother pay the rent. Taking a sudden and dramatic stance before the groups resting on Boardwalk benches or lolling on the verandahs of ocean-front hotels, he would take off his cap, bow low and launch into a "recitation." His repertoire included such gems as:

> When you see a man in woe,
> Walk right up and say "Hello."

Or in a more personal vein:

> I hate the pants that Mother makes
> That leave me room to grow.
> That's why they hang around my legs
> That's why they wobble so.

At the finish of each gratuitous performance, he'd bow again, smile and pass around his little cheap cap, and more often than not was able to return home with as much as a dollar for his mother.

That lady had need of any extra dollar. Even the extra dimes, nickels and pennies her small son brought home were welcome. She was supporting herself, her four children and her own mother on the ten dollars a week she was earning as a compositor for the Atlantic City *Daily Union* and the Egg Harbor *Gazette*, two local papers published by her brother. This weekly income was augmented once a month by a stipend of six dollars, her mother's pension as the widow of a soldier who had fought in the War of 1812.

The small boy was later to become known as Howard Lindsay. The last name, a *nom de théâtre*, was adopted from his grandmother. In those early days he was known as Herman Nelke, his father being a German immigrant. Nelke was a man of great charm, a Baron Munchausen imagination and an inability to tell the truth. He always found fantasy more worthwhile than fact.

According to him he had, during the Franco-Prussian War, won a crucial battle single-handed. In this colorful yarn he claimed that he had been sent on ahead of the German lines to reconnoiter, that he had spied the enemy on the far side of a hill, had leapt up onto the bare summit, deliberately exposing himself to enemy fire, and thereby enabled his battalion to locate and destroy the French gun-emplacements. This deed of valor resulted in a wound of which he claimed to be inordinately proud. Howard Lindsay, recalling his boyhood, wrote, "Father did indeed have a scar, but it had all the appearance of a hernia operation." A further boast of Nelke *père* was that, during the same war, he deliberately disobeyed his general's orders to lead a detachment of artillery down a certain road which he knew to be impassable. Aware of another road that was clear, he led his men down that one instead and the Prussians won the day. For this act of patriotic disobedience he was court-martialed, given the lightest possible sentence, reinstated as an officer and decorated with the Iron Cross. Needless to say, no member of the Nelke family ever saw a trace of the Iron Cross.

His favorite story, and one which he repeated frequently, was that he was directly in line for the throne of whatever German principality he came from. It seems that in this Graustarkian realm there existed a law whereby if twin sons were born to the reigning Prince and Princess one of them was farmed out to a bourgeois family to be brought up in happy ignorance of his royal birth. The reigning Princess happened to bear twin sons and, not surprisingly, he was one of them, the less fortunate, who was relegated to the foster family. A few years later, as he was out playing in the royal park, the Princess, looking from a palace window,

○ ○

caught sight of him and, sensing with emotion his identical resemblance to his twin brother, sent an equerry to find out what family he came from. On being told, Her Royal Highness fainted dead away.

Mr. Nelke recounted these fabrications with such conviction, plus the allure of a European accent, that his listeners believed them, if only momentarily. The person who didn't for a moment believe a word of them was his wife. A no-nonsense Down Easter from the state of Maine, a lady of excellent education and high principles, she had a passion for the truth. The gradual realization that she was married to a compulsive liar must have come as a cruel trial. She had a strong sense of thrift, and a further blow to her marital happiness was the discovery that her husband was not only hopelessly profligate but unable to hold any job for more than a few weeks.

It had been a whirlwind courtship. The romantic-looking young man with his European manners had turned up in her home town as a traveling salesman, and the local girl had been completely swept off her firm New England feet. The wedding was hasty and she had ten years in which to repent at leisure.

With all his shortcomings she must have loved this charming good-for-nothing, for during those ten years she bore him four children, two girls and two boys . . . the youngest, Howard. Eventually the mismated couple came to a parting of the ways and the mother with her children and her own mother moved to Atlantic City to live off that weekly ten dollars her brother paid her as typesetter for his newspapers plus the small change little Howard brought home from his daily rounds. Life for this family of six must of necessity have been austere, yet Howard Lindsay wrote that somehow, miraculously, they were never hungry. Days when there was no food in the house other than bread, his grandmother would serve it up fried in bacon fat, seasoned with sage, and they all found it satisfying. However there were other times when the Nelke family was not obliged to subsist on fried bread alone. Howard's uncle helped them out from time to time. In the world of small-town newspapers, it was the custom that advertisers who could not pay for their ads were allowed to issue due bills in lieu of cash to the publisher. Whenever this occurred, the uncle generously turned over such due bills to the sister, who used them for maintaining the household. For several years they lived off and on by free orders on grocers, butchers and dry-goods stores.

His grandmother did more than cook. She ran the house and looked after the children. Wise, warm and generally wonderful, she took the place of the mother, who had to be off at work the greater part of every day. Young Howard adored her. She was his loving mentor and ever-available consolation. When during later adolescence his face broke out in mortifying splotches of acne, she soothed his distress by telling him that when he got older he could grow a beard. She was the one who completely understood him and seldom reprimanded him. If a spanking was in order, she turned the distasteful duty over to her daughter . . . and Howard's mother didn't believe in sparing the rod. When, at the age of nineteen, he announced his intentions of becoming an actor, his mother's reaction was one of shocked disapproval but his grandmother remarked with a quiet smile, "I think Howard will make a very good actor. He's so fond of staying up late at night."

One of the attempts Howard's uncle made to help out his sister and her family involved an elocution teacher, one Miss Alice Rutter, who set up a tatty little "studio" on the Boardwalk and took out a daily ad for pupils in the personal columns of his newspapers. As none was forthcoming, as was no money for the teacher, the publisher allowed her to take off her debt in trade. The trade was young Howard, to whom she gave free lessons twice a week. She made him memorize innumerable "pieces" (including the two he performed on the Boardwalk). At the end of four years of this thespian training, he had acquired a repertoire of over a hundred recitations. Moreover, he proved to be an avid reciter, who would put on his act at the drop of a hat, or even if no hat was dropped. As he wrote of himself, "Anytime two or more people were in the same room with me, they were in danger." He recited in school, at Bible class, at WCTU meetings, to which he was taken by his teetotaler mother. His family encouraged these juvenile histrionics, thinking that he was very cute, and he obviously thought so too. In time he became, he said, "the nastiest little exhibitionist on the Atlantic Seaboard."

He continued to peddle his newspapers and, there being no newsstands along the Boardwalk, always did very well. One morning he did so well he never even reached the Boardwalk. This was February 15, 1898, and the front page of the extras he was hawking bore the news that the battleship *Maine* had been torpedoed and sunk in Havana Harbor. Excitement was rife. Flags were unfurled. In no time all the souvenir shops were selling large lapel buttons reading:

Remember the Maine.
To hell with Spain!

The nine-year-old news vendor never had need of being reminded to remember the *Maine*. The public intoxication plus his personal rapture over selling all his newspapers in record time was too much for his youthful kidneys, and before he reached home he had wet his pants.

Another sartorial disaster had occurred some years previously on a warm and sunny Sunday. Howard, like all nicely brought-up little boys, was dressed in his "Sunday

○ ○

best," which in his case was a Peter Thompson suit, brand-new and all white except for the braid on the sailor collar and a dark blue nautical tie. His shoes and socks were also pure white. During the course of the day, he joined up with a group of small fry acquaintances who, like him, found themselves with little to do on an idle afternoon. Someone hatched the inspired idea that a fine form of amusement would be to go down underneath the Boardwalk, find a good location amid the steel pillars and iron supports and hold an endurance contest as to who could "skin the cat" the greatest number of times on one of the horizontal bars. After skinning a fair number of cats, young Howard happened to glance down at his formerly spotless attire and realized to his dismay that from neck to toe he was a mess of red iron rust. The dismay was tripled by the realization that this would result in a spanking after he reached home. Furthermore, he knew he was already late, and made a hasty dash from his companions. Bursting through the front door, he rushed in before his assembled family, struck a melodramatic pose and cried out, "See what a plight I'm in!" The family's joint reaction was to explode with laughter and for the first time Howard Lindsay tasted the rewards of giving a good comedy performance.

Even as a little boy, he seems to have had the instincts of a born performer. His repertoire of dreadful little recitations took on more and more of a histrionic quality. There was one which must have been a beauty. Written in verse, it depicted a wronged wife falsely committed to an insane asylum by a cruel husband who wants to be rid of her. Howard, needless to say, depicted the wronged wife. Each verse ends up, "I am not mad! I am not mad!" until the final heart-rending stanza in which the poor creature eventually does lose her reason and cries out, "I'm mad! I'm mad!" followed by a wild shriek and a burst of maniacal laughter.

○○

For all the child's enthusiasm for exhibiting his talent before an audience, Howard Lindsay's first appearance on a legitimate stage was a definite comedown. This was as a reluctant stooge in a "lightning calculator" act. One of the many get-rich-quick hopefuls to set up shop along the imagined El Dorado of the Boardwalk was a mathematical expert calling himself "Professor" somebody, and claiming that he could teach even the most backward child the rudiments of arithmetic in record time. He installed himself in a cubbyhole which he dignified by the name of "classroom" and took out sizable advertising for pupils in the *Daily Union*. Like the elocution teacher, the poor man was unable to meet the cost of this publicity and again Howard's publisher uncle allowed his creditor to take out his debt in trade. And again his nephew was the pawn in the trade, having to go twice a week to the Professor for a torturous arithmetic lesson, learning very little and hating every minute of it. There being no other pupils, the Professor in desperation hired the local Academy of Music and apprised the public that he would give a single matinee exhibition of his "lightning calculation" skill . . . admission free to anyone who came accompanied by a child. The exhibition was hardly spectacular. A handful of Boardwalk strollers, attracted by the word *free,* drifted in, dragging along vocally protesting children. The Professor gave a short lecture on the beauty and mental stimulus of mathematics, at the finish of which he demonstrated his genius by doing some difficult calculations in his head and then writing the results on a blackboard. By way of an added attraction he announced that his prize pupil would come forth and give a demonstration of the fruits of his remarkable instruction. At that, his prize (and only) pupil, dressed in a little boy's velvet suit, short pants, white socks and a flowing tie long enough to trip over, walked out onto the stage. The Professor wrote down two numbers of four digits each, told

○ ○

his prize pupil to multiply them in his head and then write the answer on the blackboard. In a flash this forerunner of the Quiz Kids wrote out the answer, which for several weeks had been inexorably drilled into his small brain. He then bowed and walked off the stage amid a flurry of half-hearted applause.

In addition to his recitations he found that a further means of appearing before an audience was by becoming a choir boy. This he did, but not before sampling a number of religious denominations. Howard's mother and grandmother were freethinkers, and although the children were expected to kneel and say their prayers every night, they were seldom, if ever, taken to any church. He found out that there was something called Sunday School, which most of the pals on his block attended, and he decided that he too would like to attend. This decision was due less to religious inclinations than to reports he had heard of a yearly Christmas party, where each pupil received a present, and an annual spring outing to the mainland, where they played games, raised a certain amount of hell, consumed the soda pop and potato salad that well-meaning parishioners had provided and which doubtless a few of the students threw up from the back platform of the home-bound trolley car. It all sounded like fun.

He persuaded his older sister Rose that Sunday School was something they should go to as a matter of prestige. They sampled a few regional sects, quickly turned down Methodist and Baptist, wavered a bit over Presbyterian and eventually settled on Episcopalian as offering the greater attraction in the way of Christmas party and lakeside diversions at the spring picnic. Moreover, the Episcopalians made it clear that, of all true believers, they were the socially elect and they looked down upon members of other denominations as being little better than heathens.

○ ○

Neither Howard nor Rose was a young person to be looked down upon, and after enrollment in the Episcopal Sunday School Howard felt very high-toned indeed. The security of his position, however, was threatened when one day in a moment of rash bravado he announced the staggering fact that he had never been baptized. To the God-fearing elite this was the equivalent of announcing that he was illegitimate and for a time he became a social pariah.

Realizing that baptism was the only remedy for this sudden ostracism, he took his problem to the minister, who agreed to perform the solemn rite one morning after service. The Sunday-School teacher was pressed into being one of his sponsors and the other "godfather" was the minister's son, who must have been of the same ripe old age of ten. "It was not as a devout Christian that I marched to the baptismal font," Lindsay later wrote. "It was as a social climber."

It is an amusing coincidence that forty years later Howard Lindsay and Russel Crouse should be reaping vast returns from *Life with Father*, the longest-running comedy in the history of the American theatre. Whoever remembers that endearing dramatization of Clarence Day's stories about his boyhood in a Victorian New York family will recall that one of the main issues of the plot arose from the fact that Vinnie (Mother Day) discovers to her horror that her husband (Father, played by Howard Lindsay) has never been baptized. This, to her, means that the family can never eventually be reunited in heaven to enjoy the amenities of eternal bliss. By means of a series of well-contrived ruses, she forces him to agree to go through the ceremony as performed by an inconspicuous clergyman in a distant uptown church where no one will recognize them. For over two thousand performances, just prior to the final curtain, Howard Lindsay stormed off the stage shouting, "I'm going to be baptized, damn it!"

Young Howard, having reinstated himself in the Epis-

○ ○

copalian hierarchy, further ingratiated himself by joining the church choir. This he enjoyed. It was almost as satisfactory as performing his solo recitation act. Besides, he received the heady sum of fifty cents a month for his services. It was fun going into the vestry and solemnly getting into the black cassock and starched white surplice. It was fun taking his place in line for the Processional — and being a small boy soprano, he was among the first in line — then progressing slowly down a side aisle the length of the church, turning and going up the main one to the altar and taking his place in the front row of stalls, singing piously and trying his best to look like a devout cherub. The service, due to the intermittent singing it involved, was happily free of tedium; the sermon was something to be endured; then after the closing Benediction it again was fun to line up in the Recessional, march again through the main body of the church replete with onlooking parishioners and end up in the vestry for the final chanted "Amen." Every Sunday he put on a good performance and, although he was merely a member of a larger cast, he felt that he was splendidly outstanding.

In addition to this predilection for appearing in public, he had a growing enthusiasm for attending the public appearances of the real professionals. To be specific, Howard Lindsay, who was soon to make his mark on the American theatre, was at an early age already fascinated by "show business." Road companies that were constantly touring the length and breadth of the United States played regular one- or two-week stands in Atlantic City. The advance man always turned up well ahead of any opening to oversee the printing of heralds, posters and press releases with their "rave reviews from the critics," most of them composed by the advance man himself. Here all the printing was made possible through the *Daily Union* presses, and the advance man, with an eye to assuring full houses, was lavish in handing out passes. Young Howard, being the editor's nephew, was able to secure a seat for every Saturday matinee he could manage. The first play he saw was *Richard III*, starring Creston Clarke, who happened to be a nephew of Edwin Booth. Clarke was an excellent actor and a modest man who took pains never to make capital out of his relationship to America's greatest tragedian. As Richard he proved to be a compelling villain and his performance made a profound impression on the boy. Years later, after Howard Lindsay had been elected President of the Players, that distinguished and venerable club housed in the former home of Edwin Booth, he recalled an anecdote regarding Creston Clarke and wrote it up as one of his contributions to Martin Levin's "Phoenix Nest" in the *Saturday Review*.

It seems that at one time Clarke had been sent for to replace a member of the touring company of Richard Mansfield, that brilliant but vile-tempered star, famous for the contemptuous manner and cruel remarks with which he habitually treated his entourage. Clarke was hesitant about accepting the job but his agent assured him that Mansfield would be courteous to a man of his talent and fine reputation, so Clarke reluctantly boarded a sleeper for Pittsburgh, where the Mansfield Company was filling a week's stand. Lindsay wrote that

he arrived at the theatre exhausted, nervous and fearful. He was met by the stage manager who gave him the part he was to play and started a rehearsal. There were just the two of them. The stage manager was delighted with Clarke and let him know how pleased he was, so that Clarke's confidence returned and he began to enjoy what he was doing. Then, out of the corner of his eye he saw Mansfield seated in the front row of the theatre listening and observing and not saying a word.

The rehearsal continued for another 15 minutes, but Clarke was now busy imagining what the silent Mansfield was going to say when he did speak. It turned out that Mansfield never had a chance to. Clarke had worked himself up to a point where finally

○ ○

he came down to the footlights and shouted, "I wouldn't act with you if you were the last actor on earth!" then threw the part into the astonished star's face, turned, stalked out of the theatre and took the train back to New York.

Why a man he had never met should come all the way from New York to Pittsburgh to insult him, Mansfield could never understand.

Haunting the theatre on Young's Pier, Howard tried to see every classical drama and comic opera. Being a normal growing boy, his preference was for the latter. A season was presented by the Wilbur Opera Company and he reveled in every performance he saw. He confessed to falling madly if distantly in love with the soubrette Grace Hazard, billed as "Five Feet of Comic Opera," whom he later summed up as being "a fascinating little bit of fluff. The leading man," he went on, "was also an object of my hero worship. I would follow him around and gaze at him like a spaniel as he tried to relax on the pier."

Young's Pier was not the only theatre haunted by young Howard. Further weekly shows took place at an auditorium dignified by the name of the Atlantic City Academy of Music. In those days one of his pals was Willard Connely, later to become a successful newspaper man and distinguished biographer of English eighteenth-century wits and writers. In a letter to Lindsay recalling their boyhood days in the New Jersey seaside city, he said:

> Every play that came to the Academy of Music from *Robespierre* to *The Katzenjammer Kids* seemed to excite your enthusiasm. A vintage melodrama you witnessed was *The White Slave.* On the morning after the performance you related to me the whole plot with such dramatic intensity that I was moved to exclaim, "You talk as if you wanted to *be* an actor." Quietly, with all the seriousness in the world, you said these words: "That's my ambition." You were ten, at most eleven.

through these two chorus girls I got a whiff of the
sense of its glamor and attractiveness.

have been earning their livings working in the
they were consumed with the desire to achieve
spectable status of "legitimate" actresses. In
most theatres closed for Holy Week, less for re-
ns than because box-office business dropped to
The two sisters had come home for the layoff,
th them a prospectus of the American Academy of
rts, which they left lying on the parlor table.
g, while waiting for his girl to finish "primping,"
cked up the brochure and started reading. He
at although to graduate two semesters of six
h were requisite, he could get a job on the stage
ne term. By going through some quick mental
he figured out that in order to be ordained he'd
nd three more years at Harvard plus another three
school. "And that," he said, "was the most deci-
in my life. The poor sinners of the world would
t along without me."

erstanding and indulgent grandmother managed to
enough money for him to go to New York and pay
for one semester. It was a rewarding six months.
my, oldest and best training school in the country,
ently run by its founder, Franklin H. Sargent. The
hat year included such theatre notables as Daniel
John Drew and Augustus Thomas, while its Advi-
d could boast of Charles Frohman, William Gillette,
lasco and William H. Crane. In his classes Howard
ht the rudimentary essentials of acting, voice train-
ical instruction, pantomime, practice in classic act-
comedy and what is classified as "dramatic" as well
rn theatre, fencing and stage dueling. This early

Lindsay's recollection of the same incident went on to Willard Connely's subsequent remark: "Huh! That's not a very
high ambition," a cut which rankled for many years until
Howard Lindsay had proved to himself and the public that to
be a fine actor was indeed a high ambition.

All this joyous theatre-going was cut short when, at the age
of thirteen, he moved with his family to Dorchester, Mas-
sachusetts, his mother having found substantial employment
in a dry-goods store. For a year Howard attended the Edward Everett Grammar School, then by good luck was admitted to the Boston Latin School. This was a fine, respected institution. Founded in 1635, the oldest public school of its
sort in the country, it had maintained its excellent and highly
respected course uninterruptedly except for a few short
months following the Battle of Lexington. The curriculum
emphasized the classics, history and English composition and
more than adequately prepared its pupils for entry into college, and Howard fully enjoyed his four years there. One of
his classmates was Joseph Patrick Kennedy, with whom he
never hobnobbed, possibly because, since the young Kennedy was rich Boston Irish, Howard felt him to be of a higher
social set. He applied himself with keen interest to the classics, both Latin and Greek, as well as history. What was
most rewarding was his growing interest in short-story writing, sometimes as assignments for English composition,
sometimes as contributions for an ambitious little publication
called the *Boston Latin School Register* and just as often for the
sheer satisfaction of putting pencil to paper and discovering
that what came forth was good prose and interesting narra-
tive. As he said in his portion of Martin Levin's *Five Boy-
hoods*:

Writing was always second nature to me . . . After I became an
actor what more natural than for me to sit down and attempt to

○ ○

write a play? . . . Whether it all stemmed from my learning to recite or whether it was something more innate I've never been sure. I've often wondered whether my father's ability to exaggerate, in fact his compulsion to lie, might somehow be connected with the fact that I, whether as an actor, a stage director, or a dramatist, have made my living telling stories.

Howard's sister Rose, always his nearest and dearest, adored her young brother, took great pride in any of his accomplishments and saved a number of his juvenile efforts. Years later, while going over her papers, he came across his first story. Commenting about it in the *Saturday Review*'s "Phoenix Nest," he wrote, "I find its concluding sentence is masterly." The setting was a lumber camp in Michigan because he would have need of a large body of water. The characters were lumberjacks — tough, crude men. The hero, whose name was John and whose admirable qualities were heightened by the fact that he had recently "got religion" at a revivalist meeting, was spreading the Word at every moment and apparently boring the daylights out of his companions, who greeted his fervency with coarse jeers. The tale ends with them all being out in a boat on Lake Michigan when a horrendous storm blows up.

> The other men were terrified at what seemed to be their approaching demise. I really do not know whether they lived or died. But John must have lived as my concluding sentence gives testimony to this. When these other irreligious characters cowered in the boat in panic and fright, John's faith rose high in his bosom, for the story ended:
> "John rose and cried out to his frightened friends: 'O ye of little faith, why are ye fearful?' Then he stepped out of the boat to walk upon the waters and became a great cynic."

Howard's intrepid hero may have ended up "a great cynic," but the fact remains that previously he himself had "got religion," not during any such ephemeral phenomenon

as a revivalist meeti
searching experiences.
tual exaltation and wit
tarian minister. In hi
"There are some simil
actors and ministers ap
and both are in a sense
He got a chance to do
in his final year when at
Prize for Declamation.
year at Harvard. It prov
At Harvard in those da
among the affluent and
looked with a certain cont
product of Groton, St. Pau
He remembered that "fello
cheat in classroom tests wo
they passed you in the Y
public school and certainly
problem of board and keep
furnace in some of the near
as the one in the boarding h
For all the shortcomings
and healthy and his spirits
rated by what he felt to be his
tion to these pious promptin
fact that he was gloriously ir
Dorchester, a short trolley r
eighteen-year-old's fascinatior
one had two skeletons in her f

> They were very pretty skeleton
> ters who had left home and ha
> that time no one would admit tl
> family any more than they woul

prison. But
stage and a

They may
chorus, but
the more re
those days
ligious reas
record lows
bringing wi
Dramatic A
That evenin
Howard pi
learned th
months eac
after only
calculation
have to sp
in divinity
sive factor
have to ge
His und
scrape up
the tuition
The Acad
was excel
trustees
Frohman
sory Boa
David Be
was taug
ing, phy
ing both
as mode

○ ○

schooling started him on the course of becoming a good actor and an even better director, while a gradual familiarity with the fundamentals of dramatic construction must have been a valuable asset to his success as a playwright.

The institution was run on the principle of turning out competently trained young performers. The year before Howard arrived, Charles Jehlinger, the Academy's director for over fifty years, had issued a statement of the school's principles that almost parallel the aims of Stanislavsky. And by that I refer to the real Stanislavsky, not the subsequent sins that have been committed in the name of that great master.

> To create an accent on naturalism accompanied by emotional recall in order to achieve a deeper more essential "truth" in performance. This approach was soon found to be an adjunct of style, but certainly not as a substitute for style. Within this context it has remained a part of the Academy's training to this day — it has never been allowed to replace the stern self-discipline of a wide tradition.

It was a tenet to which Howard Lindsay was to adhere during his entire career. In 1956, by then a Vice-President of the Academy's Board, he voiced some of his own theories:

> An actor must find the simple meaning of a part. He must attack it emotionally. What would your emotional reaction be as the character under the circumstances? However one mustn't overanalyze.
>
> The theatre is an emotional medium. Acting intelligence is not related to other forms of intelligence. One must try to reach the audience's mind. Acting is to mean what you say sincerely in order to tell the audience what you mean. That is technique.
>
> An actor doesn't learn how to act until he is in front of an audience. Everything that is done on the stage must be heard and seen. The theatre is a luxury item.

He could never take seriously the disciples of the purely cerebral "think" or, as some say, the "grunt and groan school," who shun intelligible diction along with any desire to communicate with an audience. In a letter to Hobe Morrison of *Variety*, he expressed his opinion of method acting, saying that it "leads to solo performing, and if you have method directing, which is little more than the honor system, the fault is compounded."

That term of 1909, he found his days in the Academy exciting and living in New York exciting. In the privacy of his small boarding-house room he worked assiduously at his studies, practicing every gesture he'd been taught in pantomime class or reciting, in tones which must have startled the other boarders, the lines of whatever part the drama instructor had assigned to him. Dorothy Stickney, his widow, has in her possession the sketchy little diary he kept that year. The entries are terse. Often as not a daily résumé will consist of the single word "Practiced." One day the line read, "Went to school. Not very well," to be followed by "Attended school. Felt better." And on Saturday of that same week the interesting information that he "attended Tuberculosis Exposition." For even at that callow age he showed signs of the hypochondria which was to plague him — or, perhaps it would be more accurate to say, in which he was to indulge himself — the rest of his life. Often the "line-a-day" says simply, "Saw girls in afternoon," although the identity of those lovelies is not made known, any more than the titles of the plays he saw are clarified by the concise record of "In evening went to theatre." However it is a notation that is made repeatedly, for the young man's interest in all matters theatrical was growing by leaps and bounds. Being an American Academy student put him into a "courtesy to the profession" status and he had free entrée, if not for a seat, at least for standing room to see most of the current productions.

It was a rich season on Broadway. Forbes-Robertson was

○ ○

reducing matinee audiences to tears in *The Passing of the Third Floor Back*. Everybody was humming hit numbers from *Naughty Marietta*, *The Chocolate Soldier* and *Madame Sherry*. Frances Starr in *The Easiest Way* had created what Brooks Atkinson calls "a scandal, a sensation and a success — the three bright 'S's' of show business," and Sarah Bernhardt was appearing in one of her many "Farewell Tours." For suspense there was *Alias Jimmy Valentine*, for comedy *Get-Rich-Quick Wallingford* and for culture there were Sothern and Marlowe in Shakespearean repertory at the experimental New Theatre.

At the finish of his first semester, there being no money forthcoming for the following year, Howard was obliged to take his leave of the Academy. Before he was formally dismissed, however, he was first summoned to recite before Franklin Sargent, who then called a meeting of the staff after which he bestowed on the young man the following accolade: "We have decided you would make a reliable actor."

Howard returned to Dorchester. He was still toying with the idea of going into the ministry, for the religious flame, if not blazing quite so brightly, was still flickering within him. The flame was considerably dampened by an actual deluge of rain, which pelted down at the precise moment that he and his grandmother were setting out from the house to call on a local Unitarian minister whose church was a fair distance away. The young man was all dressed up in what was known colloquially as an "ice-cream suit," a natty light-colored outfit that showed every spot and blemish, and he owned no raincoat. He never called on the parson. God lost out and the "Devil's Workshop" took over in the form of a Boston stock theatre in which he worked as an extra at three dollars a week.

This unspectacular beginning gave him enough courage to take a chance on finding work in the New York theatre. He was able to get a theatre job but not in New York. It was to

○ ○

tour in Margaret Mayo's *Polly of the Circus,* a play which had
scored such a long and successful Broadway run, four road
companies were being sent out. Howard was in the fourth,
his contract calling for forty-two and a half weeks of one-
night stands. This was a pleasant little play saved from sac-
charine banality by a spectacular last act in two scenes, the
first being outside a circus tent, the second inside under the
canvas while a performance is going on. Such Belasco-like
realism called for trapeze artists, clowns, musicians, barkers
and further extras, which in those union-free days could be
hired for circus peanuts. The plot was what one might sur-
mise. Polly, a bareback rider, is a pure and lovely girl and,
needless to say, the darling of the troupe. She is descended
from a long line of eminent equestrian acrobats, most of
whom seem to have been killed during their acts. The setting is in a small Ohio town, where, for purposes of dramatic
convenience, the Big Top has been pitched on an open lot adjoining the parsonage of a young and handsome minister.
The first night in town, Polly, in landing from a hoop jump,
falls from her horse, seriously injuring both her ankles. The
local hospital having (again conveniently) recently burned
down, she is carried into the house of the young clergyman,
who agrees to put her up until she recovers. To keep everything on a respectable level, there are two faithful Negro re-
tainers, Mandy and Hasty, who take loving care of the in-
jured girl. Certain narrow-minded parishioners are openly
shocked by the situation of the pretty circus performer living
in the house of their unmarried parson, although Polly has
endeared herself to others of the community through a
number of altruistic activities, among them taking on a
Sunday-School class of small children. Love burgeons in the
hearts of Polly and the minister but, realizing that her presence might be a stumbling block to his clerical career, she
resolutely says good-bye and goes off to rejoin the circus.

Months pass. The troupe again turns up in town and the young parson cannot resist coming to see the opening performance. During her act, Polly, suddenly setting eyes on him standing by the ringside, loses her footing and starts falling off the horse's back, only to find herself in the arms of the minister. There follows a change of scene and some dialogue, after which we see the lovers in a tender embrace. They then stand hand in hand watching the diminishing lights of the circus wagons slowly wending their way off toward distant hills.

Casting for this little drama had hardly been done according to type. Being very young, Howard was given the part of a very old doctor. In the tent scenes he doubled as a clown and later he was assigned the additional role of an elderly deacon with no increase in his salary, which was far below the minimum eventually stipulated by Actors' Equity. Nor was there extra emolument forthcoming when he found himself again doubling as assistant stage manager.

To be plunged into theatre life in the raw was hard work but excellent training. He found out all about actors — not the topflight elite of Broadway, but the travel-toughened "pros" of "the road," who knew the shortcuts to frugal touring. They could ferret out all the cheap but adequate lunch counters that stayed open after show time. They kept lists compiled by former troupers of the best theatrical boarding houses. They gave him useful tips on further economies, such as how to save on laundry by wearing special shirts of a depressingly drab color which didn't show the dirt and were known in the trade as "thousand-mile shirts," and they were not above hinting that an easy way to augment one's supply of make-up cloths was simply to purloin one of the skimpy towels from a hotel wash basin. Best of all, he gained a wide knowledge of actors and their many-faceted natures, their virtues, their foibles, their kindness, their pettiness, their

○ ○

generosity, their parsimony, their ego and easily wounded vanity. And with it he developed a deep affection for them all — not only for the seasoned veterans who had been in the profession most of their lives and would remain so until death or the Actors' Fund Home claimed them, but also his contemporaries, the struggling beginners. Howard Lindsay was always to have an interest in his fellow players, young or old, successful or deadbeat, and an unflagging concern for their well-being.

He became familiar with the life of one-night stands — its hardships, its inexplicable fascination. Most departures took place well after midnight, which meant waiting in half-deserted, dimly lit stations, the troupe in various states of weariness, some inside warming up by a coal-burning stove, chatting in groups, with a few stretched out on battered benches catching a fitful nap. Others outside in the smoky air pacing the platform or staring hopefully up the rails for the headlight of the oncoming locomotive. The higher-up members of the company traveled in Pullmans. Howard, along with the bit actors, extras and crew, learned to sleep in coaches. Seldom able to afford a meal in the diner, he subsisted much of the time on stale sandwiches, peanuts and soda pop peddled by the candy butcher.

Often as not, arrival in the next town would be brutally early in the morning. The other actors hurried off to various hotels and boarding houses. Not young Lindsay. As assistant stage manager, it was his duty to go with the crew directly from station to theatre and wait for the vans to pull up with the trunks, the scenery and the property cases. It could be a long wait and he got acquainted with that specialized stratum of labor, stagehands — genial and kind-hearted men, most of them, all of them compulsively talkative. They covered every known topic during these waiting hours. During one wait, they got onto the subject of being broke in a

○ ○

strange town. The fellow to whom this had happened told of his awkward experience in going to the house of a clergyman to ask for assistance. The parson took him into his parlor, made him give an account of his life, of his sins (in vivid detail), then forced him to get onto his knees and beg forgiveness, while all he wanted was some food and a cup of coffee. After the clergyman had also prayed at length for the poor sinner's salvation, he allowed him to rise, and gave him two dollars. After this sorry tale one of the other stagehands came out with a bit of sage advice. "When you're flat broke," he said, "never go to anyone like a clergyman. There are only three kinds of people who will hand you money without giving a damn why you need it. Go to a whore, a gambler or an actor." Lindsay, writing up the incident, said:

I was shocked to hear myself bracketed in that company. Then slowly it dawned on me. These were all precarious professions. (Whoring was a profession in those days, its practice confined to professionals.) Being in need was a desperation all these people knew intimately. Out of harsh experience came a quick sympathy for others in trouble and a generosity that didn't ask questions. Then the young man that I was at this time discovered that he was rather proud of being classed with gamblers and whores.

In his later years Howard was to manifest the instinctive liberality of actors. His kindness and generosity to friends or even mere acquaintances in trouble were boundless. People didn't need to ask for a handout; he'd offer one before they could broach the subject. Frequently he'd interrupt a hard-luck story, saying, "Don't you need some cash?" Russel Crouse told Howard Teichmann, the author, that "Lindsay not only lends money, he delivers it. Someone calls up and says, 'I need a hundred dollars in a hurry. I'll come up,' and Howard says, 'No, I'll leave it at your house,' then adds quickly, 'But don't print that because it's tough enough to be

○ ○

a soft touch without letting everybody know about it.' " If his secretary informed him of the death of some fellow actor or playwright who had been hard up, often as not he'd say, "Send his widow a thousand dollars." One day the Lindsays' friend Gladys Hurlbut happened to come into the room when he was talking over the phone to a former press agent who was in desperate financial straits. "Never mind the costs," he was saying. "I'll be responsible. I'll pay the rent and the doctor's bills. They can all be beholden to me. Don't worry." Then as he hung up he sighed and said, "Well, I've just lost another friend." When Bertrand Robinson, who had been his collaborator on his first three plays, became bedridden with dreadful arthritis, Howard paid practically all his hospital costs. After Robinson's death, his widow fell ill and Howard sent his sister Rose to take her down to Florida. Rose was his reliable standby, who helped him out with many of his charity cases. Howard was a modest man and never talked about his private philanthropies, nor did he want anyone else to mention them.

Even during his early, struggling years, Howard Lindsay himself was never to ask for a handout, although there were many times when he might well have felt he'd have to, many times when he needed not merely extra cash, but money with which to pay for the bare necessities of living. After his tour in *Polly* he returned to New York and joined that ever-present body of actors who, sparing themselves the humiliation of admitting themselves jobless, say that they are "at liberty." Putting on a brave front, they wear out shoe leather along Broadway, haunting the airless offices of agents, bracing themselves for the inevitable "Sorry, nothing for you today," called out by an office boy. Young Lindsay would have accepted any sort of job and it was a rugged one that he eventually did accept. He was booked to go on tour again, this time with the Stair and Havelin Circuit, which specialized in cheap repertory outfits sent on tour mainly throughout the Midwest. These outfits, heralded as "celebrated stock productions," were extremely popular with local citizens, many of whom attended every performance. The bill varied. Monday night they opened with a farce. The next four nights they'd present versions of Broadway favorites somewhat revised and outlandishly retitled, as well as sure-fire old "mellers," in which the plain but stalwart country hero routs the villain and wins the girl. Saturday night usually wound up with a Western, complete with cowboys and Indians, a long-suffering horse or two and a horrendous amount of blank cartridge shooting. This was followed by a farewell "olio" made up of burlesque acts so "risqué," the more respectable townsfolk would leave with their children before it began. The children got their innings on Saturdays at special matinees of *Uncle Tom's Cabin* or *Little Red Riding Hood*, given a happy ending in which Grandma calls in a passing woodsman who kills the wolf in the nick of time.

A brass band went with the show, and between acts various "artistes" would oblige with a song or two, either a tear-jerker like "Over the Hill to the Poorhouse" or a "scream," such as "I play in the fields with the daffy-dills . . . I'm going crazy, don't you want to come along?" Singers and musicians were recruited from among the actors, who had to be versatile and literally "double in brass" — an expression stemming from the days of the *Uncle Tom's Cabin* touring companies, when members of the cast were called upon to play instruments in the parade which marched through the town advertising the arrival of the "Tom Show." Howard was engaged to play bit parts in the stock repertory, heaven knows what in the "olio" and, lacking in instrumental talent, doubled not in brass but as utility boy and bill poster.

*

○ ○

One season of such touring was enough for the ambitious young thespian. This carnival-like set-up was hardly giving him the genuine theatre training he longed for. Nor did the next job he was able to get, although this did give him the opportunity to appear in public before an audience. A picture company which specialized in one-reel movies of an educational nature sent him out as lecturer to accompany their film of the durbar in Delhi. This was a "Kinema-color sensation" depicting the coronation of George V as Emperor of India in flickering red and green. It was booked in various cities at small so-called art movie houses, which strove bravely against the competition of *The Perils of Pauline* or the Keystone Kops showing in the larger palaces. Lindsay had to appear pointer in hand and wearing a dress suit. The pointer was supplied by the management. The rental for the dress suit came out of his pittance of a salary, which scarcely allowed him three square meals a day. Sometimes he'd type out menus for some cheap restaurant in payment for a dinner. Other times he'd stay in bed in his shoddy hotel all day in order to quiet his appetite while he read the *Saturday Evening Post* from cover to cover, including every word of the ads. The producers of these "two-color sensations" increased his repertoire with two more illustrated travelogues, one on the situation in the Balkans, the other on the Panama Canal. Just what the young speaker had to say about the struggles of Bulgaria, Greece, Serbia and Montenegro against the Ottoman Empire is subject for speculation. His talk on the Panama Canal must have been equally enlightening. During his opening lecture on "the Big Ditch," he was giving out such accurate and vital statistics as the mechanism of the locks, the number of feet in the length and breadth of the Culebra Cut and the exact number of miles from deepwater in the Atlantic to Pacific deepwater when a kid in the front row startled him

○ ○

and delighted the audience by calling out, "How do you know?"

This brief speaking tour in some way led him to a job in Hollywood. It too was brief. He played a number of minor parts in a few Grade B pictures. In those days, films had to be sent East for processing and it took almost six weeks for the finished products to return to California. By the time the films in which he appeared were shown, Howard Lindsay usually ended up on the cutting-room floor.

His career as a screen actor thus fortuitously nipped in the bud, he left Hollywood and joined McKee Rankin's repertory company on tour. Rankin, former star of the romantic school, matinee idol, hailed in London as "the American Apollo," was by then demoted to the ranks of "old-timer." He was sixty-seven years old. The dark wavy hair that ladies longed to stroke was grizzled. The godlike figure had become paunchy. Forty-four years had passed since he had first burst upon audiences at Niblo's Gardens as the breathtakingly handsome leading man for Lydia Thompson. Thirty-two since he swaggered onto the stage of the Union Square Theatre as Jacques Frochard, the fascinating villain of *The Two Orphans,* and not too many since his stormy liaison with Nance O'Neill shocked and titillated the theatre-going public. During his career he had known great success, had lost several fortunes and was now reduced to taking out cheap companies on barnstorming tours mainly through the Far West.

Lindsay played every variety of part in Rankin's repertory, which had been thrown together in a haphazard fashion. *Magda, Oliver Twist, Julius Caesar, The Danites, A Kentucky Colonel* and a comedy called *The Bachelor's Baby.* In this last there was a scene in which Howard was directed to place a sugar bowl in the middle of a mantelpiece, he failed to figure out why. Eventually he got up nerve enough to ask the star himself. Rankin, who was in a good mood, cheerfully explained: "One time a stagehand left that sugar bowl on the mantelpiece by mistake and when I suddenly saw it, I remember doing some comedy business that brought down the house. What I don't remember is what that business was but I keep hoping it will come back to me." Now and then the company would put on a current Broadway hit, happily ignoring any royalties or credits. Using a pirated script, Howard had to type out the parts, distribute them and put the cast through a first rehearsal. This must have been his initial experience in stage directing.

In lieu of salaries, hotel bills, theatre laundry costs and a weekly allotment for food were met by the management, with the indefinite proviso that if, during any stand, the show "caught on" the players would receive certain shares of the profits. Theirs was what was known as a "wildcat tour" — through the gold-mining centers of Nevada, the San Joaquin Valley and the recently discovered oil fields of California. They played a moderately good week in the newly settled desert town of Las Vegas, had a highly successful run amid the red mansions and crowded saloons of Virginia City, which was enjoying its final boom as "Queen of the Comstock Lode," and they struggled through five disastrous days in the half-abandoned settlement of Goldfield in the Mojave. In Fresno they came to grief and were literally stranded to the point where they couldn't even get out of town. Nevertheless they kept on playing, hoping that business would pick up. As Lindsay said of such professional optimism, "What has kept the theatre alive all these centuries is the elemental fact that actors like to act."

For the second week's bill in Fresno, a melodrama called *The Mountaineer's Daughter* was advertised. It proved an awkward choice when it was discovered that the list of char-

○ ○

acters required one more actor than they had in the troupe. This was for the short but essential role of a sheriff, who, having found the hero's knife beside the body of a murdered man, enters at a crucial moment, claps his hand down on the shoulder of the innocent hero (played by Howard Lindsay) and announces in ringing tones, "Young man, you are my prisoner!" As an emergency measure, the director called in a workingman named Charlie, whose acquaintance with acting was limited to sweeping out the theatre every morning, and offered him five dollars to go on as the sheriff. Charlie proved to be not very bright. His single line, "Young man, you are my prisoner," came out in a low mumble which couldn't be heard close to, let alone across, the footlights. Remembering the occasion, Lindsay wrote:

> The only way to make Charlie audible was to get him mad — slap him or kick him in the shins. We knew on the opening night that our fortunes were at stake and we were desperate. If we didn't catch on this week, we were stranded in Fresno. This was before the days of the Actors' Equity Association. Offstage with Charlie, before our entrance in Act 2, I did what I could to rouse his ire. I couldn't slap him because that might dislodge the gray mustache and goatee we had pasted on him, but I could kick him in the shins and I could push his head against the brick wall.
>
> The second act was laid in the home of my parents. It opened with my father, mother and sister discussing what a fine boy I was and how they all loved me. I made my entrance, gay and affectionate. We were a happy family. Then Charlie came in. He came in fast and determined. He slapped his hand down on my shoulder and spoke up loud and clear, "Young man, you are my murderer!"
>
> It was no fun being stranded in Fresno.

The company disbanded in that town, and from there Howard made his way to Los Angeles. Then came his first good break. Hearing that Margaret Anglin and her touring company were playing in Santa Barbara, he took a train to

that town and arranged for an interview with her. Pleased
with the young actor's manner and looks, she handed him a
copy of *Twelfth Night,* which was included in her current repertory, told him to study up on the minor role of Valentine,
"an attendant on the Duke," and come see her the following
day. Howard, in a state of elation, stayed up all night memo-
rizing Valentine's few lines, most of which he forgot at the
next day's audition. Miss Anglin heard him through, then
with an indulgent smile said, "His voice has quality," and
took him into her company as a super at fifty cents a performance. It was hardly a position he hankered after but for the
time being he was content to be under the aegis of this remarkable star and to become a member of her excellent entourage.

In 1913 Margaret Anglin was at the height of her distinguished career. After her glamorous years as leading lady for
Charles Frohman's light, popular plays at his Empire Theatre,
she had branched out into more serious fields with Henry
Miller in William Vaughn Moody's *The Great Divide.* Her
triumph in this established her in the front ranks of the country's emotional actresses, after which she formed her own
company, playing in New York and on the road in a repertory
of the best of modern plays and eventually the classics —
Shakespeare and the Greek dramas.

Soon after his fifty-cents-a-performance apprenticeship,
young Lindsay progressed to playing bit parts at a minimum
salary. In *The Taming of the Shrew* he cowered effectively as
one of Petruchio's intimidated servants. In *As You Like It* he
sang "Under the Greenwood Tree" until it was discovered
that he sang off key. And in *Antony and Cleopatra* he distinguished himself in an offstage battle effect, the noise of
which had so drowned out the voices of the actors that Miss
Anglin told the stage manager to cut it. The stage manager
gave the order to everyone except Howard, who was in the

wings on cue and went through the violent rattling of chains, the clashing of sword against shield, the blood-curdling war cries and further bellicose sound effects. The star, from stage center, waved frantically at him to stop, but, thinking she was cheering him on, he redoubled his efforts. Eventually the curtain came down. Margaret Anglin forgave him. She was an understanding woman who had grown to take a warm interest in this intelligent, stage-struck young man. After a few months she gave him a further promotion. Instead of raising his salary, she made him her stage manager and his name was printed on the program.

In addition to this duty and his stint as a bit player, he'd sometimes be called upon to jump in if a member of the cast was taken ill or had been forced to leave the show. The troupe carried no understudies. Those were the golden days of tough theatrical training before Equity ruled that an actor playing a part could not also stage-manage. As Lindsay commented, "Youngsters had a better break. We weren't protected against working too hard." On these emergency occasions, Miss Anglin would send for him and announce, "Lindsay, the worst has come to the worst." And he'd know, with a thump of his heart that was half dismay, half delight, this meant "Get up in the lines right away." Her interest in him was not based on his acting talent, which she found to be reliable, though not extraordinary. But she recognized the fact that he seemed to have an instinctive knowledge of how a scene should be played, how an actor should say a line — a sense of theatre which, prophetically, she felt would grow with the years.

Lindsay said of her that she was one of the greatest directors and teachers of acting he ever knew. Yet she was not above asking his opinion of some tyro who might be trying out for a place in her company. During a Chicago engagement of a play called *Beverly's Balance* (Anglin was as deli-

○ ○

cious in comedy as she was magnificent in drama), her leading man suddenly gave notice and an immediate replacement
was needed. Someone recommended a young actor from
Waukesha, Wisconsin, who was summoned to read for the
part. There arrived a tall thin youth of twenty-one, nervous,
gawky and so self-conscious about his height that, instead of
making an asset of it by standing straight, he crouched.

Anglin sat in the darkened house while on a bare stage, lit
only by a glaring rehearsal bulb, Lindsay, holding one script,
ran through her lines and the young man read the replies
from another, his hands and knees shaking, his voice squeak-
ing uncontrollably. After fifteen minutes the kindly star put
him out of his misery, thanking him and saying she'd let him
know by telephone. On their walk back from the theatre,
Miss Anglin asked, "What did you think of him?" Howard's
instant reply was "Terrible." He later recalled that "there
was a long silence while this wise and sensitive woman considered what I had said and then rejected it: 'Make no mistake, Lindsay,' she said. 'That boy has quality. We will try
him.'" The young man's name was Alfred Lunt. He was
signed up for the remainder of the season.

Alfred Lunt still has a clear memory of that tryout session.
He remembers Lindsay too as a very serious young man and
so dedicated to his job as actor and assistant stage manager
that when he read Miss Anglin's lines he went so far as to
give an imitation of the acting of the star herself and even put
on the "prop" apron she wore during the scene. Later, after
Lunt was taken into the Anglin company, he and Lindsay
saw one another on a pleasant basis "but," said Lunt, "I
never knew the lighter side of Howard. I still regarded him
as the serious, dedicated young man. A real scholar. I remember being very impressed that he was familiar with the
Greek classic drama which he had studied in the original language."

○○

That summer of 1915 Margaret Anglin presented her triumphantly successful classical festival at the University of California's open-air Greek Theatre in Berkeley. She made
theatre history with her staging of the three great Attic mas-
terpieces, *Iphigenia in Aulis, Medea* and *Electra.* They opened
with *Iphigenia.*

Lunt was cast in a minor role. Howard, who was stage
manager, wondered if this emaciated-looking youth could be
heard in that vast open-air theatre, which seated ten thousand spectators. He needn't have worried. The Berkeley
acoustics were on a par with those at Epidaurus and the
young man's voice carried to the topmost row. In a 1956
Good Housekeeping article entitled "Lindsay and Crouse and
the Fabulous Lunts," Howard described Alfred's apprenticeship in Greek tragedy:

> We had one reservation. Could those seated at a distance *see*
> him? He was painfully thin. After some padding of his waist
> and chest, it was decided he would be visible as well as audible.
> In the next play, the *Electra* of Sophocles, everything was re-
> versed. Lunt had no lines and almost no clothes. He was told
> to stroll about the stage at one point pretending to be a decadent
> youth. He wore vine leaves in his hair and they managed to look
> suitably awry. No one worried that he would not be seen —
> only that he might be.

Anglin was superb in all three of her Greek roles but she
seemed to surpass every other in her *Electra.* She was to
revive this in New York during the early 1920's and the critics
were ecstatic. Walter Prichard Eaton said that she "epit-
omized the noble grief, the rankling passions, the fervent
apostrophes and the comprehensible, if unholy joys of
Sophoclean drama." Alexander Woollcott, heading his review "Anglin the Great," wrote that in the recognition scene
"she forgot the modern world and the last three thousand
years, a mighty glow was on her and I had known what I had

known before, that here at last was an actress whom one could call great, one who, from Sarah Siddons and a long thronged past, caught up and handed on the torch of a great tradition." The critic of the *Telegram*, in less rhetorical but more graphic words, wrote that "Margaret Anglin brings a surging thrill to Sophocles' tragedy of the Snyder-Gray case of Greece."

Young Lunt made an unexpected hit in *Medea*, filling in for the actor who had broken his ankle shortly before going on in the important role of the messenger who comes running down a ramp with the loud cry of "Get thee away, Medea," followed by the news that her revenge on the faithless Jason is accomplished and that his young bride is dead. Lunt, who knew the part, rushed on letter-perfect and delivered his horrendous message in ringing tones, which electrified the vast audience and gave Miss Anglin confidence in his ability. The engagement was extended a week and she decided to fill it with a repeat presentation of *Iphigenia in Aulis*, entrusting Alfred Lunt with the part of Achilles. Tired out after playing her exhausting roles, she turned the company over to Howard to rehearse while she took time off for a rest. In the same *Good Housekeeping* article, Howard recalled:

> I worked very hard with Lunt. I made him throw back his shoulders and hold his head high, take the long stride that befitted his height, throw out his chest instead of his hips, spread his feet apart when he stood shield on arm and sword in hand. He was somewhat slight for a warrior, but we knew that in the performance he would wear armor and the result should be sufficiently impressive, if not classically heroic. The result was just dreadful. No one had anticipated what the weight of the armor would do to him.
>
> A striking Achilles strode on to the stage. In the helmet, Lunt looked eight feet tall when he first appeared. Then something strange happened. Achilles kept growing shorter. By the time he reached stage center, that famed fighter was less than Lunt's

natural height of six feet three. He spread his legs and locked his knees as I had taught him and his knees held firm. But there are those who swear that before he had finished his first speech, his legs were bowed. But if he made a bowlegged and bowed-down Achilles, it was an Achilles of high spirit, and for a lad of twenty-one a creditable achievement.

The Berkeley experience and Howard Lindsay's five years as Margaret Anglin's stage manager and occasional actor from 1913 to 1918 gave him, he always claimed, his ultimate schooling in the trade, or the craft, of acting. He told the students of the American Academy how he had learned:

> . . . by watching Miss Anglin, seeing that great woman, with that wonderful sense that she was up on that stage to tell a story to an audience; that she was up there for the benefit of the audience. And it was my observation that most actors have to be in the profession about five years before they realize that. It is a lot of fun to be up there in costume and make-up, and indulge yourself in characterizations. But it takes you some time before you really sense that you are there for a definite purpose that has something to do with an audience.
>
> The audience should be considered. I am not of the school that think they should be ignored. It seems to me that when they have spent their time getting tickets and coming to the theatre, and spent their money, and are going to have a difficult time going home, there should be some reward. And, in some way, the actors are connected with that.
>
> And it is the rapport that you finally achieve between being true to your character and, at the same time, making it explicit to the audience what the purpose of that character is and his relationship to the show, it is in that, that you finally profess the theatre.

In the late autumn of 1917, Emily Kimbrough received a postcard from Howard Lindsay. As a young teen-ager she had met him when he was stage-managing the plays at the Greek Theatre and her family had allowed her to appear as one of the garland-bearing maidens in the chorus. The pic-

○ ○

ture postcard marked "Camp Devens" shows Corporal Lindsay in AEF uniform, complete with baggy trousers, puttees fitting loosely over his shoes, and broad-brimmed hat, staring through pince-nez with a splendid look of determination to make the world safe for democracy. On the back is written: "Dear Emily Kimbrough, I have mailed one of these to the Kaiser. You may expect Peace very shortly."

After basic training at Camp Devens, he was shipped overseas with members of the 76th Division on a troopship known as the *Poona*. As this converted passenger tub zigzagged its course across the Atlantic, Howard whiled away the time putting out a news sheet he called the *Poona Blast* (member of the Latrine News Association). Its daily entries gave out such varied information as:

> Our reporter has interviewed several fish along the route. For the first time they are satisfied with the quantity of food they receive but complain of its quality.

At another time, he published his own panegyric on the *Poona*'s food:

> Break, break, break
> On the biscuit's crust, O teeth.
> And I pray that my tongue won't utter
> The curses that lie beneath.
>
> Oh, well for the sailor man
> If he's used to this kind of grub,
> But if that's his idea of a biscuit, Lord!
> What's his idea of a club?
>
> And the camouflaged ships sail on,
> Approaching the zone of war
> And oh for a taste of Devens bread
> And a Devens meal once more.
>
> Break, break, break
> Pray tell me what I should do,

○ ○

I've broken my teeth, I've broken my knife
I've broken my bayonet too!

Howard Lindsay was overseas for thirteen months. Instead of being sent to the front to help load the guns at Château-Thierry or the Argonne, he was kept most of the time in American headquarters at Brest, where he was ordered to supervise the entertainment section of the YMCA. He organized a group which he glorified with the name of the Brest Stock Company and which he directed in a series of successful comedies.

He had no trouble in finding talent. There were any number of actors who had enlisted in the American Expeditionary Force. In a foreword to a program for one of his productions he wrote that "Mr. Holbrook Blinn has announced that investigation has proved the theatrical profession to have contributed in proportion to its personnel *more men* to the army of the U.S. in the present war than any other profession or any department of business life. The present cast of actors who came to France in the AEF lends testimony to that fact of which the American theatre is justly proud."

Lindsay ran into a few difficulties during rehearsals when certain sergeants in his cast openly resented being bossed by a mere corporal and refused to follow his directions. In despair he appealed to General Smedley Butler, who issued a directive that Corporal Lindsay's stage directions were as binding as army orders and deliberate disobedience was cause for immediate court-martial. This subdued the recalcitrant sergeants, and things went even more smoothly when Pershing appointed Corporal Lindsay a Second Lieutenant.

The biggest hit of this corps of soldier-actors was Lee Wilson Dodd's dramatization of Harry Leon Wilson's amusing story, "Bunker Bean." This was heralded on posters throughout the camp as "The Comedy Scream," with the

added attraction that "your uniform is your pass." It went
so well in Brest that official arrangements were made for a
short run in Paris, where the troupe appeared at the Théâtre
des Champs-Elysées to the delight of Yankee officers
and doughboys on leave and the polite bewilderment of the
French. Lindsay received the following commendation from
the U.S. Overseas Director of Entertainments:

> The Brest Stock Company has justly earned the distinction of
> being the most popular comedy company of the AEF to appear in
> Paris and this office knows that a great deal of its success is due
> to you.

The Armistice was signed. Second Lieutenant Lindsay was
kept on in Brest for a few more months in charge of entertainment for the home-bound troops, then he too received his
honorable discharge from the army. Once back in the States
he lost no time in rejoining Margaret Anglin's company. She
had kept his job open and was waiting for him. Also waiting
for him, although he was unaware of it, was a quiet, unob-
trusive girl named Virginia Frölich.

They had met during the festival at Berkeley when Howard
was a stage manager and Virginia was a dancer in the Greek
chorus. Her mother was the Anglin wardrobe mistress — a
woman superior to her position, for Madame Frölich, who
had had a European training, enjoyed a thorough knowledge
of historic and period costuming. For a number of years she
had been in the employ of Sothern and Marlowe, who had
taken an interest in her daughter. Julia Marlowe in particular
helped out in the girl's education and tried to instill in her a
love of Shakespeare and English poetry. Virginia was a
sweet, vague young thing with a moderately pretty face and
very little personality. She and Howard had met casually at
rehearsals and, without his knowing it, she had fallen in love
with him.

Howard Lindsay was hardly one's idea of a knight in shining armor. Nor would anyone meeting him for the first time have taken him for an actor. He was not tall and his frame was thin. His hair was straight and sandy. His features, anything but romantic-looking, were not augmented by the austere addition of pince-nez. His general appearance plus his manner, stiff and at times brusque, was that of a scholar, which, fundamentally, he was.

He and Virginia had been thrown together in the peculiar intimacy of a theatrical company. She was appealingly worshipful and Howard married her. It is doubtful if it was an impulsive, all-consuming love on his part. Throughout the country there was a wave of postwar weddings among the returning military and possibly Howard felt that it was time for him to join in the stream. It was a brief marriage and they were divorced before Howard's first play was produced. Recalling Virginia, Nedda Harrigan said, "She was a shadow. She could never have kept up with Howard."

He must have felt certain compunctions about Virginia, for even after they were separated he continued to keep in touch with her and was concerned for her welfare. It is characteristic of a good man's kindly if sometimes misguided impulses that shortly after Howard and Dorothy Stickney were married, he got a notion that it would be friendly to invite Virginia to their flat for dinner. He did. It is to be assumed that the first Mrs. Lindsay failed to have a riotously good time. As for Dorothy, she says that afterward she cried herself to sleep. Virginia had poor health. She also had a poor sense of economy and lived well beyond the modest alimony that Howard was able to pay her. During the years between *Anything Goes* and the bonanza of *Life with Father*, Howard and Dorothy were not at all well-off. At one point, they were just about to go broke. To tide them over, Dorothy borrowed $2500 from the bank in her home town of Dickinson, North

ooo

Dakota. For the first time in his life, Howard had to turn
down a request for a loan from his former associate Bertrand
Robinson, who was even worse off than he. But he managed
to scrape up enough to help out Virginia. She had developed
T.B. While Howard was away on some minor Hollywood
business, her illness was complicated by blood poisoning and
Dorothy got her admitted to Presbyterian Hospital, where she
died on New Year's Eve in 1938.

As early as 1913, American players had formed themselves
into an association they called Actors' Equity. At its outset,
Miss Anglin was all in accord with the idea, regarding it in
the colorful light of a trade guild of sorts. As the AEA grew
more union-minded, she became increasingly alarmed and
when in 1919 they came out not only for a closed shop but for
membership in the American Federation of Labor, she was
irate. A newspaper interview quotes her as saying, "I am
violently opposed to a closed shop for the professional stage.
Artists are not bricklayers. They cannot be controlled by a
union or rules . . . Art is something spontaneous which
flows freely and uncurbed . . . My ability as an actress would
be impaired if I were to be held down by iron-clad rules."
No member of her casts had ever found fault with her generous and fair-minded management. It was with a sense of
wounded incomprehension that she aligned herself with a
small group of players who were dead set against unioniza-
tion, the Actors' Fidelity Organization, known somewhat
jeeringly by the strikers as "the Fidos."
Howard Lindsay did not share his star's point of view.
Why shouldn't actors have the ability to stand up for their
own abused rights? More and more they had become the
victims of the purely commercial if not indeed rapacious
managements like that of the Shuberts or the firm of Klaw
and Erlanger. These powerful syndicates were out to make

○ ○

money, not to bother about the injustices to those who made it for them. Actors were required to play extra matinees and, in certain cities, Sunday nights without extra pay. It was nothing for a cast to rehearse a new play for as long as five or even six weeks (with no such thing as rehearsal money) and then to have the producers decide not to put on the show. On the road a production might close without notice, leaving the company stranded and without return fares to New York. Often players were required to meet the cost or the partial cost of their own costumes.

Equity's demands for a revised contract with the managers were moderate. They didn't ask for any raise in basic salaries; they merely wanted the limitation of eight performances a week with the understanding that actors receive compensation for extra matinees, that touring companies which closed on the road should be given a week's notice plus return railroad fare and that rehearsal periods should consist of four weeks for straight plays and five for musicals with pay for additional ones. The managers refused to agree and on August 6, 1919, a half hour before curtain time, a hundred actors walked out of their respective theatres, with more to follow in the next forty-eight hours. It was a gay and colorful strike. Well-known stars paraded up Broadway and around Columbus Circle, led by Marie Dressler and a bevy of chorus girls carrying banners reading, "No more pay. JUST FAIR PLAY," followed by a band playing "Over There" and a group singing "And we won't come back till the managers are fair!"

Strike orders were sent out to all Equity members of road companies, and Howard Lindsay, although he was under the benign actor-management of Margaret Anglin, felt that he must side with his fellow players. He handed in his notice. This was a shock to the star and an outrage to her husband, Howard Hull, who reacted in a belligerently ugly manner.

○ ○

Howard Hull had been an actor, but an unsuccessful one, who had watched his two more talented brothers, Shelly and Henry, climb to the upper echelons of Broadway. He then became a newspaper and magazine writer in a desultory fashion. After his marriage to one of the most important women of the American theatre, which took place amid considerable publicity in St. Patrick's Cathedral, he gave up all pretense of working. His wife paid for everything — the rent, the food bills, his tailor, the $2500 touring car she gave him as a wedding present (and on which she paid the damages to a victim of a subsequent accident), and she gradually settled with his creditors after he went into bankruptcy in 1914. Hull was a man of easy wit and considerable surface charm. Fundamentally he was a wastrel — arrogant, selfish and very often drunk. Yet Margaret Anglin indulged him in many ways. She humored his assumption of an air of importance in her affairs. At rehearsals she encouraged him to sit beside her and she deferred to his judgment just enough to satisfy his ego, then quietly carried out her own ideas, leading him to think they were his. Apparently she loved him.

Lindsay left the road company for New York with a heavy heart. The rift was a bitter one for the young actor and looked to be irreparable. However, in later years, Anglin softened in her attitude and made overtures to repair it, and Howard, who still worshipped her as an actress and as a person, was quick to respond. By then he himself was becoming a celebrity. He went to tea with her a number of times and their meetings were warm and gay. She did her best to induce him to call her by her first name, but he could never do it. He still felt a humility in the presence of this remarkable woman who had started him on the right road to all that is best in the theatre.

Howard may have left the Anglin company with a heavy heart but there were bright prospects waiting for him in New

○ ○

York. Word of his proficiency as a director had gotten around theatrical circles, and George Tyler wanted him to join his staff in the capacity of stage manager, director, head of casting and occasional actor. Loyal to Equity, he refused to go near the office of any producer until the strike had been settled, a gesture of independence which annoyed Tyler, but an agreement between actors and management was signed and Howard Lindsay joined the Tyler establishment.

This was a big advancement for Lindsay, who always claimed that George C. Tyler was one of the greatest producers of the American theatre — greater even than Charles Frohman, who at that time was popularly known as "the Napoleon of the stage." Frohman produced sure-fire plays with well-known stars. He was also an importer of European successes performed by internationally famous talent. Tyler dared introduce new writers as well as foreign drama new to this country. Frohman employed a press agent, a startling innovation in publicity. Tyler never had a press agent, but depended upon the freshness and excellence of his productions to keep his name before the public. Tyler was a quiet man, but audacious in his hunches, which usually proved sound. He considered himself a gambler, but his risks were well-calculated ones and many of them turned out to be successful. He made three fortunes and lost them all because he invested them in further theatre ventures. He was keen on the works of American authors. In addition to producing the popular melodrama of Paul Armstrong's *Alias Jimmy Valentine* or the Glad Girl treacle of *Pollyanna*, he created new playwrights by persuading Alice Hegan Rice to dramatize *Mrs. Wiggs of the Cabbage Patch* and Robert Hichens to do the same with *The Garden of Allah*. He was the first to realize that Booth Tarkington could write good plays as well as brilliant novels, and it was through Tyler that the theatre-going public would rejoice in *The Man from Home, Monsieur Beaucaire* and

o o o o o o o o o o o o o o o o o o o o o o o o o o o o o o o o o o o o o o o o o o

Seventeen, to name only a few. He liked good theatre, and in later years he deplored the radical changes that were taking place in modern drama. "When the matter of woman's honor became unimportant," he wrote, "playwrights lost their greatest emotional asset. The only climax was murder and the only thing left to do with sex was to kid it."

Upon joining this producer's office, Howard was handed a play to direct but he didn't like the script and asked instead to be sent out with one of the Tyler road companies as stage manager and actor. Acting was still his first love though Howard Lindsay was never more than an adequate actor. There was a certain stiffness about him which of course was a great asset in his magnificent performance of the elder Day in *Life with Father.* And there were other minor roles in which he scored, but his real gifts lay in other theatre channels, writing and directing.

On his return from the road he got his first chance to direct a Broadway play when Tyler again handed him a script. It was by two new playwrights and it had been written expressly for a little-known actress. The names of the playwrights were Marc Connelly and George S. Kaufman, the actress was a newcomer named Lynn Fontanne and the title of the play was *Dulcy.*

Tyler had been intrigued by one Dulcinea, a character invented by Franklin P. Adams and mentioned frequently in his "Conning Tower" column of the New York *World.* She was a blithe, meddling featherbrain, full of cheer and good intentions, who talked incessantly in bromides and obvious "wall-mottoes" ("Every cloud has a silver lining if you only look for it" or "Laugh and the world laughs with you, I always say"). One of Tyler's hunches was that a comedy could be built around Dulcinea, or Dulcy. He also had a hunch as to who could most deftly act this exasperating yet lovable goose. He had already put on a few plays written by

○ ○

J. Hartley Manners for his wife, Laurette Taylor. In his auto-biography, *Whatever Goes Up*, Tyler recalls that "on her re-turn from England Laurette Taylor brought with her a star-tlingly capable beginner named Lynn Fontanne . . . shy and awkward enough . . . always turned her toes in (and a time she had breaking herself of the habit!). But through all her shyness you could see she was blessed with the grand man-ner even then!"

When Miss Fontanne was signing her contract in the Tyler office, she met young Howard Lindsay and suggested that in addition to directing the play he also be given the role of Vin-cent Leach, an egomaniacal Hollywood scriptwriter. Howard was delighted to get the part. Hitherto, he said, he had usually played either colorless or very precious people, and the scene in which Leach outlines the plot of his forthcoming picture had the potential of being a show-stopper. Happily it turned out that way.

Howard was somewhat new at directing and the authors somewhat new at playwriting but rehearsals went well. Kaufman spent most of the time silently pacing up and down the darkened theatre aisles, listening to the lines and think-ing up new ones. Connelly, more articulate, was helpful with suggestions, for he himself was an instinctively good director. The cast, which in addition to Lynn Fontanne in-cluded Gregory Kelly, John Westley, Wallis Clark and Elliott Nugent, was cooperative and all worked smoothly together.

Dulcy was scheduled to come into New York in early au-tumn. Before that there was a spring tryout in Indianapolis with a week's further test in Chicago. During the course of the Indianapolis first night the audience became increasingly disturbed by a tall, weedy young man who kept pacing up and down the center aisle. When the house manager finally stopped him to ask what the hell he thought he was doing, he replied, "I'm worried about that last exit of Lynn's. We've

○ ○

got to get her a laugh to go off on." The young man, of course, was George Kaufman.

Dulcy was warmly received in Indianapolis and had an equally gratifying reception in Chicago. Then the play and cast had a summer layoff, which was usual in those non–air-conditioned days. Lindsay, young, ambitious and always in need of cash, went the rounds of the Chicago theatrical agents in search of a short summer job. What he got was hardly destined to add to his training in the drama, but it was a colorful experience. The leading man for Jack Percy's traveling tent theatre had given notice and Howard was hired to replace him. This meant that he had to get up in six parts within ten days before joining the company. Being cast as the leading man was not as impressive as it sounds. Jack Percy's bills were all "Toby" shows. The Toby was a character peculiar to the rural American theatre in the early part of this century, although he may have appeared earlier than that. He was portrayed not as an out-and-out clown but as a good-natured yokel, complete with red wig and farmer clothes. When things go wrong, it is Toby who straightens them out. When the hero and heroine find themselves in danger, it is Toby who rushes to the rescue. The leading man hardly scores. Howard in that role found he could score even less when he was informed that when Toby (played by the manager Jack Percy himself) came onto the stage, all the other actors were expected to "fade" (a tent show term for underplaying). The rest of the time they could overact and yell their lungs out, which they did. Jack Percy, secure in his position as boss and "Toby player," gave some good advice for anyone appearing in his sort of show. Realizing that Howard's acting was too legitimate, he told him that "the man with the biggest gun and the loudest voice is the hero."

Howard had a busy eight weeks. In addition to having him play six leads, every afternoon Percy would drive him in his open touring car around the main streets and squares of every town, so that he could ballyhoo through a megaphone, "Great show at the Big Tent tonight!" When he wasn't on the stage he was obliged to put on a white coat and sell Cracker Jack through the audience. And if, at the end of the Toby play, a straight sketch followed, he'd be assigned a part in it.

Howard loved every minute of his experience "under canvas." He said that he learned the difference between "theatre" and "show business." "In the theatre," he said, "actors do not feel any personal responsibility for the success of an enterprise. In show business you quickly learn that unless the customers are pleased, you are going to be out of a job, and that you are there to serve the audience."

It is characteristic of Howard's warm loyalty to the people who had been part of his early theatre life that thirty-five years later, on hearing that Jack Percy, old and retired, was living in a Florida mobile home park with his wife, now an invalid (she had played the heroines opposite him), he wrote his former boss a nostalgic letter saying, "I have very warm memories of you, Jack . . ." adding modestly, "You may have seen my name in the theatrical news, but I do not know whether you associated it with the young man who joined your company for the summer of 1921 . . . Looking back, I realize that I was something of a misfit as far as the acting went. I had learned in a different school. I can remember your dear wife being very uncomfortable at my habit of turning my back on the audience." Then, after some brief news of the other members of the tent show company whom he had run into from time to time, he wound up with: "You might be surprised how often I boast that I was once with a tent show — the Jack Percy show" and regretted that he had not known that the Percys were living in Sarasota when he was there as he "would have enjoyed seeing you and Mrs. Percy

○ ○

and reminiscing." In letters of this sort, Howard Lindsay meant every word that he wrote.

DULCY

a comedy in 3 acts by George S. Kaufman and Marc Connelly
(with a bow to Franklin P. Adams)
staged by Howard Lindsay

opened at the Frazee Theatre at the end of August 1921 and was an immediate success. It was the making of Kaufman and Connelly while overnight Lynn Fontanne became the proverbial toast of the town.

A lesser but definite hit was made that evening, and one paper next morning stated that "one of Tyler's most brilliant strokes was to assign the double choice of directing the play and acting the role of a movie writer to a young man in the cast, Howard Lindsay." His brief scene might have been considered "actor-proof" but, as Alan Dale wrote, "It would be ungracious not to acknowledge that he seemed to do wonders with it." It was an actual tour de force. Dulcy, after assembling her guests, delightedly informs them that Mr. Leach is going to tell them all about his forthcoming picture. At that the absurd scenarist, starting with the profound statement (and taking the words right out of Dulcy's mouth) that "the art of motion pictures is only in its infancy," goes into an elaborate monologue with appropriate gestures and a piano accompaniment reluctantly played by a disgruntled guest. The title of the film is *Sin Through the Ages* and it traces the progress of evil down the centuries. At one point in this recitation, to indicate the passing of half an hour, the curtain is lowered. When it rises we see Dulcy, still in a state of delight, her guests in varying states of restlessness or somnolence, and Leach still talking. By now he is describing the last reel in which "Fred kisses Clara and, to preserve the symbolism, Marc Antony is immediately shown kissing Cleopatra

○ ○

and George Washington kissing Martha Washington." Heywood Broun wrote that "the whole scene of Leach's recital and its effect upon the composite house party is the most successful portion of the play and as deft and happy a piece of satire or possible burlesque as the stage has known in our time."

The theatre by now was Howard's life. His interest in writing grew. It was more than a casual interest. Unlike many writers who work laboriously and find it torture to sit down and face a blank sheet of paper, Howard Lindsay loved to write. He enjoyed composing amusing short articles for the Players Club *Bulletin* or the *Saturday Review,* as well as one-act skits. He was an avid correspondent and took pleasure in turning out a spirited business letter. Friends jokingly accused him of answering advertisements with whimsical notes — "Dear Messrs. Abercrombie and Fitch: I am sorry that a sprained ankle prevents me from attending your private sale of sport shirts on April 15th. Thank you for the kind invitation. With every good wish, Your devoted customer." His head was teeming with ideas. He began outlining potential plots for plays and decided he had nothing to lose by trying his hand at turning one out himself. Being a tyro in the field, he felt he needed a collaborator and hit upon Bertrand Robinson.

Robinson was an ex-actor. Born in Denver and from childhood mad about the stage, he had been a bellboy in the Brown Palace, at which job he earned enough money in tips to go to Los Angeles and enroll in a dramatic school. Between classes he supported himself by running an elevator in a local hotel. After making his way to New York, he was given a few minor parts in a few minor productions. Then, realizing that acting was not his forte but still stage-struck, he turned to playwriting, specializing in short playlets and

○ ○

sketches for vaudeville. At this he had a marked success. Robinson had a good knowledge of the technique and mechanics of playwriting and Lindsay found that he himself had a facile gift for plot, situation and comedy, and the two men worked well together.

Their first venture was a pleasantly innocuous comedy that went by the simple title of *Tommy*. George Tyler liked the script and agreed to produce it. Howard was the director and it opened at the Gaiety Theatre on January 10, 1927. That night the two authors, in an advanced state of nerves, sat with bated breath and crossed fingers in the back row of the balcony. The first act went smoothly enough but during the second act there occurred a few minor mishaps which to them seemed nothing short of disaster. Among them, the property man forgot to place on a table a sewing basket and a piece of embroidery work with which the actress playing the mother had an important bit of business. Then at the end of the same act there was to be, it was hoped, a big laugh, followed immediately by a quick curtain. The laugh came with a gratifying roar, but the curtain remained stationary for what seemed like an eternity until someone shook awake a stagehand to lower it. This was the first and last time Howard Lindsay ever sat through an opening night of any of his plays. In future he made it a practice to pass those agonizing hours in the pool room of the Players Club.

Tommy, though hardly a smash hit, was pleasantly received by audience and press. It dealt with a simple "home-town" romance, and Alison Smith of the *World* called it "a naive, disarming and thoroughly ingratiating comedy" written in "just those bright colors which decorate the cover of the *Saturday Evening Post* which the play greatly resembles." The *Times* found in it "innocuous and mildly diverting entertainment belonging distinctly to the John Golden wing of the

American drama, but it is also not without its pleasant moments."

Nineteen twenty-seven was a year when a group of puritanical citizens were campaigning for cleaner drama and inveighing against wicked plays like *The Shanghai Gesture*. Their pressure was such that *The Captive* and Mae West's *Sex* were each closed by police and the actors taken off in the paddy wagon. Heaven knows *Tommy* was morally above reproach. Percy Hammond of the *Tribune* said:

> Those playgoers who with Bishop Manning and Rabbi Wise feel the urge for unstained drama have a chance to indulge comfortably that somewhat rare emotion in the new comedy at the Gaiety . . . which managed last evening to keep its audience in the best of good humors. Genial, witty, shrewd and intelligent, it is as blithe a racket as has been seen since the spotless days of *Clarence* and *The First Year*. This soiled critic left the theatre refreshed, sanitary and a little amazed. No first-nighter had walked out on the salutary proceedings! — the fable was pleasantly routine but the manner of its relation was craftily satiric. Moreover the acting was delightfully humorous, though real, and the stage direction by Howard Lindsay was a masterpiece of theatrical gerrymandering.

For Howard Lindsay, 1927 started out auspiciously with the agreeably successful production of his first play. It culminated in late summer with his marriage to Dorothy Stickney. They had first met in 1924 in the office of Al Lewis and Max Gordon, the producers for whom Howard was then working. They had given Dorothy a contract to replace June Walker in Owen Davis' *The Nervous Wreck*. She lost out on the job when Davis, after taking one look at her skinny little body and pinched little face, refused to have her in his play. This was a bitter blow to her. For three years she had been trying to break into Broadway, making persistent and fruitless rounds of the offices of managers and agents. Eventually she was engaged to play a bit in a vaudeville sketch for which she rehearsed for eleven weeks without pay and which lasted six performances and then closed. She continued to haunt the offices of managers and agents but always received the proverbial turn down, *"You're not the type."* In her frustration she wrote a poem, using their words as its title.

YOU'RE NOT THE TYPE

I looked for work in early fall,
And could not find a part at all.
I looked and looked and looked and then
I looked and looked and looked again,
I looked and looked and now it's Spring,
And still I haven't anything.
Too fat, too thin, too short, too tall,
Too blonde, too dark, too large, too small.

An office boy my dreams would thwart,
"You're not the type," I'd hear him snort,
So then I asked a big producer,
"Oh, let me play a part for you, sir!"
And as my eye he saw me wipe,
He yawned and said, "You're not the type."
A playwright next I interviewed,
My heart with highest hopes imbued.

He turned away and lit his pipe,
And shortly said, "You're not the type."
To see an agent then I went,
My shoes worn out, my money spent.
The agent smiled, and said, "My dear,
You're not the type, come in next year.
For doubtless then I'll be engaging."
And I departed, madly raging.

So here within my furnished room,
At last I face my awful doom.
I'll starve and go (I hope) above,
And this is what I'm dreaming of —

○ ○

> Perhaps if I am very good
> And play my harp as angels should,
> Saint Peter will be kind to me
> And lend me once his Golden Key.

> I hope to see upon the stair
> Imploring for admittance there,
> Producers, playwrights, agents too,
> And all the deadly office crew.
> When my familiar face they see
> They'll say, "Don't you remember me,"
> Then from the Pearly Gates I'll pipe,
> "Oh, go to hell! You're not the type."

In later years Howard Lindsay and Russel Crouse had a large framed copy of these verses hung on their office wall.

Her meager funds were running out, and when they did, she knew she'd have to go back home. In her misery over losing out on the job in the Owen Davis play, she turned to Howard for advice. This surprised him, as their meeting had been a perfunctory "Mr. Lindsay, this is Miss Stickney," but he took her out to lunch. In an article entitled "I Knew Dorothy Stickney When . . ." he remembered that

> she could have been a pretty girl except that her face was too drawn and taut, partly due to unfulfilled ambition, partly to her present despair . . . She wanted to act. It wasn't a case of wanting to be an actress. She wanted to act. There is a vast difference.

Her stage experience was practically nonexistent. She had started out as a member of a quartet called The Southern Belles, four girls whose only claim to the name "southern" was that one came from South Dakota, another from South St. Louis and a third from South Bend, Indiana. Their act, Dorothy explained, was "fiddling, dancing, heavy dramatic sketches, piano-playing, costume mending, crying and acute homesickness." They played such towns as Rosebud, Montana; Whitefish, North Dakota; and Cutbank, Utah. Their

○ ○

tour was called off after a performance when the audience consisted of the ticket-taker and one usher.

It is remarkable that she could have been able to go on tour at all. From the age of three to seventeen, she had been periodically incapacitated with corneal ulcers. After seven eye operations she gained enough vision to go to Minneapolis, where she trained in the North Western Dramatic School.

She told this in bits and pieces when she sought out Howard for advice. That advice, given in a kindly but firm manner, was that she give up any idea of the stage and return to Dickinson, North Dakota. She thanked him, but never followed it. Shortly after this, she got her first break when she was engaged as the ingénue in a summer stock company at Skowhegan, Maine, where she proved to be a good little actress and a great favorite with the local theatre-goers. She had been there two seasons when Howard Lindsay came up as director. The management agreed to give him the choice of plays for the summer repertoire and also the selection of an all-new company — with the exception of Dorothy Stickney, who, they stipulated, must be re-engaged for the ingénue roles. He balked at this. To him she was an unknown quantity and he had no confidence in the management's praise of her talent. His objections were overruled and he grudgingly accepted the verdict. In addition, he again took her out to lunch.

A season in summer stock can be hard work, with its weekly change of bill which means rehearsing the new show during the day and playing the current one at night, and doing matinees on Wednesdays and Saturdays, all the while endeavoring with zeal and desperation to memorize lines. However, a summer stock experience can be richly rewarding not only in training but in its sense of freedom, uninhibited by the restraints of Broadway management or the menace of dramatic critics. If the weather is good and the company

○○○

congenial, there is a pervading holiday spirit. In whatever spare time there can be, older actors take leisurely walks in the sun or read, while the younger ones, including the college student "apprentices" employed as stagehands, scenery painters, errand runners and purveyors of Coca-Cola, can catch an occasional swim or a game of tennis during the day and after the evening show foregather in dedicated groups to discuss the play, their parts, Art, Life and further topics dear to starry-eyed youth.

Howard enjoyed it all. He enjoyed being in charge, running the playhouse on a community basis, seeing that they all ate together at one long table off the main dining room, discouraging any undue mingling with the hotel guests as being unprofessional. He enjoyed directing. He enjoyed the fact that he was free to choose the plays, and those he chose were usually ones in which he could cast himself. And did. In some he was good. In others he was not. There was still a certain reserve in his stage presence. It was as though he were hesitant to reveal his warm, humorous and friendly nature. There were even times when he was not completely dependable, as when, during a performance of *The Poor Nut*, in the middle of a scene with Nedda Harrigan he suddenly forgot his lines. Instead of the traditional reaction of freezing with horror, he broke up into uncontrollable giggles and kept saying, "Stop laughing!" to Nedda, who remained perfectly calm and kept throwing him lines. Yet he persisted in his determination to be an actor, although the season he directed *Hamlet* with himself as the melancholy Dane, his performance must have been little short of deplorable.

Howard Lindsay seldom swore. His most frequent expletives being "Well, I'll be a son of a bitch!" or a very loud "OH, DAMN!" (even before he immortalized that expletive in *Life with Father*). Yet in Skowhegan one afternoon, someone caught him, after things had gone wrong at the theatre,

○ ○

in the process of attacking a tree with vicious kicks and emitting a stream of profanity. After some ten minutes he managed to kick much of the frustration out of his system and became his pleasantly contained self again.

More and more he enjoyed the fact that Dorothy Stickney
was in the company. He found her to be a tireless worker,
eager to learn and grateful for his advice. Frequently they
played opposite each other and this he enjoyed too. As he
wrote in the article about her:

> Toward the end of the season we did *Outward Bound*. Dorothy
> and I played the "half-ways" . . . the pathetic young couple who
> have committed suicide on earth, and who drifted through the
> play clinging to each other.
>
> We discovered that we were clinging to each other off-stage
> too. In the scene-dock there was a large comfortable chair by a
> window where the scenic artist used to sit waiting for the paint to
> dry. We'll never forget that chair because sitting in it we fell in
> love.
>
> I had been married before, and it hadn't worked out. I told
> Dorothy I had been a failure as a husband, that I thought I would
> always fail as a husband. I strongly advised her not to marry me.
> Did she take my advice?

Fortunately, of course, she did not. However, at that time
neither of them had enough money to warrant getting married. In the meantime, they became engaged. In their exuberance they could not resist announcing the news to the
world in general. The company was delighted, as were the
local theatre-goers. It was written up in one of the Bangor
papers in the fatuous words of the women's page:

> The sweethearts make an interesting picture as they stroll about
> the grounds in their sport clothes, rehearsing or discussing
> "shop" as they go. The dainty and vivacious little ingénue wears
> a blouse and knickers, with her blond hair bobbed and confined
> by a ribbon. Mr. Lindsay's costume is not dissimilar (except for
> the bob!). He also wears knickers and a sportshirt open at the
> throat.

○ ○

It was two years before they felt they could afford to get married and during that time their professional careers began to prosper. Dorothy through determination and Machiavellian ruse managed to bag herself a show-stopping part in *Chicago*, Maurine Watkins' melodrama about the underworld in that gang-harassed city. Another actress had already been signed up to play Crazy Liz, but dainty little Miss Stickney yearned to impersonate this elderly, demented scrubwoman. Dressed in items she found in her wardrobe trunk, shabby clothes and a battered hat perched on top of her skinned-back hair, she haunted the offices of Sam Harris, the producer, kept waylaying him, offered to understudy for nothing and badgered him until, out of exhaustion and the kindness of his heart, Harris said she could watch a rehearsal provided she sat in the back row of the house and let no one know she was present. There follows the theatrical fairy-tale ending. The girl due to play Crazy Liz failed to show up. Dorothy was summoned from the dark to come up onto the stage and read the part — result: Dorothy Stickney made her first Broadway hit. Howard was beamingly proud of her performance. "When friends or strangers would mention having seen 'Chicago,' " he wrote, "I would chime in, 'My fiancée is in that company. She plays Crazy Liz.' Their minds would go back to the toothless old scrubwoman they had seen in the play and their congratulations would be faint and forced."

During those same two years, Howard Lindsay kept busy as an actor playing not very important parts in not very important plays. What was of real significance was that gradually he was growing in stature and was more in demand as a director. Throughout his career as one of the country's most capable practitioners of that métier, his methods never varied. His instructions were never indirect. Never, like the producer Arthur Hopkins, did he leave his actors to fumble about on their own, making their own moves, finding their own places, interpreting their lines as the fancy took them. Nor did he go in for the deep soul-searching analysis of the later more cerebral directors. Howard Lindsay was primarily a "pro" who loved *good theatre* and who demanded "pro" perfection from his actors. Before a first rehearsal, he went over the script time and again. He figured out every position, every move. He knew just how he wanted each line delivered. If an actor failed to give him the reading he wanted, he'd act out the line for him. If the actor still said it the wrong way, Lindsay would imitate his faulty reading, sometimes to the point of caricature, which might have been a bit tough for the actor but showed more clearly where his fault lay than any analytical correction. He had an uncanny way of expressing what he wanted. Once when he was directing his wife in a love scene and it was not coming across he said, "Dorothy, be starry-eyed," and she caught on right away.

With every passing year, Howard Lindsay was to become more and more established as a reliable director. Other actors relied on his judgment, even such seasoned ones as the Lunts. In 1924 these delightful experts were the top players for the Theatre Guild and found themselves having trouble with their rehearsal performances in Molnar's *The Guardsman*. They were also having their personal troubles with the bigwigs of the Guild, that highly self-confident board of directors who were not the easiest lot to get along with. The Lunts were unhappy and sent for Lindsay to tell them what was wrong. His analysis was simple. "This is a comedy," he said, "and you aren't having any fun." They began having the sort of fun that only the Lunts can conjure up and *The Guardsman* was the hit of the Guild season.

For all his strictness, Lindsay got on well with his actors. Being one himself, he knew the agonizing insecurities of the average player. He knew that each needed a pat on the back now and then — chiefly now. In contrast to that inscrutable type who says little to the cast but whispers in consultation with author or producer, then dismisses everyone with a cryptic "come back at two," letting them file out like condemned criminals, Howard was generous with words of commendation when deserved or clear in directions for improvement when required.

Nothing could deter his determination to produce a "good show" — even his not infrequent spells of hypochondria. An actress who played under his direction and knew him well tells of one time when he arrived for rehearsal feeling acutely faint, or imagining that he did. After calling the cast to start the first scene, he tottered out into the front, where he sat slumped in a seat, brooding about the precarious state of his health. "Suddenly," said the actress, "one of the performers read a line the wrong way. With a cry of 'No! No! that's not at all the way it should be said!' he sprang from his chair and bounded onto the stage with the agility of a teenager, took over the entire scene and put the cast through their paces with the vigor of a tireless martinet."

At the finish of the Skowhegan season in 1927, Howard and Dorothy pooled their resources and decided that their joint finances warranted matrimony. They were married in the nearby town of Waterville. From that day on, they looked upon Maine as their favorite state.

For a short time they lived in what was called an apartment but was little better than a bed–sitting room, kitchenette and bath on East Sixty-second Street, but they soon took up more commodious quarters in a two-room duplex at 41 West Tenth Street. Later, in 1936, they bought a house at 50 West Eleventh Street. It was a delightful old New York brownstone, charmingly furnished by Dorothy, whose taste ran to the Victorian especially after the success of *Life with Father*. Here

○ ○

they lived for eighteen years. Then Dorothy again felt the urge to move, her chief excuse being that she was a late sleeper, seldom getting up before noon, and their neighbors had four yelling children and two barking dogs. A large townhouse was for sale on East Ninety-fourth Street and she persuaded Howard to buy it. He would have been happy to remain where they were, especially as it was within easy walking distance of the Players Club. When he gently protested that Ninety-fourth Street seemed a long taxi ride uptown, Dorothy blithely replied, "But, Howard, we'll be going against traffic!"

Dorothy always had her way. At the same time it was she who had to attend to all the practical details. At the time of one of their *déménagements,* Howard took a room in a hotel, to write a play, he said, while Dorothy stayed on amid the mess and confusion of departure. What must have been the greatest trial was that the movers arrived at seven A.M., an ungodly hour for her. In the midst of the turmoil Howard rang up with the consoling words, "Don't worry, darling, I've taken care of the newspapers. They'll send them all to the new house." "And that," said Dorothy, "was Father Lindsay's contribution to the job of moving."

To Howard it was a highly essential contribution, for he was a compulsive reader. He perused every news item, every editorial, every obituary, every ad of every paper — and he subscribed to them all. One Christmas Dorothy presented him with a huge pile of old newspapers prettily tied with a red ribbon and he read each one of them with relish.

Their existence together was warm and beautifully congenial. They shared the same interests, the same tastes. They were fond of the same friends, of whom there were many and to whom their door was always open. Wherever they lived, although there were never to be any children, there was a sense of "family." Theirs was a mutual communication as

○ ○

established as that of two persons who have spent most of their lives together. Their conversation often included those shortcuts to explanation that become "family sayings." Two of them were culled from vaudeville comedians. One was a line from a monologist telling about trying to rescue a cat from the top branches of a tree. After climbing up, he found himself confronted by a snarling wildcat and he also found it almost impossible to get down. His account ended with, "I never got so tired of one animal in my life." The other was delivered by Harry Kelly, whose specialty was a skit called *The Deacon*, in which he wore a Prince Albert, a top hat and a mournful expression. In one bit, as he is sitting at a table in a restaurant, he is approached by a waiter, who inquires if he is enjoying his soup. His sorrowful reply is, "I'm sorry I stirred it." Howard was to write, "Whenever Dorothy tells me of some unpleasant experience she has been through and says, 'I never got so tired of one animal . . .' I know just how she feels. And when I report to her about some activity in which I've gotten myself involved and say, 'I'm sorry I stirred it,' she knows at once about my despair and regret."

They loved to have their friends drop by of an evening. They loved to be by themselves, often reading aloud to each other. Many times their evenings extended through the night. Once during their early married days in the Tenth Street duplex, Howard startled Dorothy by announcing that he was going to bed as he had an early business meeting the following morning. "But, Howard!" his bride protested, "you and I always watch the sunrise together!" In spite of this moving plea, he was adamant. Next morning as he was about to leave, Dorothy, leaning over the upstairs newel post, called down to him, "Howard Lindsay, you are a stranger to me!" He still went on his way.

Dorothy was notoriously extravagant. Howard was never overly careful with his money when he had it; he knew less

○ ○

than nothing about investing it, and there was always his lavish generosity in helping friends who were down and out. Acquaintances used to predict that the Lindsays would end up broke. However, if they cast their bread upon the waters, it came back rich cake. As an example, the farm they purchased in New Jersey in 1932 seemed a wild expenditure, yet today it could sell at quadruple the cost.

The Lindsays were essentially city people and yet they loved their place in New Jersey. Dorothy especially enjoyed fixing up and refurbishing the charming old Colonial house and entertaining their friends there for weekends. What she enjoyed less was when Howard chose to drive their car. She herself was an excellent driver. Howard was an abominable one. When they were cruising about the country, he'd more than once go off the road and end up in some open field or wooded grove, at which his only comment would be, "How did we get here?" A more amazing comment would arise when Dorothy would see a car coming from the other direction and seemingly heading straight for them. In reply to Dorothy's panic-stricken "Watch out, Howard. Here comes another car!" he'd simply say, with the utmost calm, "He sees me." And when she asked him to slow up going around a curve on a slippery road he'd say, "I know it's dangerous. That's why I want to get around it in a hurry."

Howard's nephew Walter Wagner tells of a time in New York when he came across his distinguished uncle standing beside a new car which he had just acquired (having also acquired a few drinks). Anxious to show off his new purchase, he hailed Wagner, ordered him to get in and announced in his most elocutionary voice, "I shall do the driving." With marked reluctance the nephew obeyed and they started, from the West Fifties to Sixth Avenue and Ninth Street, going through every light, red or green, on the way.

○ ○

They ended up triumphantly crashing into a stanchion of the Elevated. While walking away from the wreck, Howard remarked with great dignity, "I don't see why Mayor La Guardia needs eight months to take down the El. I can do it in two or three days and at a nominal fee."

Then there was the time when he had been summoned to Hollywood to help out on a script. He had bought a new Ford roadster and had rented a house on Vermont Avenue on the side of a hill, the front entrance and garage door being on the uphill side, and the back of the house supported on stilts overhanging some sixty feet of precipitous height. One of the first things Howard did after arrival at his new temporary habitat was to drive through the back wall of the garage, leaving the rear of his car dangling over the mountain drop. He immediately called the dealer, who reassured him that there would be no problem and came over at once to collect the vehicle, which he repaired and brought back within a few days. A week or so later, the same thing happened and Howard again called the dealer, who said in some astonishment, "But Mr. Lindsay, we fixed your car," at which Howard explained, "I know. But the car seems to have done it again." Luck was sometimes on Lindsay's side. A lawsuit was brought against him by someone whom he had run into. Howard's lawyer won the case by pointing out the fact that although his license read "Must wear glasses" the words "while driving" were not included.

Dorothy's extravagant spending went in part for clothes, but more particularly for antiques, with which she all but cluttered the rooms of wherever they were living. Whenever the Lindsays were out in their New Jersey house, she scoured the countryside in her never-ending quest. One day as she, Howard and Russel Crouse were racing along a side road with Howard at the wheel, a traffic cop stopped them and

asked what their hurry was, at which Crouse informed him
that "the lady is in a rush to buy some antiques and we want
to get there before they become any older."

There were to be special occasions when Dorothy's charming collection of *objets d'art* were not put on display. She
took care to hide them whenever Howard's mother came to
visit. That lady was described by her son as "a small, deli-
cate-looking woman, a wisp of New England granite." She
had a native sense of strict economy. She disapproved of the
young Lindsays' having a part-time maid and she always
asked how much they had paid for every Christmas present
they gave her. It was six months before she met her new
daughter-in-law and in one of his "Phoenix Nest" contributions, Howard wrote:

> She knew I had married an actress. I am sure she had imagined
> her to be somewhat like the lush female on the poster of "The
> Girl from Rector's." She was not prepared for that wide-eyed
> chit of a child stretched out on the couch, her pale forehead con-
> tracted in pain. I explained to mother that Dorothy was not well.
> She had a severe headache. All her life, mother had been subject
> to what were then called "sick headaches" and she was instantly
> sympathetic. What we could not tell mother was that Dorothy
> was suffering from her first hangover.

The night before, the Lindsays had been at a party in the
Village given by Miriam Hopkins, where they talked and
laughed and sang old songs and drank more than either was
accustomed to. "That Dorothy was to meet her mother-in-
law the next day seemed unimportant," Howard wrote and
went on:

> I had ordered a simple and frugal dinner which mother seemed to
> enjoy. Dorothy sat with us at the table, ate little and contributed
> little to the conversation. After the coffee had been served,
> mother held Dorothy's eye and asked, "What do you do with
> your old coffee grounds?" The throb in Dorothy's temple jumped
> into high gear. Had my wife been in perfect health and high

spirits I submit this was an unfair question. "I don't know what we do with them," she stammered, looking very guilty. "I guess we just throw them away." "You can use them for flavoring," mother said smugly. "Make your own coffee jello."

I too had been bewildered by mother's question, but now I knew that mother had accepted our marriage and was trying to contribute to it.

It was an ideally happy marriage. Dorothy loved her husband with a devotion that was almost worshipful. And he adored her. Yet his adoration of her as a wife never interfered with his judgment of her as an actress. He knew, perhaps better than she, what she could play and what she couldn't. The only period of stress between them came in 1945 with *State of the Union,* the Lindsay and Crouse play which won the Pulitzer Prize. Leland Hayward was producing it, Ralph Bellamy was to star and Dorothy was determined to have the feminine lead. Howard was equally determined that she shouldn't. She was not right for the part. (It was eventually played by Ruth Hussey.) Dorothy was hurt and bitter. It was some weeks before she would even speak to Howard and the atmosphere in their house was one of acute tension. It was a difficult situation for Crouse and Hayward as well. However, Lindsay was convinced that if he allowed love for his wife to sway his better judgment, he would be disloyal to the theatre, and he stood by his decision with the firmness of Richard Lovelace telling Lucasta that he could not love her so much, loved he not honor more. The rift, in time, healed itself.

Except for this one trying interlude which, after all, was caused by a professional situation, the private life of Howard Lindsay and Dorothy Stickney continued on its joyous way. On May 12, 1968, the Mary MacArthur March of Dimes Award was given to the Lindsays. Howard had died three months before, so the honor was handed to his widow as

○ ○

meant for them both. A résumé of their joint existence was read by David Wayne and me before a large audience in the New York Hilton ballroom. It started off with a poem Dorothy had written to Howard not long after they were married:

By way of the park on a misty night
We enter the country of heart's delight;
Away from realities dross and drab
My love and I in a hansom-cab.

The clock in a neighboring tower shows two,
The hurrying cars in the park are few,
So we jog along on our hansom throne,
The king and queen of a land our own.

We're out from under the city's roofs.
The soothing rhythm of horse's hoofs
Are beating a song on the asphalt wet
The curves like a river of gleaming jet.

And stretching away on either hand
Are lighted vistas of Fairyland.
Against the sky is a castle tall
A glamor and glory has touched it all.

We talk a little of that and this,
We hum a tune and we lean to kiss,
And laugh that a man in a taxi stares
At love's-young-dream-in-a-cab, who cares?

So hand in hand in a sweet content
We drive and drive till the money's spent,
Then we drive toward home when it's half past three;
The horse is sleepy and so are we.

He delighted in Dorothy's acting when she was correctly cast and he was dotingly proud of the program she later worked out completely on her own, "A Lovely Light," consisting of short readings from the poems and letters of Edna

○ ○

St. Vincent Millay. He came to see it time and again, and when he did, he laughed and cried unashamedly over her touching performance. Sitting one evening in her dressing room and watching her make up her face, he startled her by asking suddenly and in the most loving of tones, "Aren't your eyes too far apart?"

In 1938 Dorothy Stickney opened in *On Borrowed Time* with Dudley Digges and Frank Conroy. Howard came to the dress rehearsal and saw his pretty wife dressed and made up as a grandmother in her seventies. When Dorothy returned to the house she found a telegram from Howard saying, "Darling, I can hardly wait!"

Howard Lindsay came into his own as a playwright in 1933 with *She Loves Me Not*. This was a dramatization of a novel by Edward Hope Coffey about some zany goings-on at Princeton when a toothsome nightclub hoofer, who is wanted as a witness to a murder, dashes into the dormitory quarters of four seniors, clad only in her spangled bra and shorts under a concealing cloak. The chivalrous students offer her refuge and there ensue complications involving the police, the Communist party, the press and eventually the motion picture industry. The producers, Dwight Deere Wiman and Tom Weatherly, who had read the book, tossed it to Lindsay, telling him that if he could get a play out of it they'd put it on. Howard took it with him on his first trip to Europe with Dorothy, and in a small Austrian hill town above Innsbruck he tackled the job. By carrying his typewriter down to a little summerhouse at the end of a garden and working all day, he finished the script in a short time.

Wiman and Weatherly were delighted with it and engaged Raymond Sovey to design the set. Sovey constructed an ingenious affair built on two platforms at the center of the stage showing the rooms of the four students, and at either side small stages for short scenes in the dean's office, Com-

○ ○

munist headquarters, and quick flashes of people in telephone booths. Howard was signed up as director and a good
cast was assembled. It included Burgess Meredith, John Beal
and Philip Ober. To play the little hoofer, the management
had picked Polly Walters from the chorus of one of their musicals. Howard told them to send her down to his house for
an interview and at the same time he asked Dorothy to listen
at the door and give him her opinion. Little Miss Walters
was sure it would turn out to be one of those lustful-
manager-helpless-chorus-girl interviews but she went cheerfully if a little cautiously. It must have come as a surprise to
find herself received by a kindly gentleman whose manner,
which was almost fatherly, put her instantly at ease.
Dorothy, listening at the door, heard her husband ask the girl
if she would like to be an actress. The answer came in the
sort of childish voice and accent typified at that time as
"chorine," saying, "Oh yes, Mr. Lindsay! I don't think
there's much future in adagio dancing." Dorothy's opinion
was, "She'll be a triumph of type-casting!"

Just before rehearsals started, Howard received a telephone
call from a young actor named Joshua Logan. Lindsay knew
him only as a member of the University Players, that talented
group of budding college graduates who had made an impression with their summer theatre in Falmouth and later
their own stock company in Baltimore and whose number included Henry Fonda, Margaret Sullavan, Myron McCormick,
Norris Houghton and Bretaigne Windust. Now arrived in
New York, Josh Logan was desperately looking for a job, any
job, in the theatre. Financially, he was down to one quarter
in his pocket. He figured that it was good for five phone
calls. If they proved unproductive, he'd give up all thoughts
of the stage and go back home. After spending four futile
nickels, he rang Lindsay, who, thanks to his concern for
young actors and his genuine desire to see them get ahead,

○ ○

said he'd find a place for him. It wasn't much of a place. Joshua Logan was hired as assistant stage manager and as understudy for eleven people at Junior Equity minimum, which was twenty-five dollars a week. It was later raised to thirty-five. Remembering Lindsay in those days and in later years, Josh said, "He was as near a saint as anyone I ever knew."

Opening night, Lindsay escaped to the Players Club for his customary therapeutic game of pool. He needn't have. *She Loves Me Not* was an immediate hit. Brooks Atkinson wrote that nothing said in his review could "convey the exuberance that roars out at the 46th Street Theatre. Last night the audience grew more and more helpless as this hare-brained comedy danced a leap-frog through imaginative absurdities . . . Staging a hurly-burly comedy as resourcefully as this involves tremendous technical skill. As his own director Mr. Lindsay has finished the job perfectly. 'She Loves Me Not' races through a blaring evening without stumbling for a moment . . . A rousing, romping junket of fun, spontaneous, guileless and tumultuous." Gilbert Gabriel of the New York *American* said: "Last night's laughter was prairie wide and fire-engine loud. We were seeing the funniest show in years," while John Mason Brown in the *Evening Post* claimed that "it forces you to check your common sense with your hat, and compels you to laugh yourself blue in the face by the ceaseless invention of its writing, by the swift excellence of its production and the rollicking spirits of its fooling." For the next few weeks Howard Lindsay was hailed by the press as the country's newest and most brilliant young playwright. All such adulation Lindsay brushed aside with characteristic modesty. Even years later he told Howard Teichmann: "I don't think of myself as a literary person, although I earn my living as a writer. I don't think of myself as a playwright per se. By being in the theatre for a number of years, I gradually came to sense how a scene was built, what a curtain of an act

○ ○

should be like, and I gradually began to sense the effect on an audience."

The New York run of 248 performances thrived on packed houses. There was one slight moment of anxiety for the management when Metro-Goldwyn-Mayer objected to one of the lines. This was when the actor playing a talent scout calls his office, saying, "Send over that picture, the one so lousy even Metro won't release it." The objection was overruled by Lindsay, who insisted that the line stay in.

The following summer Gilbert Miller imported the production and cast to London for what looked to be a sure-fire success. The company arrived with high hopes. Joshua Logan was promoted to first stage manager with only two parts to understudy. He and most of the men in the company went off immediately to Savile Row to order new suits. Unfortunately, the orders had soon to be canceled. This totally American farce was incomprehensible to British audiences and it closed a week or two after it opened.

Among Howard Lindsay's many interests and activities were numerous ones which show the man's keen public-spiritedness and his knowledge of current politics. At one time he was elected chairman of the Arts Division of Americans for Democratic Action and, as spokesman for the committee, sent telegrams to Truman calling for the exclusion of supporters of States' rights, for changes of congressional rules to prevent filibusters and for checking the power of the House Rules Committee to strangle progressive legislation.

Another public-spirited endeavor to which he gave much of his time was the New Dramatists Committee, founded in 1950 by Howard Lindsay and Michaela O'Harra. Its purpose was to give new and unestablished professional playwrights a sense of identity with the theatre. The committee was an

ooo

impressive one, comprising as it did Richard Rodgers, Russel Crouse, Moss Hart, John Golden, John Wharton, Oscar Hammerstein II. They met every Tuesday in conference around a large table in a room over the Hudson Theatre, with Lindsay presiding like a benevolent parent. Michaela O'Harra wrote of him:

> A lot has been said about Howard Lindsay playing Father Day on stage. But there has been no word about his being Father Lindsay in "real life," the private life of the theatre family, and it's here, I think, that he gave the best of what he was most, as a man; to being to the "family's" new generation of playwrights what fathers are everywhere. What most men try to give to children of their own blood. Howard gave to our theatre's bloodstream . . . what, more than anything else, keeps the theatre alive and effective generation after generation . . . its continuing supply of new, gifted, produceable playwrights. Before 1950 a writer might "get his toe in" by way of an option or a first production, and if it wasn't a hit, where was he? Just an obscure associate member of the Dramatists' Guild.

That organization held a meeting at the Adelphi Theatre which got out of control as these frustrated playwrights started shouting demands: "Abolish agents!" . . . "Kill the critics!" . . . "Produce our plays!" "Suddenly," continued Miss O'Harra,

> a member of the Guild rose. Thinning sandy hair, wearing glasses. He wasn't very impressive from where I sat. Except for his courage. But suddenly he had them calmed down. He listened, peering down over those footlights, quietly getting articulate, sensible questions from some, articulate if impossible demands from others. He listened a long time (and Lindsay was a man who "listened with his heart") . . . and I thought, "That man cares!" It was Howard, of course.
>
> Then other professionals listened and at once many acted. Robert Sherwood for the Playwrights' Company said, "For years we've been looking for a way. This is it!" John Golden wrote

complaining, "All I've tried to do for playwrights . . . and this is the best way yet — and you haven't even asked me for money and I'm mad, but here's my check for $3000!"

Howard was somebody who was somebody in the theatre; and in one man he was every knowing professional who must pass judgment on a script before a curtain can ever be raised on it, he symbolized the whole . . . he cared . . . not just about playwrights as such, but about the theatre, first, last and always it was the *whole* theatre to which he gave.

He gave so much . . . season after season, to successive groups crowding round tables in the big shadowy rooms up above the Hudson or Empire or City Center theatres he gave continual stress to what he believed was the most vitally significant function of the playwright . . . and theatre . . . in the larger scale of things. He said, "Your job is to give to the audience. No matter what kind of play you write, give the best. The audience may be enraged, divided, engaged, transported, insulted or enchanted, but they must never be bored." Mr. Lindsay's unbreakable rule, writ large, is what the New Dramatists can continue to hold up as a beacon before the eyes of today's and tomorrow's playwrights. Father Lindsay took seriously his parental responsibilities. I can still see him standing there, peering down behind those footlights, still caring like hell about the whole theatre, and still — at any self-indulgence of us even dreaming we can live without the others — exploding with, "OH GAAHD!"

Those first months of the New Dramatists were rewarding ones for their founders and sponsors. They helped launch and promote the careers of Robert Anderson, Paddy Chayefsky and William Inge, among others.

Paddy Chayefsky wrote of his beginnings and the help and support he got from the New Dramatists Committee and especially Howard Lindsay. Remembering those meetings, he says:

I don't want to present Howard as a benign headmaster of a preparatory school. There was nothing paternalistic or undergraduate about it at all. Howard was the most incorrigibly professional man I ever knew. He evaluated the professional atti-

○ ○

tude to the austerity of an art. He was entirely concerned with the craft, the technique, the architecture, the manufacturing art, the actual writing and performance of a play, the presumption that drama was an art and anyone affecting to its practice was an artist. To him the practice was an art. It was all meat and potatoes. His way of saying it might be, "If it's a comedy, your curtain should be laughs. If it's a drama, your curtain should be dramatic. Wherever your biggest laugh is, it ought to be your second act curtain. If you're in trouble in the third act, take some dialogue from a secondary character and give it to the lead." Howard's workaday reflections are truer to the aesthetics of drama than anything I've ever read on the subject.

He gave to the New Dramatists many things, his time, his energy, his money, his theatre, but more than anything, he gave those qualities that celebrate him as a man, his substance, his self-respect and his integrity.

Howard's integrity and his compulsion to do the public-spirited thing prompted him to take a stand against the injustices of those "plague years," when innocent Americans were blacklisted as "Commies" in *Red Channels*. He wrote a letter condemning that vicious publication to the New York *Times* and was immediately smeared by *Counter-attack*, a similar hate-leaflet, at which *Variety* rushed to his defense, later saying, "But the transparent absurdity of the charges as well as the public stand he had taken did much to discredit and ultimately destroy not only the authority of *Red Channels* but the whole lynch-law movement it typified."

Lindsay openly championed the actress Jean Muir when her contract to play the mother in the radio series *The Aldrich Family* was canceled by the network on the same flimsy pretext of purported Communist leanings, and his letters to both Clifford Odets and Howard Fast show his concern when they too were senselessly persecuted.

It was not alone the theater which kept Howard Lindsay happily occupied — there was the Players Club. The Players

○ ○

Club, to Howard Lindsay, was sacrosanct. The fact that the gracious old dwelling on Gramercy Park had once been the home of Edwin Booth, that its members represented not just "Broadway" and "show biz" but the aristocracy of the American theatre, plus many of the country's best writers and illustrators, that it was the New York equivalent of London's Garrick Club, filled him with a certain awe and pride. He had been elected a member in 1918, and he loved the sense of tradition he felt whenever he made his way through the front door. He enjoyed taking an active part in the occasions which were unique to the Players. Edwin Booth's birthday, celebrated with the placing of a wreath at the foot of the Saint-Gaudens statue in the center of Gramercy Park. Founders' Night, when the members assemble in the Great Hall before the large fireplace under the superb Sargent portrait of Booth and pass around the loving cup bequeathed by Joseph Jefferson. And the various Pipe Nights, enlivened with dinner and brilliant speeches throughout the year.

On the retirement of Walter Hampden in 1955, Howard Lindsay was elected President of the Players. He accepted, of course, but with the stipulation that his term of office be limited to ten years. His fellow members accepted his terms but insisted that he retain the title of President Emeritus. They also wanted to emblazon his name across the arching lintel of a room, but that he declined, choosing instead a modest plaque, and explained, "You see, I haven't had much experience in being a room."

The Lindsay Pipe Night was held on October 30, 1960. Besides the customary dinner and the attendant speeches, it was the evening when his portrait, a fine likeness by Gordon Stevenson, was presented to the Club. Members who could not attend the celebration sent messages. Frank Sullivan wired:

○ ○

I am sorry I won't get to your hanging Sunday . . . I hope you'll let me say that I'm sorry I can't come to your Varnishing on Varnishing Day this Sunday . . . I doubt very much if you need a coat of varnish; you were manufactured in the days when the artist took some pride in his work. You can't get that kind of material these days.

Sight unseen I will say that you are fortunate to be done in oils by Gordon. I have always thought the portrait he did of Mark Twain, from photographs, was a masterpiece, and yours should be one, too, since he didn't have to do you from memory but had the original script right there in front of him . . .

Congratulations and love to you and Gordon.

The messages wound up with a reading of

The Verdict of the Players
to Howard Lindsay

In commemoration of a birthday which shall be ageless, and in recognition of a devotion to The Players which is timeless:

We, your fellow Players, honor you for your distinguished service to the theater as an actor, playwright, director and producer; for your stature as a man and your contribution to the world of men; for your wisdom and your wit and the ability to temper one with the other.

And by presenting to ourselves this portrait of you, we take this occasion to express our gratitude to you for your leadership as the fifth president of The Players, a true keeper of its traditions, a worthy successor to your illustrious predecessors, and a constant recipient of our love and affection.

The Pipe Master that evening, as might have been foreseen, was Russel Crouse. He started off his introduction saying, "I think it is an open secret that I am in love with Howard, in a nice way . . . but it's all right . . . everybody else is too."

Crouse was right. How the members of the Players loved Howard Lindsay! During his last illness when he was usually in his home confined to bed, he took it into his head

one evening to go down to the Club and make an unan-
nounced entrance into the bar. Every Player in that crowded
room, seeing him coming down the stairs, jumped to his feet
and joined the others in spontaneous applause.

PART II

○ ○

Russel Crouse

W hen the Kansas City *Star* was about to celebrate its eighty-fifth anniversary in 1965, a letter from the Anniversary Arrangements Committee, addressed to the "Secretary of Russel Crouse" and asking for "some vital statistics about your boss," arrived at the Crouse home. Within a few days the committee received the following reply:

Dear Anniversary Arrangements Committee,

I have your inquiry about my boss, Russel Crouse, and I will give you the real low-down, only I trust you will keep it confidential, as I wouldn't want him to know I ratted on him.

Russel Crouse is the typical Continental boulevardier-type — handsome, dashing, devilishly clever, quick on the *bon mot* and a little nuts. He is about two weeks younger than St. Augustine, Florida.

He flies his own plane, runs the one hundred yard dash in one hour and 17 minutes, makes all his own clothes, plays the glockenspiel with assorted symphony orchestras, and his pastime is making fudge, a sport popular in his youth. He paints pop art, being known in avant-garde circles and his family as Pop. He loves operettas, especially telephone operettas.

○ ○

You ask about his titles. I believe he has been knighted because he is called "Sir" by his two children, Timothy, a student at Harvard, and Lindsay Ann, a student in the Chapin School in New York, and by his two valets, three butlers and one footman, or chiropodist. He lives in New York on the sunny side of the street and has a summer villa in Villadelphia.

He is a playwright and some of his better known works are "Hamlet," "Abie's Irish Rose," "East Lynn" and "Ladies' Night in a Turkish Bath."

I must close now because I see him coming back from lunch with egg on his face. Anything else you want to know about him can be found in "Who's Who" under C. Also in "Who's Who in the Theatre" under C.

Yours Surreptitiously,
(I'm sorry I'm not allowed to give out my name to strangers)
Secretary to Russel Crouse

Needless to say the document was written by Crouse himself. One can imagine with what glee he described himself as the "typical Continental boulevardier-type." Certainly he dressed like anything but a boulevardier. His suits often gave the impression that he had slept in them. Seeing a snapshot of himself which glaringly showed up his rumpled trousers, he said to his wife, Anna, "Send back the negative and have my pants pressed." His jacket hardly ever fitted because he had a habit of stuffing his pockets with clippings, memos, uncashed checks and loose change. When sending one of his suits to the cleaners, Anna once found an uncashed check for $20,000 in an inside pocket. Howard Lindsay said, "Crouse is a human filing cabinet," and once when Crouse consulted a doctor, complaining of constant fatigue after climbing up steps, the doctor's sole prescription was, "Get some of that stuff out of your pockets."

As for his shirts, until he married Anna Erskine, they were a disaster. Of the drab gabardine ones Lindsay said, "He doesn't have to send them to the laundry. He can always

○ ○

have them sand-blasted." And of the others Frank Sullivan recalled: "Crouse's shirts!! They were never just brown. They were half a dozen colors like whatchacallit's coat of many colors in the Bible. They were awful. One of the reasons I think Anna is a great woman is because she made him quit wearing those goddam shirts after they got married."

Crouse's letter reveals one innate characteristic, his uncontrollable compulsion for punning. Goldsmith might have been writing about him when he described a friend as "That rare compound of oddity, frolic and fun / Who relished a joke and rejoiced in a pun." When his friends heard them they either laughed or emitted the traditional groan. Some of his puns were rather distressing, as when he announced that he was going to Saratoga to the spa, and added, "with my spa-ing partner." Others were captivating, like the one he made when he and his first wife, Alison Smith, were enjoying drinks at a sidewalk café in Paris, she having cocktails and he, who was by then a teetotaler, regaling himself on water. Russel hailed a waiter and said, "The lady will have another martini and I'll have a little more of the Seine."

Bad or good, his puns were part of the quietly humorous side of his nature just as his clothes were an indication of his complete selflessness. Charles Brackett, the author and film producer, said of him, "Buck is the most flawlessly gentle, tactful and witty being I know." And John Mason Brown at the Crouse memorial in May 1966 said in his tribute: " 'Enter smiling' runs the old stage direction. Buck always entered smiling. I think his wrinkled clothes were merely an extension of his smile."

Most of Crouse's friends called him Buck. Some say it derived from a successful prize fighter named Buck Crouse; others claim that it came from his ability, when a party was at its height, to spring to his feet and execute an astonishingly proficient buck and wing. Whatever the origin, it was a

○ ○

curious choice of nickname. As Abe Burrows said, "I never considered the name really suited him. 'Buck' sounds like a rugged cowboy and Buck was one of the gentlest human beings I've ever known. Of course he dressed as badly as a cowboy. Buck could take a $500 suit and make it look as though he'd made it himself."

Much of Russel Crouse's sunny nature, his interest and concern for his fellow man may have been an inheritance from his father. Hiram Powers Crouse was a born newspaperman and, in his way, a brilliant one. He had started out as a cub reporter on the Findlay, Ohio, *Republican* and had done his job so commendably that the owner, an elderly man on the point of retirement, gave the paper outright to young Crouse and an equally alert youth who went by the interesting name of Homer Eoff. Together these enterprising boys brought out an excellent daily — one which is still going today.

Hiram Powers Crouse's first and second names had been bestowed upon him by his father, who had a predilection for the works of the American sculptor Hiram Powers. He especially admired the artist's well-known and much-discussed *Greek Slave,* symbolizing "Greece enslaved by Turkey" — a female figure in a supplicating attitude and, except for a few chains and manacles, quite nude. It had achieved an immediate success at the London Crystal Palace Exhibition and some years later reproductions of this Victorian triumph began cropping up in American homes, the nakedness of the subject being mitigated by the noble appeal of the cause it depicted.

That the elder Crouse so admired this work of art to the point of naming his son after the sculptor sheds an interesting sidelight on the man's character, for he was a Lutheran minister. To be exact, he was an itinerant preacher, the sort known as a "circuit rider." Ohio in those days was sparsely settled, and churches in the little towns so inadequate, no community could afford a resident clergyman. The result was that the Reverend Mr. Crouse was obliged to cover his spiritual circuit on horseback. He'd ride to one small parish, deliver his sermon, then ride on to the next one and the next with whatever endurance his religious zeal and his horse's stamina could bear.

It was a migratory life, because the parson's headquarters were always temporary and every few years the ecclesiastical powers in charge would move him to a different section of the state. Hiram, his son, spent his childhood and adolescence in a variety of small Ohio towns. When, for a time, the preacher and his family were settled in Mount Cory, they bought their milk from a neighboring farmer named Schumacher, whose pretty daughter Sarah had the duty of delivering the cans every morning. Hiram Crouse told his son, Russel, about how he used to wake up early and lie in bed waiting for the delight of hearing the patter of Sarah's little feet on the back stoop. Hiram Powers Crouse and Sarah fell in love when Hiram was in his late teens and Sarah in her early ones, but they waited to marry until after the Crouse family had moved to Findlay and Hiram had landed his job on the Findlay *Republican*. The young couple settled in a modest house; then, after Hiram took possession of the paper, they moved into a more extensive one and life was good. Hiram, an outgoing, roly-poly, genial young fellow, was immediately popular with all the townspeople. His wife, a pretty though highly nervous woman, was liked well enough. Their first child was a daughter and the neighbors were politely congratulatory. When, however, in 1893, a boy made his entrance into the world, most of the local populace seems to have rejoiced, as one may gather from the newspaper clippings.

∘ ∘

Bro Crouse of the Findlay *Republican* rejoiceth exceedingly over the birth of a son . . . The *Republican* must be enjoying great success to afford such luxury.

The persevering editor of the Findlay *Republican* was presented with an eight pound boy last night, and this morning the paper came out with its two regular columns of bright and spicy editorials just the same as if nothing had happened.

It's a Boy!

When he came down late last night, Editor H. P. Crouse wore a smile so broad there was just room enough at one side of the street for his friends to come up in pairs and accept the "Green Seals" [cigars] which the gentleman was passing out recklessly. It's an eight-and-one-half-pound boy, looks like his father and is in favor of McKinley and protection.

"A high tariff is what we need!" cried a boy who arrived at the home of editor H. P. Crouse this week. Brother Crouse has a boy and a girl and with his new house is the happiest man in town.

The baby was christened Russel McKinley Crouse — the middle name the result of Hiram Crouse's admiration for William McKinley, who, though yet to be elected President of the United States, was an able governor of Ohio and the instigator of the McKinley Protective Tariff Act.

Russel's memories of Findlay were never very clear as he lived there only through his seventh year. He did, however, remember going to grade school and he also remembered one of his schoolmates. She was the postman's daughter, a little girl with long golden pigtails and the prettiest legs in Findlay. Even at his tender age he admired them as together they rocked to and fro on the swinging gate outside her father's house. Those legs were to dance their way from Ohio to Broadway, where they were hailed as "the loveliest legs in America" while their owner whirled enchantingly through *The Passing Show, Sunny* and *The Ziegfeld Follies.* Her name was Marilyn Miller. According to the press agent Richard

○ ○

Maney, when in later years Miss Miller and Mr. Crouse met on Broadway "they made vague plans to return to their home town one day in a coach drawn by four white horses, but somehow they never got around to it."

Pleasant as life was in Findlay and successful as he was as its leading publisher, Hiram Crouse felt the need to branch out into wider fields. As a desirable locale, he chose Toledo, a city whose two daily papers, the *News* and the *Bee,* he learned, were rapidly going downhill. Through loans from banks and friends he was able to buy up the two papers, merge them into one and produce the Toledo *News-Bee,* which in no time became the city's leading daily.

Those first years in Toledo were easy ones for the Crouse family. They had a comfortable, fair-sized house. They lived well and with little worry about expense, for Hiram Crouse, notwithstanding his brilliance as a journalist, had no sense of economy. He was a self-taught bibliophile and one of his extravagances was collecting rare books; in due course he built up a fine library, which was the pride of his heart. Few people realized the intellectual side of this affable man, who in Toledo enjoyed the same sort of small-town popularity he had in Findlay. He was a person of charm and wit and his nature was a sunny one.

If the gene theory is valid, these happy characteristics must have been passed on to his son. Throughout his life, Russel Crouse had a gentle humor and an affectionate concern for everyone he knew. After his death, Norman Nadel, the critic of the *World-Telegram,* referred to him as a man blessed with an abundance of love. "I have never known anyone," he wrote, "who could greet a friend with such gladness. When he asked you how you were, the world paused until you answered him you were all right. To him everyone mattered."

In contrast to his father, Russel's mother was a little woman with an uncontrollable temper, which not infrequently cowed

ooo

her children, particularly her son, who lived in apprehension
of committing some misdemeanor that might "make Momma
talk loud." A few of Sarah Crouse's genes may also have
been passed along to her son. As a very little boy Russel too
had a temper — although in the light of his later years this is
hard to believe. In 1954 he wrote an endearing letter of reminiscence to his children for the purpose of acquainting them
with family history. In this he told of one of his own juvenile
tantrums.

> . . . I remember very clearly we had just finished lunch and were
> in the dining room. I wanted to do something . . . I can't re-
> member what it was . . . but my mother said no. I flew into a
> violent fit of temper and I remember slamming a dining room
> chair on the floor. At this point I happened to look up and catch
> my mother's eye. I will never forget the look of heartbreak and
> anguish I saw there. It changed my entire life. I think from that
> moment on I have tried to have a consideration for others. I tell
> you this because I hope you will both learn this without having
> to hurt your mother.

However, in between those outbursts when "Momma talked
loud" Sarah Crouse was soft and feminine and had a deliciously infectious laugh and Russel later recalled that their
household rang with laughter most of the time.

Generally speaking, it was a warm and happy family and
one that had a strong sense of "togetherness" years before the
embarrassing word made a mockery of that estimable emotion. When most small Midwestern children ate their meals
early or out in the kitchen with the cook, the three young
Crouses (there was a second daughter by then) sat at table
with their parents, who went on the theory — extraordinary
at the time — that children should not only be seen, but also
heard. Conversation was general, animated and covered
many topics. Everyone, including the son and two daugh-

○ ○

ters, was encouraged to express views on whatever subject arose: never to be dogmatic about them, but to express them purely as personal opinions and open to discussion.

Russel went to an average public school where his grades also were average. He attended Sunday School every week, and, what's more, he enjoyed it. He was, in a few years, to teach Sunday-School classes himself, and all his life he attended church regularly. For Russel Crouse was a devout Christian in the best sense of the term although he never imposed his piety on anyone or even mentioned it. At the memorial ceremony after his death, Dorothy Stickney was to say, "Russel was a deeply religious man, but he didn't talk religion, he simply lived it."

Life in Toledo for the Crouse family was agreeable and thoroughly American. There were the usual holiday and birthday celebrations. Spring and summer there were outings to the country, excursions on a Lake Erie pleasure boat and, as a special treat on certain fine Saturdays, the three young Crouses, accompanied by their parents, would board an open tram and ride out to the local amusement park known as the Farm. After an hour of squealing rapture on the roller coaster, ferris wheel and further delicious panic-producing diversions, they would foregather in the picnic area to devour the contents of a well-stocked picnic hamper. Then would come the greatest treat, at least for Russel: attendance at the matinee of the park's Vaudeville House, which during the summer months presented a weekly variety bill.

From his own account, Russel at the age of eight met his first actor. The actor was all of six. They met by accident. Russel, having finished his last sandwich and downed his last bottle of pop, was working off meal and pent-up energy by cavorting over the empty benches and picnic tables. Suddenly he was joined by a boy smaller and obviously younger than he, on whom he instinctively looked down until he noticed his companion's extraordinary acrobatic agility. While Russel was clambering onto the benches and tables and then jumping off in lumbering awkwardness, the little fellow was either leaping from table to table in a single bound or turning an occasional cartwheel in the intervening spaces. Pausing to catch his breath, Russel asked him where he lived and the child, whose face, old for his years, had a deadpan expression, answered in equally deadpan tones, "Lots of places." Then he explained that he and his parents were in the vaudeville show the Crouse family were about to attend — information which enraptured Russel, who said he'd be sitting down front and asked the boy to wave to him. That young Roscius, clearly shocked at the mere idea of such theatrical unprofessionalism, said he could never do that but he agreed that, when the act was finished, he would lift his hat. At the matinee, Russel, shining-eyed with anticipation, was hardly aware of what went on during the opening numbers. Then finally a bizarre trio appeared — a lady in a spangled gown, a tall man in baggy trousers, battered stovepipe hat and Irish tramp make-up of semibald head and red beard; with them was an urchin, whom Russel recognized as his friend of the picnic grounds in spite of his make-up and costume, which was a diminutive replica of the man's. Their act was one of energetic clowning in which the little boy was used as a violently handled stooge (he was billed, it turned out, as "the Human Mop"), being dragged about the stage, swept up by a large broom and tossed off into the wings, whence he'd instantly run back for further good-natured manhandling. Throughout the entire act, the child wore an expression of intense solemnity. Russel watched with breathless wonder. Finally, to a flourish from the orchestra, the three lined up to take their bows. Recalling the event, Russel Crouse was to write:

○ ○

The man and woman were smiling. The boy's face was deadly serious. I thought he must have been hurt . . . and why not after what he'd been through. Then suddenly he lifted the silly little hat he wore and I remembered it was a signal. I waved but he didn't wave back. Just a stone face bowing. Then I noticed an easel at the side of the proscenium which read: "The Three Keatons . . . Joe, Myra and Buster." I never did see Buster Keaton again except on the screen. I never did see him smile.

The Crouses lived in Toledo for eight years and it was during that time young Russel acquired his interest in journalism. Whenever possible he spent his afterhours from school hanging about the *News-Bee* plant. Fired by an ambition to become in time an editor and publisher, he went so far as to publish his own newspaper. This he called the *Herald*. With access to type which had already been set up, he was able to cull enough previously printed items to fill four small pages of brown paper. He said that the only creative effort that went into this juvenile publication were the words "edited and published by Russel M. Crouse." He was eleven years old. The items he gleaned were hardly of national or international interest and the fact that the Russian fleet had been sighted off the Japanese coast was tossed lightly aside. He went in for more colorful excerpts: "Farmer swings to doom by suicide rather than face a mob in Albuquerque bent on lynching him as a cattle-thief." Or from Berlin, the astonishing announcement that "a brood of chickens has been hatched by a cat which attacked the hen each time it ventured to approach and continued to sit on the eggs until the chickens appeared. The chickens now follow the cat wherever it goes." One may also learn that Carrie Nation "looking for something to smash met a man too big to smash but open to adverse criticism. He was smoking a cigarette. Carrie objected to the cigarette and spoke out. The smoker objected to Carrie and knocked her down." Each copy of this

○ ○

enterprising little publication sold for one cent. How many editions of the *Herald* came out or how wide was the circulation is subject to conjecture.

Inspirited by his debut into the Fourth Estate, the young journalist three years later brought out a more ambitious newspaper. This was when he was a student at the Monroe High School. It was a weekly, the first public-school publication in Toledo. It is typical of Russel Crouse's quiet humor that he named it the *Monroe Doctrine*.

Hiram Powers Crouse had run his paper with unflagging public spirit. His editorials were perceptive and fearless and through them he brought about a number of civic reforms which for long had been glaringly needed. He had the courage to realize that Toledo needed a complete political clean-up, one which should totally break with the professional politicians. As a consequence of his campaign efforts, the city elected its first nonpolitical mayor in the person of Brand Whitlock, who went on to distinction as an eminent diplomat and American Ambassador to Belgium during the First World War. Hiram Crouse was by now one of Toledo's most respected citizens and, being an amiable man with a warm smile, he had a host of friends. Under his excellent guidance the *News-Bee* was running successfully — so successfully, the Scripps-McRae newspaper syndicate bought up a half-interest. It also bided its time until Crouse went on a trip to Europe. During his absence the syndicate, through some clever finagling, bought enough further stock to put it in the powerful position of being able to dictate the *News-Bee*'s policies. These policies were at complete variance with those of its high-principled editor, who in disillusionment and disgust sold off his own remaining shares and resigned.

His many friends plus a number of civic-minded citizens, distressed at the prospect of the city's losing an editor of such integrity, banded together, raised enough funds to buy the

○ ○

Toledo *Press* and placed Hiram Crouse's name at the top of the masthead. The Scripps-McRae syndicate, regarding this paper as an upstart challenge, launched an overwhelming assault on the Toledo *Press,* which, helpless against such competition, simply expired.

Its unhappy editor-publisher all but expired with it. He had lost one quarter of a million dollars of his own money and owed a similar amount. Hopelessly bankrupt, he was forced to sell his house and possessions, including every book in his beloved library. His health gave way and he had a complete physical and emotional breakdown.

This Toledo fiasco was the first of a series of financial disasters which, throughout his professional life, plagued this kindly, brilliant but improvident man. He was eventually to die owing thousands. How many no one ever knew, with the exception of his son, Russel. It was characteristic of Russel Crouse, who was then married to his first wife and struggling along on seventy dollars a week, that somehow in time he was able to pay off most of his father's liabilities.

After the editor's recovery, his friends begged him to stay on in Toledo and go into another business. But Hiram Crouse was first and foremost a dedicated newspaperman and he decided to stick to his trade, pull up stakes and move to some other and more distant part of the country. The part he chose was Oklahoma, which was indeed new and more distant territory, having just that year of 1907 been declared a state by Theodore Roosevelt.

For Hiram, the move meant starting out all over again on a clean slate — if that dust-blown prairie land can be compared to a clean slate. He settled in a town called Enid whose leading paper, the Enid *Daily Eagle,* was a pedestrian sheet with mediocre editorials, sadly in need of general overhauling. With his journalistic skill and his genial personality, he had no difficulty in acquiring requisite loans from the local banks.

ooo

He bought the paper and published it in a completely new format. It was an immediate success. The citizens were delighted that their town could boast of such a "citified" paper, and one enthusiastic subscriber wrote, "It would serve Enid's poky old editors right if Mr. H. P. Crouse of Toledo, Ohio, just put their hick sheets out of existence."

Enid is located in north-central Oklahoma. In 1907 the section was known as the Cherokee Strip, a fertile area that had once been the proud possession of the Comanche Nation. It goes without saying that the Comanches never forgave the White Man's intrusion. The atmosphere was still that of Frontier America. Most residents remembered the famous "Run" of '89 when, two million acres of choice land having been declared open free to homesteaders, one hundred thousand persons had lined up along the militia-controlled border waiting for the cannon fire which would be the signal for them to dash forth and stake their claims. They had dashed in every known sort of vehicle. Some even made the stretch on horseback and a few hastened and eventually limped along on foot.

Enid, little more than an Indian trading post before the Run, had mushroomed by 1907 into a sizable town. Most residents still lived on their claims in plain frame houses which, though two-storied, in place of inside staircases bore outside iron ladders as connection to upper floors. A few wealthy families were housed in more pretentious residences in the center of town while a number of settlers still lived contentedly enough in sod shacks on the outlying prairie land. Life centered on a five-acre main square surrounded by crude business buildings — dry-goods emporiums, hardware and harness outfitters, two banks, a twenty-four-hour lunch counter, a barber shop, the newspaper offices and plant and a rather ramshackle hotel. The sidewalks were made of wood and the awnings above them were made of wood too. The square itself had little shade except what filtered glaringly down from a few scraggly cottonwood trees. Dusty, sun-baked and wind-blown, the only vegetation of which it could boast was buffalo grass and a sad little plot of scarlet sage. All around the area ran an iron tie-rail to which were tethered

rigs of all kinds; buggies and carriages, tops up and tops down; farm wagons of all kinds, from light spring wagons to big red and green Studebakers; enormous hayracks, movers' covered wagons, closed town hacks, the weather-beaten yellow stage which ran only from the Square to the Rock Island depot at train times; buck-boards, carts, broad-tired drays, the splendid brewery trucks . . . and oh yes, the Moore phaeton with its colored driver handling the bays and the colonel's daughter, Miss Mabel, lean-ing back with a folded parasol on her lap, looking like a picture in a book.

The words are those of Marquis James from his book *The Cherokee Strip: A Tale of an Oklahoma Childhood.* James was later to become not only a distinguished journalist but twice a Pulitzer Prize winner for his biographies of Sam Houston and Andrew Jackson. He had lived in Enid since babyhood, his family having been among the first settlers. His father, in fact, alone in the saddle had made the historic Run of seven-teen miles in fifty-eight minutes without in any way injuring his horse. He had set up his stake in Range 6 west of the In-dian Meridian, built a house and sent for his family. The house was a substantial wooden structure painted yellow, double-storied. What's more, it had an interior staircase. Houstin James was a successful lawyer who soon rose to local fame as City Attorney. He also dabbled in journalism. His son Marquis was an alert young fellow, himself avidly keen on getting into the newspaper world. Having finished eighth grade, he managed to land a cub reporter job on the personal column of a weekly called *Events.*

After the Crouse family settled in Enid, the two boys became fast friends. Russel was impressed by the fact that Marquis was not only two years older than he but was actually working on a paper. And Marquis was impressed not only by Russel's smiling wit but by his middle name (William McKinley had been President, and, what added considerable luster, had been assassinated). Marquis called him "Mack" and so did his other schoolmates until they began to feel more mature and called each other by last names.

The two boys, fired by their journalistic ambitions, hit upon the idea of reviving a defunct high-school daily known as the *Evening Squeak*. They asked the elder Crouse if he would consider setting this publication on one of his linotypes at a cut rate. The editor told them kindly but definitely that he wouldn't begin to consider such a proposition. At another time Marquis James must have approached him about getting a job, for in his *Cherokee Strip* he wrote: "Mr. H. P. Crouse was an extremely affable man and so fat he couldn't see his feet. He would lace his fingers on his paunch and be vague so agreeably that it took some time to get on to the fact that he had no place for me on his paper."

Poor Hiram Crouse was soon to wonder if he had a place for himself on his own paper. Again financial disaster overtook him. As a matter of history, financial disaster overtook the entire country by way of the Panic of 1907 and banks were unwilling to advance any risky loans. The president of Enid's First National sorrowfully turned down H. P. Crouse's request for aid. But again, as had happened in Toledo, friends rallied to finance him in another publication and he established the Enid *Morning News*.

Although Russel was only fourteen, he still hankered to be a newspaperman — so much so that his father allotted him an off-hours job as assistant sports writer, covering chiefly the games out at the baseball park and occasional trotting races at the county fair. Again, to quote from the letter he

○ ○

wrote to his children some forty-three years later, "It was a great thrill and I am afraid that the moment my first literary effort, such as it was, appeared in print, my life's pattern had been set."

Frustration over their inability to republish the *Evening Squeak* didn't dampen the ardor of either young Crouse or James. They succeeded in bringing out a monthly magazine on their own without benefit of the elder Crouse's linotype. It bore the less frivolous title of *The Quill* and its masthead proclaimed:

Russel McKinley Crouse — Business Manager
Marquis E. James — Assistant Editor

The Quill was a success not only among the students and faculty of the high school but with the citizens of Enid. One paper paid it a special tribute, saying, "*The Quill* is an admirable example of student work . . . It is in magazine form, thirty-two pages, neatly bound and with many artistic headings . . . Many short stories, rhymes etc. make the *Quill*'s pages shine." A number of those short stories were contributions from Russel McKinley Crouse. One in particular, in a 1909 issue, called "Susan's Success," tells of a young woman from a small town coming to New York with scant funds but high hopes of becoming an eminent author. The simple tale is related in the first person singular as coming from one of Susan's admirers. It winds up: "Dear, impulsive, noble little woman! How successful an author she might become by that will of hers! Yet how much greater a wife! I know it's early . . . but I fear I must make a confession . . ."

Besides these budding indications that Russel would in time become a writer, he even then exhibited a sense of showmanship. Whenever entertainments were put on at the Enid High School, it was he who was the manager and pro-

ducer. He was the impresario of a highly successful entertainment "rendered" by the Demosthenean Society. It consisted of musical numbers, a recitation (in Latin) of "Mary
Had a Little Lamb" and the reading aloud of an essay, " 'The
Geography of Our New State' by its author McKinley
Crouse." The following year he arranged another bit of high
jinks, transforming the school gymnasium into what he
termed a "midway," with booths selling food or offering a
variety of simple entertainment. His special creation was an
attraction labeled "Seeing Enid by Night. Admission one
cent." It was written up in the paper the following morning:
"Opening the door to this room a cold wind met one and the
room was in total darkness. 'Seeing Enid by Night' was
managed by McKinley Crouse and was one of the huge sells
of the entertainment. The wind did blow through an open
window and the room was dark and looking out of that same
open window Enid in all her beauty was viewed by night."

For all Russel's success in amateur theatricals, his main interest, his passion, was always journalism. His father by
now was allotting him further assignments than sports on the
Morning News and it was after hours that the young fellow
began to develop a sense of the colorful, even the romantic,
aspects of working for a morning newspaper. This small Oklahoma metropolis was at night a sleeping town. The square,
by day a-swarm with activity, was ghostly in silence. The
shops and business buildings surrounding it were dark,
made darker by the deep shadows cast by the overhanging
wooden awnings. The intense heat of the day had, at sun-
down, been diminished by a dry breeze blowing in from the
vast prairie land. By twelve o'clock the only sound to be
heard was its rustle in the dry leaves of the cottonwoods, interrupted perhaps by the single sharp hoof stamp of a Comanche's horse tethered to the rail for the night. One or two
lighted windows might be visible — Cap Bond's restaurant,

○ ○

where a sleepy handyman was stacking chairs onto the empty tables prior to mopping up the sawdusted floor, or the all-night drugstore, which thrived mainly on a bootlegging business, for Oklahoma was one of the first states to go bone dry. One light that was certain to burn into the wee hours came from the windows of the *Morning News,* behind which staff and employees worked over the layout of the early editions.

Young Russel found this a magical experience. Throughout his career as a newspaperman he felt it a rare privilege to belong to the night people. He was at his best and most alert afternoons and evenings. Later, during his playwriting years, this was a quality he was to share with his partner, Howard Lindsay. Essentially a city man, he had no special love for the country and once announced blandly to a reporter, "My idea of a country estate is the Ritz-Carlton in Boston." This ordinarily sweet-tempered man went on to say that rural sounds irritated him. "Especially birds," he complained. "They get up early and wake me up. I don't like to get up early and I don't like to be waked up. That's why I stay in the city."

Russel graduated from high school if not *summa cum laude* at least sufficiently *laude* to have made a fine impression. Even at seventeen, Russel McKinley Crouse had definitely left his mark on Enid. In 1969, three years after his death, the high school posthumously honored him with its Pride of the Plainsman Award, a distinction singled out for the town's most distinguished citizen. It is pleasant to learn that Russel's pal, Marquis James, received a similar glorification.

After graduation, Russel had his heart set on continuing his education at Western Reserve in Ohio, but again family funds were in arrears and Father Crouse couldn't meet the expense. Instead, the good man, through some political friend, arranged for his son to apply for an alternate's appointment

○ ○

in the United States Naval Academy. This meant first trying to pass those terrifying, brain-breaking examinations. With high hopes, he went to Annapolis and for several weeks underwent rigorous cramming courses at Wilmer and Chew's Preparatory School. The day came around for the first examination, which was in geometry, and Russel filed into the impressive hall along with the other apprehensive candidates. The boy sitting directly in front of him took one look at the questions and fainted. (The list led off with: "If a quadrilateral inscribed in a circle is a parallelogram, prove that it is a rectangle. If a quadrilateral circumscribed about a circle is a parallelogram, prove that it is a rhombus.") Russel didn't faint. He simply didn't pass.

"And that," he said, "was one of the nicest things that ever happened to the United States Navy. During World War Two I would have been an admiral and I am sure that at some time during that struggle the Navy Department would have received word from the South Pacific that my flagship was up a palm tree."

Meanwhile his family had again undergone the financial reverses that seemed to be the scourge of the elder Crouse. In spite of his brilliant and courageous editorship, the Enid *Morning News* went bankrupt and the family was again forced to move on, this time to a town called Pawhuska in the Osage territory of Oklahoma. The place had barely emerged from being merely the guardian seat and chief trading post of an Indian reservation. By the time the Crouses arrived, there had grown up an urban community boasting five general stores, four hotels and rooming houses, three banks, four meat markets, four livery stables, three blacksmith shops, six eating places, three barber shops, four "millinery parlors," three wagon yards, two photograph galleries, two bakeries and two "Gents' Furnishings" establishments. The statistics are culled from a pamphlet about the Osage Nation entitled

○ ○

The Last Reservation. From this we gather that Pawhuska was still primarily an Indian community. The banks were governed by reputable officers of Osage birth who were well primed on tribal affairs. The public schools, although run by the government, were open only to fullbloods. For their education, young whites had to make do with whatever parochial schools were available. The Osage Council met every two months in the main hall of a municipal building which housed the offices of a judge, a U.S. Commissioner, two lawyers, a dentist, a real estate and insurance agent, the "Blue Point Restaurant and Young Mister Blanc's Barber-Shop." The Council meetings were summoned by Chief O-lo-ho-wal-la or his assistant, Chief Bacon Rind.

The atmosphere may have been colorful but life was a far cry from the worldlier existence of Toledo or, for that matter, Enid, and Russel must have been happy to forget this dismal interlude. Certainly he makes no mention of it in his letter to Timothy and Lindsay Ann.

Even in this frontier settlement, the usual financial disasters continued to plague Hiram Crouse and again he moved — this time to the more civilized locale of Kansas City. There he went to work for the Kansas City *Journal*, not in an editorial position but in some minor capacity. And that too must have been a further blow to the poor man's already battered pride.

In loyalty to this father whom, despite his shortcomings, he so loved, Russel told his children: "Your grandfather had passed the peak of his career and the rest of his life was not as successful as the early part. However, through all his adversity, I never knew him when he couldn't smile and when he didn't hold his head high. He was a wonderful man and I hope I have been able to give you a picture of him that will at least warm your hearts a little."

After the Naval Academy fiasco, instead of following his

family to Kansas City Russel stopped off in Cincinnati to visit an uncle who was a reporter on the Cincinnati *Post*. This helpful relative managed to get his sixteen-year-old nephew a job on the Cincinnati *Commercial Tribune*. It was a six-day-a-week job of hard work and excellent training. The *Commercial Tribune* being a morning paper, he worked afternoons and usually most of the nights and his duties were diversified. Sometimes he'd be called in as assistant reporter to rewrite clippings from the afternoon papers, sometimes he'd be given the gory eight-hour assignment of covering the cases brought into the emergency ward of General Hospital and sometimes he'd be ordered to spend the greater part of the night wandering about the city, stopping in at hotels, flophouses, railroad "depots" and police stations to see if he could pick up any news. And he usually did, drawing up his reports with insight, compassion and, whenever possible, humor. His items caught the eye of the managing editor, who wrote that "a few flashes of human intelligence convinced me that he had the nose for news and he showed remarkable facility in expressing himself, dropping naturally into language and diction which usually comes to reporters only after long years of experience and training, and, in too many instances, not at all."

Guy Fowler, then a fellow reporter, later the editor of a California paper, wrote to Anna some of his reminiscences of her husband:

Back in 1910 a couple of cub reporters used to play pitch and catch in the alley beside the *Commercial Tribune*. They drew about the same pay, around $9 a week. They were learning the trade. One of them learned a great deal beside and the other learned nothing but his trade. I was the unlearned guy and Buck Crouse was the genius. Buck never allowed anything to interfere with his humanitarianism. He believed first in human beings, then in his writing and last of all in making money . . . On one side of the *Commercial Tribune* was a narrow little bar called The

○ ○

Hole in the Wall. They served huge mugs of beer for a nickel and huge free lunches for nothing. Buck and I usually ate there . . . On one pay day we met a couple of young girls in front of the office and asked them for dinner. Neither Buck nor I was much of a lady's man. So on the way to the home of one of the girls we paused at grocery store for supplies.

"Mama's a good cook," the hostess told us.

Well, Mama was. She set out a meal for us and disappeared into the kitchen. I rather think that Buck and I both appeared to be harmless and were. We played the old Victor phonograph and sat in the shabby little parlor. No romance resulted from the encounter, for we never saw the girls again.

"They could use those groceries," Buck observed when we departed. The milk of human kindness ran through his heart even then.

Crouse remained on the job, loving every phase of it, for nearly two years. Then when he was eighteen, his uncle managed to get him a scholarship at Western Reserve and he tendered his resignation to the newspaper. The staff was sorry to see him go and the managing editor presented him with a to-whom-it-may-concern letter of commendation saying:

R. M. Crouse is one of the few "cubs" I am proud in having had a hand in starting on their fell career. When I took charge of the *Commercial Tribune* staff I found him chasing those minor items which usually fall to the lot of the youngster mounting the first rungs of the ladder of journalistic fame.

As opportunity has arisen, he has been pushed forward and given an opportunity to develop his natural ability. In every instance I have found him truly worthy of trust. He has a high sense of honor and his loyalty is unquestioned.

While I would not say a word to discourage him in his laudable ambition to secure a better education, I would be perfectly willing to keep him just as he is, knowing full well that even now he is capable of creditable and intelligent work.

Just before the academic year at Western Reserve was scheduled to start, Russel came down with some sort of viral

○ ○

illness which was incorrectly diagnosed as tuberculosis. When he recovered, the first term was well underway so there was nothing for him to do but join his family in Kansas City. "Findlay, Toledo, Enid, Pawhuska, Cincinnati, Kansas City!" Richard Maney was to write. "It becomes evident that Crouse has made as many stops as a milk train." He never did get to college, but in the long run it was no great loss. He pursued his self-education with tireless enthusiasm. As one of his fellow journalists said, "He possessed one of the great assets of a good newspaperman . . . intellectual curiosity." It was an asset which, far from lessening, increased throughout his life.

Thanks to the letter of introduction, he was able to land a job on one of the country's most important papers, the Kansas City *Star*. He was taken on in the capacity of "relief watch" to help out other reporters on night assignments. One of his first news stories came to the notice of a coworker, E. B. Garnett, later to become chief drama critic and Sunday editor but in those more youthful days known affectionately as "Ruby" Garnett. What struck him was Russel's account of an incident taking place in police headquarters. "I cannot recall what the story was about," he wrote, "but I do remember it was clear-cut writing . . . terse, direct and *dramatic*."

Russel was eighteen years old. In a short time he was promoted to assisting the sports editor by writing up the minor prize fights and wrestling matches held in the old Convention Hall. One block away was Kansas City's leading burlesque theatre and this became the young reporter's favorite haunt. If he finished his sports assignment in short order, he could catch the last half of the evening show at the Gaiety. He even went so far as to send in an occasional write-up of the Gaiety's weekly bill — that is, when he felt such reportage would be acceptable for the dignified pages of the *Star*. Nineteen hundred to nineteen fifteen was "the Golden Age of Burlesque" and Russel became a dedicated patron. He was little attracted by the voluptuous contours of the "beef trust" girls or the libidinous gyrations of the striptease artists, those fat, coarse wenches who were the forerunners of such artistic perfectionists as Ann Corio and Gypsy Rose Lee. What he reveled in was the excellence of the comics. An early awareness of good theatre made him quick to spot a true professional and in those days "burlicue" was the breeding ground for comic talent, the last training school for farce. He might have delighted in the brilliant clowning of Henry E. Dixey in his superb spoofing of one of the standard classics, often far more entertaining than the classic itself. Or he might have watched the early antics of the boy actor Eddie Cantor or watched another aspiring kid named Al Jolson peddling water in the gallery and singing songs as he made his way up and down the aisles. In burlesque the true comics were truly funny, not just indecent. He must have subconsciously studied their techniques in putting over their acts. Sumner Blossom, the editor-publisher who was then on the *Star* and had become a fast friend, claimed that he "picked up a lot of tricks of the trade, some of which I have recognized in his long and brilliant career as one of the most successful playwrights and producers of his day. It never occurred to any of us, and probably least of all to Crouse, that he was being educated in what was to be his life's work."

Through the Gaiety's manager Bert McPhail, Russel had the entrée backstage where he delighted in talking with the performers, finding out about their interests and ways of life. McPhail knew every minor show person who came to town — circus "artistes," carnival barkers and minor film actors sent out to make personal appearances before the

○ ○

showings of their Grade B pictures in the cheaper movie
houses. Russel met many of them. One tough and genial
lady whom he found cheerfully winning was publicizing a
Western in which she played a bronco buster. This was more
than a decade before she became what Brooks Atkinson was
to call "the symbol of revelry during the Prohibition Era" —
New York's most insulting and best-loved nightclub hostess,
Texas Guinan.

A step up from burlesque was America's version of the English music hall, vaudeville. The Keith and Orpheum circuits
booked top attractions in all major cities and at the Kansas
City Orpheum, Russel saw the best of variety shows. In addition to the opening acrobats, trained seals and further "Bill-
Toppers," he enjoyed the fine comedians, the expert song-
and-dance teams and every so often an excellent one-act play-
let performed by big stars: Ethel Barrymore in *The Twelve
Pound Look,* John Drew and Mary Boland in *The Tyranny of
Tears* or perhaps Elsie Janis singing, dancing and giving her
delicious imitations.

In addition to the zany joys of burlesque and the higher-
grade entertainment of vaudeville, the amenities of real, or
"legitimate," theatre became one of Crouse's greatest de-
lights. At that time, countless road companies toured the
length and breadth of the States and Canada, most of them
with their original Broadway casts. Kansas City was always
good for an S.R.O.-week or, possibly, a two-week stand.
Russel, thanks to his press pass, was able to see practically all
the visiting shows once if not several times. He told Ruby
Garnett that he took in eight performances of one musical
which went by the histrionic name of *Hanky Panky.* It was
advertised as a "Jumble of Jollification" in which Florence
Moore delighted the audience with her comic dancing, Harry
Cooper had them in the aisles with his clowning and the
Wriggle Sisters soothed their ears with "Where the Edelweiss

Is Blooming." Other musical stars who came to town were Julia Sanderson in *The Sunshine Girl*, Billie Burke in *The Mind-the-Paint Girl* and, not to run out of girls, Ina Claire in *The Quaker Girl*. There was Weber and Fields with their "Jubilee Company of 100 Players" which included Fay Templeton, Lillian Russell and Willie Collier. And there was more serious fare . . . Laurette Taylor in *Peg O' My Heart*, Sothern and Marlowe in their Shakespearean repertory, Forbes-Robertson's *Hamlet* and possibly Sarah Bernhardt on one of her numerous "Farewell Tours."

Crouse's immediate boss, the sports editor, had a wide acquaintance in theatrical circles and would take him along to join a few members of some cast for late suppers at the Hotel Edward. These were dazzling experiences for the young reporter. Although not yet twenty, his outgoing friendliness, his keen but kindly wit made him an asset to any gathering. Alert, widely read and well informed without ever seeming precocious, he immediately attracted people. He probably had little chance to meet the high-up celebrities but he made friends with many of the lesser show people . . . particularly with the company managers. Through them, he was able to wangle the job of Kansas City correspondent for *Variety*, an appointment which he relished because, although it brought him scant prestige and almost no money, it gave him the chance of writing short notes about all the productions that came to town.

He managed to maintain this extracurricular job because of his youth and enthusiasm. But at the same time his zeal as a conscientious reporter for the *Star* never wavered. He was blessed with an invaluable reporter's asset — the ability to write fast, and to write well. He could handle every type of story although he was most felicitous when his wit and easy turn of phrase, what was known in the trade as "the light touch," came into play.

○ ○

Not every assignment that came his way could be tossed off with the light touch. He dreaded ever having to write up any sordid or tragic event, and being obliged to interview a bereaved person all but broke his heart. Therefore it was very painful one day to be told that he must go out to the house of a woman whose son had just been killed in a downtown street accident, talk to her and bring back a photograph of the unfortunate young man for reproduction in next morning's paper. The youth had attained local celebrity by way of being a *magna cum laude* scholar as well as a football hero for a leading Kansas City high school and rated at least a quartercolumn in the *Star*. In deep depression Russel made the long trolley ride out to the house of the stricken mother. After a few words uttered in tones of profound condolence, Russel realized that the poor woman wasn't stricken at all. In fact, she hadn't even been informed of the accident. The prospect of having to be the one to break the tragic news appalled him and for a time he floundered about miserably, uttering banalities, saying what a fine fellow her son was and how the *Star* wanted to publish his picture. The mother, elated by such praise, pointed proudly to a framed photograph of her boy on the mantelpiece, and at that, Russel saw his chance. Feigning a sudden and violent coughing attack, he asked, between choking gasps, if he could please have a glass of water. While the kindly lady was out of the room, he leapt to his feet, grabbed the picture and fled. Next morning's *Star* carried the sad announcement complete with photograph, but Russel's part in the story was not finished. Conscience-stricken over his theft of the photo, he made certain that it was neatly put in its frame, did it up in a tidy package, journeyed back to the lady's house, placed it beside the front door, rang the bell and again fled.

More and more often he'd be called upon to do a rewrite job on some sloppily written report. Then again he'd be kept

○ ○

overnight on routine staff work essential to a morning paper. This he relished. No matter how tiresome the day might have been, he was alert and ready for whatever night work might be at hand. Any late job was a stimulus and a challenge.

This proved itself during the early hours of April 15, 1912. The morning edition had been "locked up." The daytime offices were dark as the blackness outside. Except for the presses, the only light in the building came from the composing room. The special wire from the Associated Press, which came through a pneumatic tube, had dwindled to such unimportant items as the fact that *The Pink Lady* was a hit in London, that President Fallières had opened the Paris Salon and that the Kaiser was off on another yacht journey — news which could wait for the next afternoon's papers. Four men lingered on in the big empty room, waiting for the checkout hour and killing time playing poker at the cleared-off end of the huge table on which the daily files were kept. They were the composing-room foreman, the assistant telegraph editor, Ruby Garnett and Russel Crouse. It was two-thirty Monday morning. The paper to all intents and purposes had been "put to bed." The page forms had been stereotyped, the plates were on their way to the presses and the predawn "bulldog" editions would soon be on the streets. Nearly time to get to bed themselves. All at once there came the sharp clicking of the pneumatic tube valve, which was the signal that an important bulletin was coming. The card players grumbled over being disturbed and called for the copy boy to go get the message. The kid was either asleep or out getting a sandwich. The four players continued with their game while the tube continued to click its insistent staccato. Russel, realizing that the copy boy was not coming, suddenly slammed down his cards and went over to the pneumatic tube. Returning with several bulletins in his

○ ○

hand, he announced, "Looks like a big story," and he read aloud: REPORTED WHITE STAR LUXURY LINER TITANIC IN DISTRESS ABOUT ONE THOUSAND MILES EAST OF CAPE RACE. There followed a stunned silence during which Russel walked over to a shelf of reference books. Finally the composing-room foreman asked where Cape Race was. Someone else ventured that it must be just east of Sandy Hook. The foreman remarked, "Don't you mean Cape Charles?" Then Russel cut in.

"No. He doesn't mean Cape Charles and he doesn't mean Cape Henry, Cape May or Cape Hatteras. He means Cape Race and I've just found it in the atlas. It's on the coast of Newfoundland."

The men grabbed the bulletins, pieced them together and sent the result along with the foreman whizzing down to the presses. Russel Crouse had saved the morning edition, and the *Star* was one of the first Midwestern papers to carry the news of the *Titanic* disaster.

After Russel Crouse's death, E. B. Garnett wrote a warm letter of reminiscence to his widow. Recalling the above incident, he said, "I have often thought of Russel's help that night. A keen newspaperman, always on the job, never to be caught asleep, knowing where to find out quickly what there was to know. That was newspaper work Russel Crouse learned in his early days on the *Star*. And I do not believe this is anything which can be taught in today's journalism schools."

Among his extracurricular activities was that of a volunteer Sunday-School teacher. In those days, Sunday School was divided into two sections, one for the boys, the other for the girls. Russel taught the boys and was popular with them. His popularity was decidedly increased when it was discovered that as a newspaper reporter he frequently covered police assignments.

○ ○

Crouse's Kansas City experience was enriching whereas the pay was anything but. His friend Sumner Blossom, in a letter to Anna, remembered him warmly:

McKinley and I (I always called him by his middle name and he called me NEWT, my middle name being Newton) being about the same age, established a rather close relationship . . . In 1912 or 1913 both of us having accumulated a few dollars from our salaries, which were around $50 a month, decided we would go to Chicago for a vacation . . . and look around to see if we could increase our earnings on a Chicago paper. [A friend on the Chicago *Tribune* suggested a trip to a certain Michigan summer resort while he looked up possible jobs for them.]

Well, we went, and rode urban trolley cars until we wound up in a place called Paw Paw Lake which, as far as we could determine, was a haven for Chicago mechanics and their girl friends who seemed to be mostly of the domestic servant class. We weren't too happy there, particularly because the room we had was so built that you could hear every movement of every other tenant in the building. So we wandered on street cars all over that part of Michigan until we began to get a little shy of money and returned to Chicago. We arrived in Chicago penniless and X located jobs for us on the Chicago Interocean, but at a price which we decided was inadequate. Next was the problem of getting money for railroad fare back to Kansas City. X, who didn't have too much money himself, couldn't dig up enough to buy transportation to Kansas City, but lent us enough to get tickets to St. Louis. We landed in St. Louis with 22 cents between us, and the man there from whom we hoped to borrow some more money was out of town. While we were walking around to find out what to do, we found a wholesale peanut roasting place and invested 20 cents of our capital in a large bag of peanuts (mostly broken shells). Then we wandered down to the freight yards and McKinley, who had covered the Union Station in Kansas City and had some acquaintances with railroad men, found a friendly conductor who let us ride in a freight caboose to Kansas City. Once there I succeeded in borrowing one-half dollar from a telephone operator at the railroad switchboard, whom I had met, and we were able to get back to our old jobs.

○ ○

Whoever knew him in his middle and later years or even during his early days in New York would be hard put to believe that there was ever a time when Russel Crouse was an excessive drinker. In New York he was known to his friends, many of whom were on the bibulous side, as a gay, amusing companion who could stay up most of the night at bar, late party or poker game and never touch anything stronger than a glass of water or a bottle of Coke. During Prohibition, he was a steady speakeasy habitué, along with such night owls as Robert Benchley, Frank Sullivan and Corey Ford, and would emerge with them in the dawn's early light as sober and bright as when he went in. He never minded his friends or anyone else drinking and he kept a generous liquor supply in his own house but he himself never touched a drop. He wouldn't allow Anna to put a spoonful of sherry into the family soup although he'd be the first to hand her a well-made predinner martini.

Russel Crouse's alcoholic interim, early and brief, started and ended in Kansas City. It may have been brought on by youthful ambition to emulate the older newspapermen who were traditionally supposed to be hard drinkers. He never came close to being a confirmed alcoholic but quite often he went on what, in those days, was termed a "bender" and, since he hadn't developed the hard head of the seasoned drinker, the results were sometimes spectacular. One morning after a particularly riotous night on the town, while he was suffering from a whale of a hangover and was fumbling into his clothes to go to work, he couldn't locate his watch. He couldn't actually recall where he'd been the preceding evening. He couldn't even remember getting home. The watch was one his father had given him and he had always prized it dearly. Somehow he got through the day, his conscience hurting him whenever he thought of his alcoholic intake, his head hurting whether he thought or not. Heavy

"The Daily Union, one cent, to help my mother pay the rent!" Five-year-old Howard Lindsay (nee Herman Nelke) in Atlantic City

Russel McKinley Crouse of Findlay, Ohio, Age 4

Yeoman 2nd Class on Michigan's Inland
Sea. Russel Crouse at the Great Lakes
Naval Training Station — 1918
(© 1918 Strauss Peyton Studio)

Wedding Portrait, 1927.
Howard Lindsay and
Dorothy Stickney

This gathering was to celebrate the repeal of Prohibition, 1933.
Front row, left to right: Marise Hamilton (now Mrs. Blair Campbell), Franklin P. Adams, Alison Smith, man unknown, Mrs. Franklin P. Adams, Mrs. Samuel Chotzinoff. *Back row, left to right:* Russel Crouse, Corey Ford, man unknown, Samuel Chotzinoff, Frank Sullivan. Please note Perrier bottle in Russel's hand.

Russel Crouse and Howard Lindsay on a North Cape cruise strike pose as Gimla wrestlers

Lindsay and Crouse starting work on *Anything Goes*
(Photograph by Dorothy Stickney)

Anything Goes (1934). William Gaxton, Ethel Merman, and Victor Moore
(Theatre Collection, The New York Public Library at Lincoln Center; Astor, Lenox and Tilden Foundations)

Red, Hot and Blue (1936). Jimmy Durante, Ethel Merman, and Bob Hope
(Theatre Collection, The New York Public Library at Lincoln Center; Astor, Lenox and Tilden Foundations)

Father and Mother Day.
Dorothy Stickney and Howard Lindsay
in *Life with Father* (1939)

Howard Lindsay in
Life with Father

Life with Father family portrait: John Devereux, as Clarence, stands behind
Dorothy Stickney

"For Anna—One for under each pillow—Howard & Russel"
(Theatre Collection, The New York Public Library at Lincoln Center; Astor, Lenox and Tilden Foundations)

Honeymoon postcard from Niagara Falls: Anna and Russel Crouse, 1945

"I just wanted to see if there was a doctor in the Crouse." Howard Lindsay as Father Day and Russel Crouse, substituting one night for an ailing actor, as Doctor Somers in *Life with Father*

Howard Lindsay at work
(Theatre Collection, The New York Public Library at Lincoln Center; Astor, Lenox and Tilden Foundations)

"Who can that be?" Alan Joslyn and Josephine Hull discover unfamiliar victim (Russel Crouse) as they pose for an *Arsenic and Old Lace* publicity still. (Theatre Collection, The New York Public Library at Lincoln Center; Astor, Lenox and Tilden Foundations)

Boris Karloff and the "Beamish Ones" celebrating the success of *Arsenic and Old Lace*

State of the Union, the 1946 Pulitzer Prize winning play. Myron McCormick (seated), Ruth Hussey, and Ralph Bellamy
(Theatre Collection, The New York Public Library at Lincoln Center; Astor, Lenox and Tilden Foundations)

Anna and Russel Crouse with their children, Lindsay Ann and Timothy,
November 1949   (Photograph by Joseph di Pietro)

On stage at a rehearsal of *Call Me Madam,* from left to right, Raoul Pène du
Bois (set designer), Leland Hayward (producer), George Abbott (director),
Lindsay and Crouse, Ethel Merman, Irving Berlin, and Paul Lukas   (Photograph by Slim Aarons)

Lindsay and Crouse enjoying their work
(Photograph by Slim Aarons)

"The Hostess with the Mostest on the Ball" toasts the playwrights and the composer Irving Berlin   (Photograph by Louise Dahl-Wolfe)

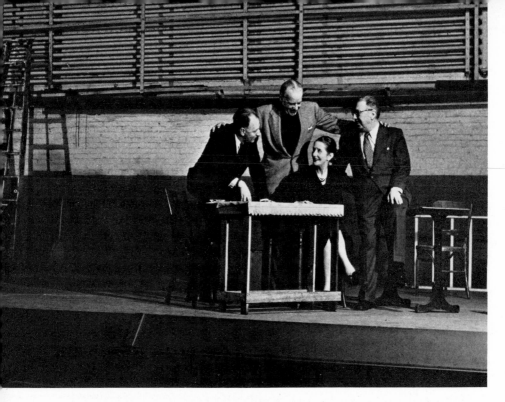

On rehearsal stage of *The Great Sebastians* with Alfred Lunt (center) and
Lynn Fontanne   (Photograph by Maxwell Federic Coplan)

Howard Lindsay stands by as Russel Crouse talks about *The Sound of Music*
at a pre-rehearsal conference. Their audience, from left to right, is
Richard Rodgers, Vincent J. Donehue, Mary Martin, Theodore Bikel, and
Oscar Hammerstein   (Photograph by Toni Frissell. Courtesy Frissell Collection, Library of Congress)

In the Great Hall of The Players Club, Dennis King, Mark Connelly, Howard Lindsay, and Charles Collingwood gather before the portrait of Edwin Booth by John Singer Sargent

From left to right, Dorothy, Russel, Anna, and Howard at the Ritz-Carlton, Boston
(Photograph by Calvin D. Campbell)

"The longest collaboration since Sodom and Gomorrah, but for different reasons."
(Photograph by Irving Penn. © 1948 (renewed) 1976 by The Conde Nast Publications Inc.)

○ ○

of heart, he boarded a late trolley for home. The conductor grinned as he collected his fare, pulled something out of his pocket and said, "Glad to see you, young feller. Here's your watch." Russel gasped with astonishment, took it and asked the conductor where on earth he had found it. The honest man answered: "You insisted upon giving it to me at two o'clock this morning so I took it to save argument. I knew I'd see you again. You take this late route most every night."

The incident came as both a relief and a rude shock and he began doubting whether heavy drinking was essential to a journalistic career. Two more incidents confirmed his doubts. The first occurred one bright Sunday morning when the befuddled fogs lifted and he found himself walking somewhat unevenly down a main city street carrying an empty beer bottle in which was stuck a single pink carnation. The culminating humiliation was when he came to at three A.M. lying prone and staring at something rough, hard and revolting, which turned out to be the gutter. From that moment on, Russel McKinley Crouse swore off liquor for life and never again fell off the wagon.

In 1914 toward the end of June when word came over the AP wires that an Austrian archduke and his wife had been assassinated in a remote Balkan town named Sarajevo, the information was of minor interest to Russel except as possible front-page stuff to be handled by the higher-ups. When in August a general European mobilization was ordered, his interest increased. Then as World War I progressed on its alarming way with daily bulletins streaming in for the extras, reporting the inexorable advance of the Kaiser's lines to be stemmed by the "six hundred taxis of Paris" and the "miracle of the Marne," the "rape of Belgium," the destruction of Rheims Cathedral, the courage of the British Tommies and French poilus in the hell of the trenches, he became vitally

○ ○

concerned. The temper of the country was changing. Popular songs changed from "I Didn't Raise My Boy to Be a Soldier" to "Tipperary" and "Madelon" as war heroes from England and France, some of them romantically wounded, made personal appearances at Preparedness rallies. Ladies formed first aid classes, many organizations were equipping ambulances to be sent overseas, intrepid young fliers were enlisting in the Lafayette Escadrille, and Sarah Bernhardt, again on one of her many "Farewell Tours," came before the curtain between acts and recited the "Marseillaise" to sharpen pro-Allies enthusiasm. When in 1917 German U-boats began making the seas a peril to neutral shipping, and Woodrow Wilson went before Congress to ask for a Declaration of War, Russel McKinley Crouse decided that he too had better do his bit.

He had first to take his leave from the *Star*. He had worked on that excellent paper for seven years and everyone from the chief editor to the most insignificant copy boy was sorry to see him go. Even his Ohio friends on the *Commercial Tribune* were stirred by the news of his enlistment and he was given the City of Cincinnati 1918 Award. The citation, composed and signed by the mayor himself, was an impressive document full of Whereases and Be It Resolveds. It commended this former member of the City Hall press (he had been merely sixteen and seventeen at the time) for "enlisting to take his place in the firing line in defense of the Flag and of Liberty"; it expressed appreciation for his having "won the friendship, confidence and admiration of the members of the City Council, and all other City Officials by his broadmindedness, his fairness, his courtesy and his pleasing personality"; and it went on record as stating its "esteem for the said Russel M. Crouse and as wishing him all possible success on behalf of himself and the patriotic cause which he now repre-

○ ○

sents." It wound up with the statement that members of the City Council "wished to remember him with a little token of our esteem upon his departure to join the forces of Uncle Sam" and that a certain distinguished citizen "had been delegated to buy the finest wrist watch in the city, or something equally as good. As we wish him Godspeed on his way to Berlin."

Russel M. Crouse never got anywhere near Berlin, nor did he even get overseas, but he served diligently as a yeoman second class on Michigan's inland sea at the Great Lakes Naval Training Station. Training for the enlisted man was rigorous and Russel's initial ordeal was learning to sleep in a hammock. The first night "on board" the stationary ship, he fell out thirty-one times, a record which, he claimed, merited the Purple Heart in that it decidedly resulted in a Purple Hip.

After the Armistice, he received an honorable discharge and returned to Kansas City, only to find that no job was waiting for him at the *Star*. He met up with a former newspaper friend his own age named Ralph Turner — known to his acquaintances as "Scoop" — and made heady plans to invade the Big Time in the New York world of journalism. In 1919 there were fourteen English-language papers circulating in Manhattan. Mornings one could read the *Times*, the *Herald*, the *American*, the *Tribune*, the *World*, the *Sun*, the *Telegraph*; in the evening one had a choice of the *Globe*, the *Evening World*, the *Telegram*, the *Evening Mail*, the *Evening Sun*, the *Journal* or the *Evening Post*. Prospects looked brighter for Russel than for Scoop. As Turner later recalled, "Buck had the recommendation of having worked for seven years on the *Star*. At that time a *Star* man could get a job in New York and there was quite an exodus of *Star* men into Park Row."

Anna Crouse has in her possession a diary her husband

kept in 1919 when he was twenty-six years old. The March 3
entry gives an indication of his feelings about going to New
York:

> The lure of New York looms again. I cover a telegraphic as-
> signment for the New York Globe. Wes Stout writes things look
> all right in the big league. I wonder whether the telegram means
> anything. I work on it with a sort of hazy hope. And yet I'm not
> sure whether I ought to go or not. But I'm not gone yet.

Then on March 17 he made his decision:

> It came rather suddenly and surprisingly but I'm going to New
> York. The Globe is a very good paper and $40 will pay expenses,
> surely, I believe. Yes, I'm going . . . but when? I leave it up to
> the Globe.

He apparently left five days later, for on March 23 he writes:

> I'm speaking as a New Yorker now.
> Good old Scoop Turner was at the train to meet me. He looked
> like a million . . . not a cent less. We "L'd" right down to the
> Benedict, my first New York home.
> Dinner at Bertolotti's. What a madhouse that place is! New
> York's so enormous that it almost overwhelms me but it can't
> overwhelm my confidence.

Scoop Turner had made inroads into the Big City some
weeks before, and found himself a job and quarters for the
two of them. He told about the latter:

> We parked ourselves in an old hotel . . . on the South side of
> Washington Square. The room was so small one roommate could
> scarcely pass the other and Buck, recalling the recent war and
> Marshal Joffre, announced that the slogan of the room would be:
> "They Shall not Pass," which he translated into proper French.

The *Globe* was a liberal daily afternoon paper with a circulation of about 150,000. It was located on Dey Street in a
rough, plain three-story building, formerly a tobacco ware-
house. The ground floor contained the presses, the second

○ ○

was divided between news and composing rooms and the third housed the offices of the editor and publisher, the business department and a few feature writers, who rated cubbyholes of their own. In spite of its somewhat shoddy quarters, the *Globe* was a distinguished and growing newspaper. Lincoln Steffens had been its city editor with a fine staff including Norman Hapgood, Philip Littell and Maxwell Anderson. Kenneth Macgowan was the drama critic and it could boast of the best syndicated cartoonist in Fontaine Fox, whose "Toonerville Trolley" delighted the entire country.

Crouse went to work the day after he arrived. He writes of it with characteristic gusto:

> My first assignment on the Globe . . . and it brought me a thrill. A committee meeting with Pinchot, Wood, Root, Garland, Kellogg and others . . . A close-up of Theodore Roosevelt Jr. and he's a live, virile young fellow.

From the start, he was obviously happy:

> The newspaper game is much the same here as anywhere else . . . except that assignments are usually on big stories. The Globe's a splendid newspaper with free and easy feature style that suits me, and an excellent standing. The gang is very congenial.

His assignments were varied and stimulating. On April 14 he went

> down the bay on a subchaser, the 418, to meet the Atlantic Fleet. A very impressive sight . . . giant dreadnaughts, light cruisers and graceful destroyers.
>
> Then to interview Admiral Henry T. Mayo, commander of the largest American fleet ever assembled. A gob interviews an admiral! It was great and I chuckled to myself all the way. Cigars, cigarettes, fudge, cushions . . . great stuff!

He seems to have been sent numerous times to write up the return of overseas troops. He met the famous 69th Division, known as the Fighting Irish, and on April 24:

○ ○

> Down the Bay again . . . it's becoming a habit . . . this time to meet the 77th Division troops on the Aquitania . . . And there was a thrill too. It was the first time I have ever filed a story by wireless . . . just a bulletin to the Office from the Patrol Boat.

On April 6 came his first big break:

> A signed story on the first page! (pardon me, book, if I stand right up and crow!) An impressionistic affair on the parade of the 77th Division. I marched from Washington Arch to 110th Street. Tired . . . well rather.
>
> It's quite a thrill to land that first signed story in New York.

Aside from its entries regarding his work, the diary sheds an occasional light on this man's essentially good and simple nature. His deeply religious sense shows in an almost weekly report of church-going, often twice in the same day:

> I'm frank . . . I like sermons. There was a time when I was held prisoner by them, but now they feed me in a strange way and I enjoy them.

> Every time I hear a talk of the kind Dr. Taylor gave tonight, I want to give up all and throw myself into some land of heathenism in the Greatest Service.

> Good Friday . . . and I didn't pay enough attention to the sacrifice for which it stands.

> Easter . . . bright, sunshiny, warm. What wonderful conditions for the day stands for warmth and light . . . new light.

Even his views on world affairs have an almost childish air of religiosity:

> What of the League of Nations?
>
> President Wilson's plan has its faults and yet can I criticize it constructively? I'm for a Brotherhood of Nations but I must admit that my plan calls for relations between all powers, large and small, that are Christian. And when that comes we won't need any agreements to bind it.

o o o o o o o o o o o o o o o o o o o o o o o o o o o o o o o o o o o o o o o o o o

He seemed at that time to have a certain amount of disarm-
ingly youthful prudery:

> If one could just forget who wrote the poems of Oscar Wilde
> and could imagine behind them a Longfellow or a Lowell, lovable
> and wholesome and yet virile and beautifully dreamy, how won-
> derful they would be. I've been reading the poems of Oscar
> Wilde . . . The short visionary ones are so wonderful, so vivid,
> so real.

Writing about some girl named Nona with whom he "trotted
the fox" at the Café de Paris until midnight:

> I can't quite understand Nona. She's remarkably refined for
> her opportunities but there are some discrepancies in her educa-
> tion along those lines. She's a quiet and pleasant companion but
> not very deep.
> She says she likes Wilde.

So much for Nona. The diary is full of references to happy
and obviously innocent evenings spent with his contemporaries at one another's apartments. The festivities included
their rolling back the rugs and dancing to a Victrola or the
music of whoever could pound out a "rag" on the upright.
"Peggy Wanamaker plays great for trotting time." There are
constant estimates of girls. "Agnes has a hot line." "Ger-
trude's a keen looker." "Ruth Gibson can dance . . . Ethel
Fritts can't dance so well." Dancing seems to have been their
chief diversion: "Dancing with the rugs rolled back; Beulah
played the ukulele." And always these carefree evenings
ended up with food, for they were young and hungry. "Late
supper at Hilda and Prue's and a very good supper it was."
Or "Home early after some hot cakes." And again, "An im-
promptu meal at Alice's for which she had to scramble. In
scrambling she scrambled a few eggs." During the hot
weather the finale to their frequent trips to Coney Island was
invariably chop suey. He and Scoop were able to move from

○ ○

their cramped quarters into a nice apartment at 67 West Eleventh Street (there had been a raise of five dollars in Russel's weekly envelope, which he considered "productive of a thrill"). Once installed, the two young men could serve up some tasty meals themselves; there are such entries as "another of our celebrated dinners. The girls ate heartily."

Russel's warm friendship with Scoop Turner was one of the same devoted loyalty he felt for others who were close to him. When, later that year, Turner accepted a more lucrative job in Mexico, he felt the loss deeply.

> There's a big empty place in me tonight. Scoop left for the City of Mexico at 1 o'clock. I can't even tell this old book how I feel about his going. He was a big part of my New York. There aren't any whiter, squarer more congenial men in this old world. I'll miss him, gee, I'll miss him.

However, there was the whole summer to enjoy together before that painful day.

They made frequent trips to Staten Island, where they had friends and which was pastoral in 1919. There they "covered considerable ground in a fine little Reo." Or they tramped through the woods, stopping to broil ham in the open. "It was a great hike. Then we hiked back and had some more food and lingered until 10:30 what with cards and a Victrola." Another Saturday: "A big fire between rocks. Good food and plenty. The knife went right through the ham and my finger but Marjorie Reed bound it very romantically." Like any normal young fellow of twenty-six his mind was very much on the tender emotions without settling on anyone in particular. During a holiday in Connecticut he wrote, "The girls are of the summer vacationy sort. They are rousing my long buried romanticism." One seemed to be making more headway than the others until she went with him to "the Methodist Church at Milford where she got the giggles and had to go out." The *Globe* gave Russel a short leave to visit his family

○ ○

in Cincinnati. On his way home, childhood memories induced him to stop off in Findlay and Toledo where he took an overnight boat to Buffalo: "A wonderful night on the water and I paced the decks without a girl to talk to . . . a terrible predicament but it was a wonderful night anyhow."

There was one girl in New York of whom his diary talked more and more and with increasing enjoyment. This was Alison Smith, who was working on the *Globe* as motion picture editor and was soon to be promoted to the post of assistant drama critic. She was also, four years later, to marry Russel Crouse. He first mentions her after one of the Staten Island outings: "It seemed rather strange to get out and wander in the wood with a big moon looking down. Jerry and Bill and young Jerry and Tad entertain Alison Smith." This winsome little person was pretty entertaining herself. She was shortly to become a favorite at that gathering spot for New York's brilliant sophisticates and literary wits, the Round Table at the Algonquin. But during the *Globe* days, she seems to have fitted easily into the activities of Russel and his gang. On one occasion they saw *39 East* together, then went dancing at the Ziegfeld roof. "Alison is interesting and yet she lacks something. I can't quite explain her. But then I don't believe I've ever yet met the woman I can explain." The two must have felt a mutual attraction which was obvious to their friends.

July 17
Jerry and Bill seem to be trying to promote a romance. They invite Alison Smith and me to Emerson Hill [Staten Island].
Alison learned fan-tan. I'm not so sure she learned at that . . . She has some strange ideas . . . some that I can't absorb. She writes great movie copy anyway.

They continued to see more of each other. They attended "a very fair vaudeville bill, some pictures and heard Arthur

○ ○

Pryor's band in the largest theatre in the world, the Capitol."
They went to Central Park, where Russel watched Alison
"pose for some outing movies with Hattie, a very docile ele-
phant" and they joined some friends for a trip to Rockaway
Beach, where "the afternoon brought forth the fact that Alison Smith holds her breath when she swims."

Alison definitely had what in those days was called "it."
Bruce Bliven, later the president and editor of the *New Republic,* was then editorial writer and managing editor of the
Globe. He recalled that "by far the most decorative member
of the staff was Alison Smith, the assistant drama editor, a
golden-haired, blue-eyed young woman from California.
She looked like a candy-box blonde until she opened her
mouth, when you discovered she had a high intelligence and
a corrosive wit." He says that all the male members of the
staff were in love with Alison, with the understanding approval, they hoped, of their wives.

In the cramped offices of the *Globe,* no reporter had the use
of any one particular typewriter although Alison Smith had a
favorite machine and it was a tacit understanding among the
members of the staff that she could pre-empt it at any time.
Coming back one day from an assignment, she found a new
young man sitting at "her" desk, fast asleep over "her" typewriter. She took one look at him, then gave him a swift biff
across the back of the neck with her umbrella. The young
man, of course, was Russel Crouse.

The diary continues to show his anxiety about finding the
"right girl" and for a short time he seems to have been quite
taken by a sweet young thing named Archie although he was
beguiled by Alison. In pleasurable indecision he wrote: "I'm
getting mighty fond of Archie . . . a peculiar situation and I
don't know how to handle it." But Alison was winning out.
In early December he speaks of a trip with her to Staten Island:

○ ○

On the way back Alison and I talk more frankly than we ever have. She pretends to be opposed to monogamy. Maybe she really is. And she can't see and feel my position.

Russel Crouse's position was that he was basically a person of what he considered to be high moral principles. Whereas Alison Smith was one of the postwar young women who was beginning to enjoy a sense of liberation. Russel wrestled with the problem, writing that, while he was more and more fond of her, he didn't believe they'd be altogether congenial in the light of their beliefs.

The diary ends with New Year's Eve and does not continue into 1920. There is no record of when the romance culminated. But culminate it did and in 1923 they were married. Alison had been married before to a Mr. Smith, of whom little is known since she never mentioned him. The man had disappeared so she assumed that he had died and felt no compunctions about the legality of her marriage to Russel.

She may have married Russel but she never became Mrs. Crouse. For all her fluttering charm, this beguiling little person was an enthusiastic member of the Lucy Stone League, a group of determined feminists, forerunners of women's lib, who were dedicated to the high purpose of persuading their sisters not to relinquish their maiden names upon marriage. They failed to explain how they reconciled themselves to the fact that their mothers and grandmothers had harbored no reluctance to take on the names of their husbands. The lady crusaders were vocal in proclaiming their aims. At times they became belligerent. One of their leaders, Ruth Hale, who had refused to go on a European trip with her husband because her passport would have listed her as Mrs. Heywood Broun, made herself conspicuous at a musical soiree when Jules Bledsoe sang "Under the Bamboo Tree." At the lines "I like-a say, this very day, I like-a change your name," Miss

○ ○

Hale hissed so loudly, Mr. Bledsoe was obliged to stop singing.

Zeal in this aggressive cause could not keep Alison Smith from being completely feminine — at times exasperatingly so. She was highly emotional and cried copiously over Irish songs or the St. Patrick's Day Parade although there was not a drop of Gaelic blood in her. Russel said that she'd even cry over card tricks. She could be scatterbrained to the point where what she scattered were her belongings — her cigarette case, her compact, her lipstick, her coin purse, her gloves — one by one as she made her way into the darkened recesses of any speakeasy. And she was a faithful frequenter of those genial taverns, for Alison Smith was a heavy drinker. One Algonquin wit, describing a gala he'd been to the previous evening, interspersed his account with the repeated observation: "Now and then Alison tiptoed across the room and had another martini."

She was woefully absent-minded. Shortly after their marriage she and Russel were at a gathering of those 1920's *literati* with whom Alison was extremely popular. Catching sight of Alexander Woollcott, who had not as yet met her new husband, she waylaid the unpredictable critic, saying, "Alec, I want you to meet my husband Mr. . . . Mr. . . ." and she drew a blank. Russel, in turn, drew a card from his wallet and handed it to her, saying, with a sweet smile, "The name is Crouse, dear."

She had nervous hands that were constantly making gestures having little to do with what she was saying. Speaking of her mother, she described a circle in the air; "So-and-so went upstairs" evoked a V-for-Victory finger gesture; and when she announced that she and Russel were going to Norway, she pointed in the general direction of the door. She had an equally mad way of talking, which she did with such conviction, her listeners accepted her remarks as if they were perfectly logical. When in 1933 Crouse collaborated with Corey Ford on a musical, *Hold Your Horses,* Ford asked them both to come up to his summer retreat in the mountains, where he had a house beside a secluded lake. On arrival, Alison, taking one look at the view, said rapturously, "Oh look! The lake comes right up to the shore!" And when the play opened in Boston and a number of their friends came up from New York to give the authors a cocktail party, Alison, at sight of the crowd, exclaimed, "Why, everybody in the room is here!"

Far from being irritated, Russel was highly entertained by his wife's vagaries. Once when a speeding motorist nearly sideswiped the car in which they were driving, she became outraged, swore she was going to have the man arrested, and that she'd made a mental note of the license plate number: 5–137–12. Russel suggested that she'd do well to write it down. She didn't need to, she claimed; she had a method for remembering things. "You see, 5 is for my five fingers, 137 was the number of my room at college, and 12 . . ." and here she paused briefly, "is for the Twelve Commandments."

Her best-known conversational blunder — and it has been quoted frequently — took place at the White House after a command performance of *Life with Father.* The Roosevelts had invited the authors and their wives to supper after the play and Alison, to her flustered pleasure, found herself seated next to F.D.R. Thrilled by this honor and agog over her surroundings, she burbled out, "Oh, Mr. President, do tell me, who was the artichoke of the White House?"

And yet for all her seeming light-mindedness, Alison Smith's mind was fundamentally a good one. She wrote with style, scholarship and humor, and her reviews of such plays as *The Front Page* or her *New Yorker* "Profile" on Fritzi Scheff still make excellent reading. She was successful in placing short stories and feature articles in numerous magazines. After the demise of the *Globe* in 1923, she went for a short time to the *Evening Mail* as literary editor, then was hired by that excellent paper, the New York *World* — first as assistant music critic and then as assistant to Alexander Woollcott in the drama department. At that time of happily thriving show business, there were frequent openings of more than one play a night on Broadway and Alison covered what was considered the second-string production. She was also responsible for the make-up of the Sunday drama page. Woollcott was fond of his assistant in a paternal and proprietary fashion and used to infuriate her by telling her he'd make a newspaperwoman of her yet. She in turn infuriated him by her occasional spells of absent-mindedness, as she had Deems Taylor when, still his assistant music critic, she had written up the performance of Elly Ney, a pianist, as a song recital. One day she sailed triumphantly into Woollcott's office and plunked down on his desk the dummy she'd made up for the following Sunday's page, saying, "There, Simon Legree, see if you can find anything to beef about in that!" What Woollcott found were the photographs of two leading actresses, one labeled "Katharine Collier" and the other "Constance Cornell." Woollcott didn't explode; he merely intoned the editorial motto of the *World*, "Accuracy, terseness, accuracy," then rose silently, called over Deems Taylor and together they pasted on a large scrap basket a sign reading: "For throwing Alison into." She had different problems when she was the assistant to St. John Ervine, the author and playwright, when he worked on the *World* as a temporary drama critic. Ervine, a volatile Irishman, was highly susceptible to the attractions of pretty women. One evening after two openings when they had both returned to their small offices at the *World* to write reviews of the plays they had just seen, Ervine, taking advantage of the late hour when most of the building was de-

○ ○

serted, suddenly invaded Alison's cubbyhole and started making heated advances. His assistant cooled his ardor with a withering look and the remark, "Look, I can fight for my honor or I can finish this review. Take your choice."

Russel and Alison hardly led the life of the average young married couple. Socially, much of the time she went her own way and he went his. An entry in his 1923 diary tells of one gathering of the literary which they attended together. Horace Liveright, who was sitting next to them, burst into loud praise of Alison's work to the point of asking her to write a book for his firm to publish. Russel's wry little notation at the end of the entry is "Who are you? Alison Smith's husband? Let me have my own career, may I?" Their twenty years of marriage must have had its ups and downs, and home life, according to his diary, appears not to have been always idyllically peaceful:

> Dinner at home and through it and after it a battle which wound up in the most imbecilic clash of obstinacies I've ever participated in. No referee could have awarded a decision for he would have gone quite insane trying to find out what it was all about.
>
> I wish she weren't so contained. When I find that something is hidden, I'm quite willing to admit, I'm something of a fiend. The answer to all this is simple. Don't hide anything from me.
>
> If that's old-fashioned, I'm one of "the boys of '76" and don't care who knows it.

And yet, the two had much in common. Both were young, witty and intelligent. Both had a zest for living, an interest in books and a keen awareness of the passing scene. Both liked people. Both were popular and both had close friends, if not always mutual ones.

They loved travel and were able to manage a number of trips to Europe. Their initial crossing was on a luxury liner in which they were allotted a first-class suite for the price of

○ ○

Russel's writing a daily column for the English section of the liner's *Ocean News*. Then, in an odd burst of puritanism, the Italian Line stipulated that they be listed by their married name as they were afraid that word of Mr. Crouse's sharing quarters with Miss Smith might shock the American passengers. It was in Italy that he started growing his mustache. He explained, he wanted to find out if he could grow as luxuriant a one as those of the women he saw on the streets of Naples. In Paris he went "to the Sainte Chapelle, a marvelous windowed chapel with its grated opening where Louis XI, who probably was as good-looking as I am, took part in worship." As was mentioned earlier, his clothes were not the glass of fashion or mold of form, yet in London "To Thomas Walls, the tailor at 106 Jermyn Street, and chose a suit of brown tweed and submitted to being measured which always makes me feel like an animal." They loved Europe and got there as often as was financially possible, each of them helping defray expenses by cabling back feature stories to their respective newspapers. From Paris one summer, Alison sent the New York *Times Magazine* a touchingly amusing profile of an ancient *cocher* as well as a review of Sacha Guitry's *Mozart*, in which the entrancing Yvonne Printemps appeared in the title role. She called it "a delicate and diverting sketch out of Fragonard" and said that "Yvonne Printemps bears about the same resemblance to Mozart as Marilyn Miller does to the lion-headed Beethoven."

In 1932 they took a cruise on the *Kungsholm* to the North Cape along with the Ralph Pulitzers, the editor Art Samuels and his wife, the actress Vivian Martin, Marc Connelly and his wife, Madeline (later Mrs. Robert Sherwood), and Edna Ferber, and had a glorious time. Russel kept them all in high spirits with his clowning, occasionally getting up on the dance floor to go into a sudden song-and-soft-shoe routine or rising in the smoking room to imitate an ornithologist giving

a lecture on birdcalls. Outside a souvenir shop at the North
Cape, he had himself photographed leaning on a stuffed
polar bear and reading a copy of the *New Yorker*. At the
ship's fancy-dress party, he enlivened the evening by appearing as one of those Finnish wrestlers who wear a number of
straps over their bare torsos for the purpose of yanking each
other about. Russel appeared in his shorts and, twined
about his chest, every belt and luggage strap he and Alison
owned plus a few lengths of heavy twine.

There is no doubt that he and Alison had fun together in
spite of their moments of stress but there was always the
shadow of Alison's drinking problem. When it became
acute, Russel was patiently forbearing, taking care of her as of
a wayward child. His protective concern was almost fatherly
in spite of the fact that she was a few months older than he.

Alison, or "Smith" as she was generally called, was far the
more worldly of the two. She liked the excitement of mingling with the brilliant sophisticates. She hardly missed a
daily luncheon at the Algonquin's Round Table. Into that
"Vicious Circle," which could have flourished only in the
'20's and '30's, she was always enthusiastically received,
along with Dorothy Parker, "that soft-spoken kitten with the
tongue of an adder," who was, according to Alexander Woollcott, "a blend of Little Nell and Lady Macbeth." Alison's wit
was quieter than Mrs. Parker's, unforced and not straining to
produce the wisecrack that would make the Gotham rounds
next day. She was to be found at most post–opening-night
parties, those noisy galas swarming with writers and stage
celebrities, sparkling with quotable banter and free-flowing
Prohibition champagne. She was sought after with invita-
tions for weekends in Bucks County, where the literary smart
set rusticated in expensive Early American simplicity. She
was among the afternoon callers at the studio of the illustrator
Neysa McMein. Here the atmosphere was easy; Neysa said

○ ○

little but listened well and would continue to work at her easel on some pretty-girl magazine cover while people came and left and above all talked. Neysa's mere presence and quiet beauty seemed to bring out the best in them.

Smith was frequently invited — or, to put it more accurately, summoned — to one of Alexander Woollcott's Sunday breakfasts in his East River apartment named, by Dorothy Parker, Wit's End. These were run in the manner of a royal levee. Here that acerbic critic, clad only in pyjamas, the top usually wide open to reveal a Buddha-like stomach, reigned from a huge armchair, never dreaming of rising for the arrival or departure of his guests, in an arrogant immobility due less to the effort of lifting his great bulk than to his intent of appearing deliberately rude. Woollcott treated his guests as he wrote his reviews, which could be viciously waspish or mawkishly sentimental. It was this unpredictable quality that made one wag say that his pen was dipped alternately in treacle and vitriol and prompted George Jean Nathan to call him "the Seidlitz powder of Broadway."

Taken along by his wife, Russel went just once to a Woollcott Sunday breakfast. It was a hot day and the imperious host insisted Buck take off his jacket, which obediently he did, revealing one of his startling shirts, at the sight of which Woollcott announced to everyone present, "Crouse is the most loyal man I know. He always sends back to Findlay, Ohio, for his shirts." Buck joined good-naturedly in the general laughter and in later years he became a good friend of Woollcott's.

He went along with Smith to a few of the gatherings of her crowd. Everyone liked him and he was on a par with the best of them in wit and party spirit, but he was happiest with smaller groups of intimate friends. Nobody impressed him simply because his name appeared frequently in the columns. It was the person himself who mattered. He was never to be

○ ○

seen at the Algonquin Round Table. He would have found the self-conscious drolleries and nonstop wisecracks strained and somewhat absurd. He told Howard Teichmann, the author, that he didn't think they ever had a serious discussion about anything. "They got together," he said, "and kidded the hell out of each other but I don't think that they ever said 'Well now, what about such and such' and discussed it seriously." And yet a few of his closest friends were charter members of that elect coterie. Three of his steady cronies were Corey Ford, Frank Sullivan and that delicious humorist and dear human being Robert Benchley, who had never had a drink until he was in his late twenties and was more than making up for that loss under Prohibition. The four of them would haunt their favorite speakeasies, which flourished under the constant shadow of a raid by the enforcement officials — Bleeck's Artists and Writers Club, which was almost an annex to the *Herald Tribune,* Tony's on Fifty-second Street, Dan Moriaty's on East Fifty-eighth and Jack and Charlie's Puncheon Club, then on West Forty-ninth and eventually to emerge from hole-in-the-wall obscurity into smart restaurant glory three blocks north as "21." In these Mermaid Taverns of New York's 1920's they happily imbibed "needled" beer, bootlegged spirits and what Frank Sullivan called that "dreadful mother-in-law of prussic acid known as the Orange Blossom," and, in the words of Gene Fowler, "applied silver polish to the linings of all our clouds." They might join up with Marc Connelly, Donald Ogden Stewart, Edna Ferber, Ogden Nash or that entertaining imposter, Mike Romanoff. Their light-hearted talk and serious drinking often lasted clear through the night, Russel keeping up a tireless share of the evening's jollity on water or ginger ale, although if ice cream or pastry was available he'd order some of that. For he had a passion for sweets which led Lucius Beebe to call him "three-dessert Crouse."

○ ○

More to his taste than these bibulous outings was his participation in a weekly card game. Frank Case, the perceptive proprietor of the Algonquin, having made capital out of the prestige of the Round Table, brought his hotel further reclamé by setting aside a special upstairs suite for the Saturday-night use of a poker-playing group known originally as the Young Men's Upper West Side Pleasure and Literary Club, then, more simply, the Thanatopsis and Inside Straight Club. How or why the name Thanatopsis, which, according to Webster's, means "a view or musing upon death" should have been a designation for these lively gatherings must have been one of their private pleasantries. Here the stakes were high and the experts, headed by George S. Kaufman, Harpo Marx and Herbert Bayard Swope, made killings off the less gifted players, who included Franklin P. Adams, Harold Ross, Alexander Woollcott and Russel Crouse. Less costly than the Thanatopsis was the weekly game of the Hoyle Club, which met at the Barberry Room after the "Information Please" broadcast. There the stakes were more modest, the players including Alfred de Liagre, F.P.A., George S. Kaufman, Heywood Broun and others. Losses or winnings meant less to Buck Crouse than the company and the game itself. He was always welcome at this table, to which he brought his particular brand of whimsicality. Here he came out with one of his more memorable puns — a remark that was attributed to Kaufman but actually uttered by Crouse — when in spite of his holding aces back to back, Ira Gershwin beat him with a hand of treys and deuces and Crouse wailed, "Trey-duced by a lyric writer!" Those sessions are still clear in the memory of the editor Herbert R. Mayes. "We played," he writes, "for as long as ten hours at a stretch; we ate, we drank, and drank and raised and called, and called, and for years survived the fumes of Frank Adams' cigars."

*

o o o o o o o o o o o o o o o o o o o o o o o o o o o o o o o o o o o o o o o o

Crouse's favorite diversion may have been poker, but his abiding interest was in whatever job was immediate for him, and as a rising journalist and free-lance writer he was never without one. After the folding of the *Globe* came a short term on the *Evening Mail,* then ten years on the New York *Post* for which he wrote not only signed features but an amusing weekly column called "Left at the Post," and a further column called "All Over New York," signed "Mann Hatton." This, although anything but a gossip piece, gave a picture of the passing scene and information about prominent visitors, including interviews with the especially interesting ones. He was by now a confirmed New Yorker and the period of an earlier and more leisurely city appealed to him. He expressed this interest in three books, *It Seems Like Yesterday, Mr. Currier and Mr. Ives* and *American Keepsake,* all of which still make nice nostalgic reading.

While remaining on the *Post,* Russel took on an extra job with the *New Yorker,* where he was given a desk and weekly assignments. James Thurber in *Life with Ross* recalled that "Russel Crouse and Robert Coates had been two of the earliest and ablest Talk of the Town writers." In addition to turning out topical items for that department, he started two of his own: "That Was New York" and "They Were New Yorkers." He had the courage to speak up about the magazine's policy of confining their "Profiles" to celebrities or successful Americans and told the editor he should print one about a failure. Ross told him he was crazy. Thereupon Crouse wrote a touching piece about a typical Bowery derelict and Ross printed it.

There came a time when the *New Yorker* had to cut down on expenses and this meant letting some of its personnel go. Thurber wrote that Ross "never had the guts to fire anybody himself." Such dirty work had to be done by the office. This cavalier treatment was meted out to Russel. Returning to

town after a vacation, he called at the magazine's headquarters to pick up the data for his "Talk of the Town" assignment only to find Thurber occupying his desk. It was
Thurber's unpleasant task to inform Crouse that he no longer
had the job. Crouse telephoned Ross to ask why he hadn't
let him know himself and that fiery yet soft-hearted editor
said, "I was too embarrassed."

He also found time to write gently humorous articles for
other magazines and to turn out some scenarios for short
films on newspaper life. And he got the opportunity to col-
laborate on his first musical.

During all of Russel's newspaper years in New York he
haunted the theatre, doing his best to meet everyone in the
profession from producers to doormen. It was one of each of
those who finally helped him get his start. Among Russel's
favorite comedians was Ted Healy. A few years earlier,
Healy had appeared in a musical comedy called *A Night in
Venice*. Russel did not have enough money to see many plays
and certainly did not have enough to see Healy as often as he
wanted to, which was every night. His friend the doorman
slipped him in for nothing. A New York producer saw
Crouse there frequently because he too was a Healy fan.
Now, some years later, the producer had signed Healy for a
musical comedy and, remembering Russel's enthusiasm, sent
for him.

His career as a playwright began with this musical comedy,
written in collaboration with Morrie Ryskind and Oscar
Hammerstein II. It was, as Russel put it, one of the most
colossal flops in the history of the theatre. It opened on February 18, 1931, and ran two consecutive weeks, during which
at most performances there were more people on stage than
in the audience. It was called *The Gang's All Here*, a rather
unfortunate title because most of the dramatic critics followed
up with the next line: "What the hell do we care?"

In spite of the disappointment, Russel decided he must be in the theatre. In September of 1931, he asked the New York *Post* for a leave of absence, which was granted. To the day he died, he always felt that that leave was still valid, and he never went anywhere without change in his pocket — just in case he had to phone in a story.

He immediately found himself hired as press agent for the Theatre Guild. While doing publicity for that august organization, he took time to write his second musical. In 1933, he again collaborated, this time with Corey Ford on a show for Joe Cook. *Hold Your Horses* was based on Crouse's *It Seems Like Yesterday*. Set at the turn of the century, the plot concerned a Midwestern cab driver who, having lost his way, arrives in New York and finds himself running for mayor. The idea, if absurd, was funny and the dialogue excellent, as was Robert Russell Bennett's score. Joe Cook as the cab driver was his deliciously comic self. The musical gave every promise of proving to be a charming hit. Then at the Boston tryout all hell broke out.

It was about to be produced by the Shuberts. Nobody from that management had so much as looked in on the New York rehearsals. But J. J. Shubert along with his brother Lee journeyed up to Boston to view the dress performance. As with all dress rehearsals, there were delays and mix-ups. The costume for the actress playing Lillian Russell had not arrived and she had to wear modern street clothes. Corey Ford, in his book *The Time of Laughter*, gives a vivid description of that night:

> Finally the curtain rose on old Rector's . . . The scene reflected the langorous mood of the period . . . the soft pastel colors, the champagne buckets, the gleam of white napery, the couples pirouetting gracefully to the strains of a "Merry Widow" waltz . . . Charles Rector moves amongst the tables greeting the celebrities of the day such as Diamond Jim Brady and John L. Sullivan.

○ ○

The charm of Old New York was captured for a magic moment.

But the moment was brief. J. J. suddenly rose from the darkness of the audience and, calling for silence, rushed down the center aisle.

> "If there's any people here not connected with this show, I want them to leave the theatre and stop talking. This ain't a picnic, it's a dress rehearsal and you folks are only here on suffrage. We're trying to put on a show tomorrow night, unnerstand? . . . From now on, I'm giving the orders around here. There's only one captain of this ship, and that's my brother Lee and me."

After shouting, "What kind of a lousy opening number do you call this anyway? Do you think people are going to pay four-forty to see a lot of statues do a waltz?" he announced that they were going to start with a parade of show girls. They not only started with them; J. J. brought them on and off throughout the entire show.

> He draped them voluptuously across steps, around tables, along balconies. He walked them in and out of love scenes, he altered plot scenes to make room for them, he chopped other scenes entirely in which they did not appear.

J. J. was in his glory, calling out, "Give me beauty! I want more beauty!" He brought in a number with cowboys and Indians to the accompaniment of "The Last Round-Up," which must have jelled nicely with the spirit of elegant Old New York. He threw out the Floradora sextette and substituted a pair of adagio dancers. For the best melody in the show, "If I Love Again," he replaced the leading tenor with a ventriloquist to sing it to his dummy, played by Dave Chasen, the future Hollywood restaurateur. Walking home from the theatre one night, Russel read aloud from his program, " 'Taken from a book by Russel Crouse.' Shouldn't

○ ○

that be changed to 'Taken as far as possible from a book by Russel Crouse'?"

And yet Russel thrived on the desperate days and nights of cutting and rewriting scene after scene. He seemed to relish all-night sessions of pounding out new comic lines on his portable. Not so Corey Ford. By his own admission, he more or less went to pieces and for most of those turbulent two weeks lay inert and miserable on the bed. Later he wrote:

> Crouse was devoted to the theatre. His energy was prodigious, and he had no tolerance for defection or weakness in a partner. *Hold Your Horses* opened at the Winter Garden to mingled reviews . . . Somehow to my surprise and Shubert's self-satisfaction, the show caught on for over half a year.

Frank Sullivan said of Crouse, "What a glutton he is for work!" and in a letter to Corey Ford:

> You are and were a diligent worker but even you caved in before the assaults of Jake. Not Crouse. He thrived on it. I suppose because he loved the theatre passionately . . . Though he never got to be an actor, he would have given his right eye to be one.

Without having to sacrifice his right eye, he did become one when he appeared briefly in *Gentlemen of the Press,* a comedy about newspaper life by Ward Morehouse. Thinking Crouse's presence in the cast would add a touch of realism to the production, Morehouse persuaded him to appear as a reporter named Bellflower, in which role he came on in a state of slight intoxication with a rolled-up copy of the *American Mercury* in his overcoat pocket and spoke eight lines. Brooks Atkinson in his review noted that "One Russel Crouse, who had been picked from the *Evening Post* staff to bring a touch of verisimilitude to a newspaper play, spoke his lines gently last evening. His performance was as muted as Duse." After

○ ○

this equivocal notice, Buck referred to himself as "the buttered toast of the town." Later, in the film version, he was cast in the same role, which by then was cut to two lines. "I took this philosophically," he said, "because I knew that with my powerful pantomime, I had little need for words. I took Marc Connelly to see the picture. Marc dropped his glasses and missed my performance."

His only other performance was an emergency one during the run of *Life with Father*. The actor playing Doctor Somers was suddenly taken ill, his understudy was not to be found and Russel, with sideburns hastily applied, was sent on, medical satchel in hand, to hurry across the stage, saying, "How do you do." Actually he said it twice because he made his entrance too early, spoke the words, then, realizing his error, retreated and came in on the proper cue. Accused of padding his part, he explained with one of his irrepressible puns, "I just wanted to see if there was a doctor in the Crouse."

His engagement in *Gentlemen of the Press* and his double entrance in *Life with Father* constituted Russel Crouse's experience as an actor. As he said with a rueful smile, "I retired at the height of my career." Unless one might count the time Richard Maney, who was acting as press agent for the Lindsay and Crouse production of *Arsenic and Old Lace,* made use of him for some publicity stills as one of the corpses stretched out on the window seat, and again when he took a bow in a line-up of those revived cadavers, who came on for a curtain call at the end of that rollicking play.

The Crouse-Smith ménage became increasingly unstable. There were times when it ceased to exist altogether. In their way they were devoted to one another and yet in 1929 they got a divorce. It was undoubtedly prompted by Alison. Possibly her dedication to the Lucy Stone canon made her feel that marriage vows were too binding for her liberated soul.

○ ○

Divorce or no, they continued to keep house together off and on for fourteen years. At one point Alison moved to a walk-up by herself. Russel immediately took a flat in an adjoining street where he could look across at her windows to see if she came in at a reasonable hour and whether or not she turned off her lights. The real estate company from whom Crouse rented his small apartment wrote to Howard Lindsay asking for a recommendation. Howard wrote them back a formal letter of endorsement, saying that Russel Crouse had been his partner for seven years, that he personally had always found him to be reliable and honest in every way but that if the picture should change in the future, he'd be glad to notify them.

The more Alison's drinking problem increased, the greater grew Russel's sense of protectiveness. Her period of independent living did not last long, and when she returned to Russel she was a sick woman. The doctors diagnosed tumor of the brain and an operation revealed an advanced malignancy. The final months were agonizing ones. She was bedridden most of the time, Russel caring for her day and night, and toward the end there were round-the-clock nurses.

Her death in January 1943 was merciful and yet it left Russel completely shattered. His friends rallied to try, unsuccessfully, to be of some help; his closest companion was Frank Sullivan. Even that shining spirit couldn't rouse him from his black despair. His personal physician, seriously concerned about him, felt that a change of scene might help. He persuaded Crouse to spend a couple of weeks at Hot Springs, Virginia, and ordered Sullivan to go with him. Frank, who would have done anything in the world for his adored Buck, was appalled by the directive. His fear of travel, which amounted to a phobia, was common knowledge. The only reason he had never fallen for the current lure of Hollywood, which had been half-depleting the Eastern writers' colony, was the horrifying thought of three nights in

○ ○

a Pullman. Even the prospect of an overnight trip to Virginia and two weeks in a strange hotel filled him with terror. The doctor pooh-poohed Sullivan's senseless anxieties and said that this was one time when he must be his close friend's Rock of Gibraltar. Frank muttered miserably, "I'll be his Rock of Jell-O," but tremulously agreed to go. The sojourn didn't turn out the way the doctor had hoped. The person in the most acute need of cheering up was Sullivan. His alarm, which during the train trip had been intense, seemed to increase when he found himself in the luxurious confines of the Homestead. At dinner only a few nights after they had arrived, Frank, looking about at the spacious walls and high ceiling, suddenly announced in genuine panic, "Crouse, the dining room is closing in on me!" Russel gave up any idea of the baths and physical regime that had been recommended and the following day they took the train back to New York. In the long run the trip may have fulfilled its purpose. Russel, in his fear that his friend was really going daft, started coming out of his own deep depression.

When Russel Crouse found himself hired as press agent for the Theatre Guild, that brilliant group was becoming, in the words of Brooks Atkinson, "the most enlightened and influential theatre organization New York has ever had. They led Broadway into the modern world." Russel was hardly the press agent type. Perhaps that was why he was so good at his job. Theresa Helburn, the most powerful, impressive member of the Guild's board, wrote of him: "He was the least showy of men, quiet, intelligent and indefatigable. I cannot conceive of his putting himself forward or doing anything in bad taste . . . I can recall no work he ever did for us that was blatant or undignified."

He enjoyed his work, which got him back in contact with the press, where he always felt comfortably at home. It also

○ ○

got him in close touch with actors and actresses, and that pleased him greatly, for one of Russel's endearing qualities was that he never ceased to be stage-struck. Not intimate with any member of the management, that awe-inspiring and self-confident group headed by Miss Helburn, he made many friends among the "talent" the Guild employed. Doubtless the most joyous relationship was between himself and the Lunts. He loved and adored them and they loved and adored him. Theirs was a friendship which lasted through the years until Buck's death. This was the time when the Guild was at its height in prestige and success. They could count among their achievements *Mourning Becomes Electra, Reunion in Vienna, The Good Earth, Biography,* to mention only a few. Yet not every play produced by those enterprising pioneers of fine theatre was a hit. One disappointing failure was *Valley Forge,* Maxwell Anderson's moving drama about Washington's bleak yet spiritually exalting ordeal during the bitterest winter of the Revolution, which ends with the line, "This liberty will look easy by and by when no one dies to get it." The cast and production had been excellent, the notices, glowingly favorable. Crouse had excelled himself in promotional outlay and yet the public stayed away in those proverbial droves. One day, after he had exhausted every possible publicity gimmick, Russel, whose spirits never flagged, rushed into the Guild offices, where the board was sitting around in a state of gloom. He was carrying a current postage stamp, which he brandished before them, calling out triumphantly, "Look! I've got Washington's picture on a two-cent stamp!"

One person of the theatre — it might be closer to the truth to say *giant* of the theatre — who became Russel Crouse's friend was that brilliant, moody genius Eugene O'Neill. How much of a friend, it is hard to say. He told Hamilton Basso, who was writing the O'Neill "Profile" for the *New York-*

○ ○

er in March of '48, "O'Neill is one of the most charming men I know, and I've known him for twenty-five years, but I can't say I understand him. His face is a mask. I don't know what goes on behind it, and I don't think anyone else does." And he went on to say that his first impression of O'Neill was that he was like someone who'd been locked in a closet for a long time, but after a while, like a suspicious dog who decides it's safe to be friendly, starts to wag his tail. It was impossible for anyone meeting Russel Crouse not to wag his tail, and right from the start there was no barrier between them. It was general knowledge in the theatre world that O'Neill liked and trusted Crouse, and people trying to get in touch with the famous playwright used to approach Crouse first. They were not often successful for Russel respected O'Neill's desire for privacy and did his best to protect him. He also did his best to keep peace between O'Neill and his wife, the beautiful Carlotta Monterey, who was, in her way, as temperamental as her husband. They often invited him to come stay at their house whether that residence was New York; Sea Island, Georgia; Seattle, Washington; or the well-known Tao House in Danville, California. Russel had a chance to study this tempestuous couple at close range. He had the feeling that Eugene and Carlotta were always fascinated and repelled by one another. Brooks Atkinson wrote of that marriage: "He and Carlotta lived together with a neurotic intensity that might have come straight out of any of several O'Neill dramas."

O'Neill relied on Crouse and respected his opinion. Anna Crouse has many letters he wrote to Russel seeking his advice. One in particular is on the subject of his acceptance speech for the Nobel Prize for literature, which was given him in 1936. When the news of this award came out, he received congratulations from all over the world but seems to have been rather miffed that none had arrived from

○ ○

home-front playwrights with the exception of Ned Sheldon, Sam Behrman, George Middleton and your esteemed self. Verily as I have always said — perhaps too loudly to expect appreciation — my U.S. colleagues are, speaking in general, cheap shitheels!

But I couldn't very well tell the Swedes that, could I? Not over the banquet plates. It wouldn't be nice. So I pour coals of bilge on the noggin of ingratitude and give them both barrels of the old akamarakus —

The Strindberg part of the speech, however, is absolutely sincere. And it's absolutely true that I am proud to acknowledge my debt to Strindberg thus publicly to his people.

O'Neill's health was not good enough for him to make the trip to Sweden so the acceptance speech was read by a member of the United States Embassy. After giving Crouse permission to release copies of his letter to the press, O'Neill continued:

If I am to be quoted, I'd like it to be exact and not have my poor speech at the memory of banquet reporters, their imaginations aflame with Swedish punch. My proxy from the U.S. Embassy — if what I've heard of U.S. Embassies is true — is quite likely to be cockeyed, too, and prefer his version to mine. He may say Sandow or Shipman instead of Strindberg — and then where would I be? Anyway write me what you think.

O'Neill further asked Russel for his opinion on plays he had written which were yet to be produced, such as *The Iceman Cometh,* and Crouse was one of the few persons allowed to read *Long Day's Journey into Night.*

The Crouse-O'Neill friendship first came about when the Guild produced the playwright's tender and nostalgic comedy, *Ah, Wilderness!,* starring George M. Cohan. If O'Neill was moody and unpredictable, Cohan was the self-appointed prima donna of Broadway. This was the first time he had ever appeared in a play not written by himself and the name of America's greatest playwright meant nothing to him. It was also the first time he had appeared under any management other than his own and the Theatre Guild meant even less. On the other hand it was the first time the Guild had ever starred any one actor, so perhaps they were even. Theresa Helburn wrote of him:

> People were amused at the idea of Cohan appearing in a Eugene O'Neill play but it proved to be, without doubt, his greatest role. Very much a star in his own right, he had to be handled carefully during the rehearsal period. Once the play was launched, of course, he was on his own and imperceptibly the play began to change.
>
> I have never known any other actor who understood an audience as well as Cohan. Before he went on the stage, he watched them, sensed their mood. He played them for laughs like a fisherman. He could stretch out a laugh as long as he wanted. By the time I caught up with the play on tour, it was running a half hour long. I was frantic.
>
> Olivier who was with me said, "Don't worry. The audience is having a marvelous time." They were too.

It took all of Russel's tact and diplomacy, and he was gifted with both talents, to keep peace between Cohan and O'Neill. Cohan not only kept on "nursing" laughs, he'd ad lib lines of his own, and O'Neill was not one to allow anybody to tamper with his dialogue. Even after Cohan's performance had been toned down in the matter of lines and laughs, the play was still running overlong and the Guild sent Russel to tell O'Neill that it must be cut by ten minutes. O'Neill's answer was "To hell with them!" They were still in Pittsburgh and the next morning Crouse was on his way to oversee a press conference he had arranged for Cohan when O'Neill phoned, telling him to come down immediately to his room. Crouse tried to beg off but O'Neill was insistent, saying he had made the ten-minute cut. Crouse, desperate to get to his appoint-

○ ○

ment, rushed to O'Neill's room and asked to take the script so he could see the cuts. O'Neill answered that they weren't in the script; he had decided to run the first two acts together and thereby omit a ten-minute intermission.

O'Neill had a genuine fondness for Crouse which continued long after the Guild years. He wrote of him that he found him "level-headed and kind, a man with a sense of humor, a sense of proportion." More than once, when he and Carlotta had had one of their seemingly irremediable flare-ups, they'd send for Russel from as far as Boston or Sea Island to come to the rescue with the olive branch he knew so well how to wield.

The happiest memory the Lindsays and the Crouses cherished of Eugene O'Neill was of an evening which went down in their family annals as the "Berlin-O'Neill Songfest." This took place in the Crouse home in November 1946. By then, Russel was married to Anna Erskine, who was expecting their first child. The O'Neills were seldom in New York, but had come to oversee the production of *The Iceman Cometh* and the Crouses had asked them to dinner, adding, as further inducement, that Irving Berlin would also be there. They knew that O'Neill was crazy about Berlin's music and had always wanted to meet him. The O'Neills were hesitant about going out for any meal, because the playwright was the victim of Parkinson's disease, with its attendant bodily tremors. Anna promised to give them a stew so that Gene would not suffer the embarrassment of trying to handle a knife and fork, and she further assured them that the Berlins as well as the Lindsays would not be arriving until after dinner. The Bennett Cerfs were also invited and their arrival as well was postponed. In the easy atmosphere of the Crouse household, O'Neill got through his dinner without any undue hand tremors. The Berlins, the Lindsays and the Cerfs

○ ○

arrived; Irving Berlin went straight to the piano, O'Neill pulled up a chair beside him and they were off on a glorious song binge. Anna, recalling it, said:

> Berlin played all his songs and all anyone else had ever written and Gene sang them all, knew the words, even songs we didn't know. Around midnight the doorbell rang. The Berlins' chauffeur, who had been told they'd be there only about fifteen minutes, wanted a chance to thaw out. The party lasted till after three in the morning . . . Berlin or O'Neill kept saying to one another "Do you remember?" and mention the title of a song and invariably the other remembered. I felt I had never seen anyone have such a good time as O'Neill did that night.

Ten years prior to the Berlin-O'Neill Songfest there had been held another event which Crouse was never to forget. This was a party given in his honor by the Lunts on the occasion of his leave-taking from the Guild. By 1936, he and Howard Lindsay had together turned out two Broadway hits and he felt that now he could safely take the risk of giving up a salaried job, which was a chore, and give all his time and energy to collaborating with Lindsay, which was a joy. Several times he handed to Lawrence Langner, head of the Guild, his written resignation, which Langner merely ignored. Then, finally, he announced to the management that he was leaving. This was during the run of Robert Sherwood's *Idiot's Delight,* which was a huge success and won the Pulitzer Prize that year. Russel had loved working on that play, mainly because it again brought him into close contact with the Lunts. Alfred, it seems, used as he was to success, hated to look out into the audience and see any empty seat. One night, Russel fixed up a dressmaker's dummy, left over from *Mourning Becomes Electra,* with a hat and jacket and placed it against the standees' railing behind the back row. Lunt was completely taken in. Catching sight of Russel after the show, he stopped him to say, "Wasn't it a glorious house

○ ○

tonight? Why, do you know there was one standee who was so interested, he never once budged during the entire evening!"

When Alfred and Lynn heard of Russel's departure from the Guild, they proposed their party for him, adding that he must stipulate what guests he'd like to have. Immediately he replied that he would like to have Noel Coward sing "Mad Dogs and Englishmen Go Out in the Noonday Sun," he would like a small orchestra so that he could dance once with Irene Castle and he would like Theresa Helburn not to be invited. The party, which lasted most of the night, was a great success. Noël Coward sang "Mad Dogs and Englishmen" to an accompaniment of sound effects by Alexander Woollcott. He danced not once but several times with Irene Castle, and Theresa Helburn was not invited. And yet there was never any feud or enmity between Crouse and Helburn. They were always very polite, very pleasant in their dealings. It was just that she was a domineering woman who wanted her own way and usually got it, and her manner at times rather cowed the gentle Russel. A story is told that once after Pearl Harbor Russel caught sight of Miss Helburn dining across the room at Sardi's and announced to the friend he was with, "I must go speak to Terry." The friend asked him, "Why?" and Russel with a sweet smile explained, "I want to say good-bye before she enlists in the United States Marines."

PART III

○ ○

Collaboration

One Friday in 1934, after his week's work at the Guild, Russel Crouse decided to relax in a poker game at the Hoyle Club. How much relaxing he did is problematical; his losses were heavy and dawn found him still trying to recoup them. He was due to leave early that morning for two days at Neysa McMein's house on Long Island but postponed going until early evening and kept on with his ruinous game. Neysa's house parties were as popular as her afternoon studio gatherings and the same "bright people" were her guests. Cole Porter had been one the previous weekend, and when Russel arrived Neysa was in the midst of telling about Cole's desperation in trying to find a collaborator to work with Howard Lindsay on an emergency script for a musical for which Porter had already composed the score and songs and which Vinton Freedley was about to produce. Russel listened politely. He didn't know Freedley, was familiar only with Porter's music and had met Lindsay a scant few times. He moved on into the next room and another card game, won back most of Friday's losses, then fell exhausted into bed. Next morning at breakfast Neysa told him she had dreamt about him and Russel remarked, "I guess that makes me the original dream-boat, although I feel more like Cleopatra's barge."

The first title for Porter's musical was *Bon Voyage*. Guy Bolton and P. G. Wodehouse had been commissioned to write the book. The setting was in the first class of a Europe-bound ship, the characters an assorted lot and the plot was to culminate with a farcical wreck at sea. On the strength of the name of Cole Porter as composer-librettist as well as the fact that the book was in the expert hands of Wodehouse and Bolton, Freedley was able to sign up Ethel Merman, Victor Moore, William Gaxton and Bettina Hall to head the cast, and Howard Lindsay to direct. The prospect was rosy and Vinton waited with happy anticipation for the script to arrive from the authors, who were then in England. It did and he read it with incredulity and mounting dismay. The thing was a disaster. There would have to be a completely new book and rehearsals were scheduled to start within a few weeks. In desperation he appealed to Howard Lindsay to take on the job. Lindsay, who was already facing the task of directing, protested that he could not possibly take on the additional one of writing.

To heighten the crisis, on September 8, when Freedley opened his morning paper, he was struck by a headline blazoned across the top announcing that the U.S.S. *Morro Castle*, returning from a cruise to Havana, was in flames off the New Jersey coast with a loss of well over a hundred lives. The idea of the play's farcical climax obviously had to be scrapped and Freedley again appealed to Lindsay, who agreed to come to the rescue provided they could find him a collaborator and find him right away.

There are several versions as to how they settled on Russel

○○

Crouse. One is that Neysa McMein telephoned Cole Porter at
seven A.M., which must decidedly have discomposed that
late-rising composer, spoke the name "Russel Crouse" and
hung up, and that Porter, after shaking himself awake, had
then called Freedley. Another version is that Neysa's Ouija
board (in which she believed with endearing naïveté, as she
believed in any manifestation of the occult) had spelled out
the name and that she had called Freedley, saying, "Russel
Crouse is your man. He works for the Theatre Guild right
across from your office." Thereupon Freedley had walked to
his window at the precise moment when Crouse happened to
be looking out one of the Guild windows; Freedley had wig-
wagged for him to come over at once with such intensity that
Russel, piqued with curiosity, had complied. The details are
unimportant. What matters is that an agreement was made
and that Howard Lindsay and Russel Crouse started on their
first collaboration. Years later, Russel asked Howard why he
chose him to be his collaborator and when Howard gave as
an explanation "Because I was told that you were the smartest
fellow in town" Buck went on, "Yes, yes, I know that but
what other reason did you have?"

This was an emergency script and there was no time in
which to pursue the creative routine they were to follow in
years to come — namely, to talk over a project, act by act,
scene by scene, before putting a word to paper. Instead, the
next two weeks were ones of frenzied writing. Russel would
leave his desk at the Theatre Guild and rush to Howard's
Tenth Street apartment where they'd immediately go to work,
keeping at it till two or three in the morning.

The schedule was especially murderous for Crouse, who
had his daytime duties, which he never shirked. But of the
two, he was the nonstop dynamo. Frank Sullivan claimed
that it was Buck who kept Howard on the alert. He remembered Crouse as a tireless martinet and Lindsay as an innate

○ ○

philosopher who, unless goaded into creatively profitable activity, would have preferred to live in modest quarters near the Players Club, turning out an occasional piece for a magazine.

There was one happy interruption to this hectic period when Cole Porter volunteered to come play the songs and part of the score for them. The Lindsays had no piano, but their neighbor, Nila Mack, a former vaudeville actress of the team of Bryant and Mack, owned an ancient upright which was in need of repair and woefully out of tune and this they wheeled into the Lindsay sitting room. Porter arrived and being always the perfect gentleman made no comment on the condition of the piano even when the ivory top of a key flew off as if on cue when the composer was playing "You're the Top." He then launched into "I Get a Kick out of You," "All Through the Night," "The Gypsy in Me" and "Blow, Gabriel, Blow." The future song hit "Anything Goes" was not written until the title for the play had been settled upon. Howard had heard the songs and words before, but they burst upon Russel's enchanted ear for the first time. George Eells in his biography of Cole Porter, *The Life That Late He Led*, describes the reaction of Buck, who claimed that "Beethoven, Bach, Wagner, Brahms, Mendelssohn, Debussy, Chopin, Verdi, Offenbach, Strauss, Haydn and Francis Scott Key could have marched into the room and I wouldn't have looked up."

After that happy session, the authors were able to turn out a general story line, a number of situations that would make for comic scenes, a rough first act, and not too clear an outline for the second. They had decided upon the characters in suitability to the talents of the actors already signed up. Lunching one day at the Algonquin, Lindsay noticed a woman at a nearby table whom he took for Aimee Semple McPherson, only to be informed by Frank Case that the lady was a popular torch singer. This inspired them to write for

○ ○

Ethel Merman the part of a former evangelist turned night-club hostess. Victor Moore, with his adorable gift for self-effacing comedy, was ideal for the role of Public Enemy Number 13 disguised as a clergyman. William Gaxton would have his usual leading-man characterization as an attractive playboy who hops onto the ship without ticket or passport in amorous pursuit of lovely Bettina Hall who, of course, would be charming as lovely Bettina Hall. Before rehearsals, Buck and Howard managed to meet separately with these four leads, each of whom they convinced had the star part.

The day came around when the cast assembled for a first reading, which turned out not to be a reading at all but a brilliant solo performance by Howard Lindsay relating the plot in detail and acting out the comic situations with great effect. The actors were fascinated as were Vinton Freedley and Russel Crouse, whose admiring comment was, "To me, it was a better speech than the Gettysburg Address." Afterward neither he nor Howard could recall more than half of the complicated résumé.

Next morning they reassembled for the blocking of the first act, such as it was. A number of blank spaces in the script confused the actors. Whenever they were faced by one of these, the authors would jump in blithely with an explanation to the effect that "now this is a very funny scene in which such and such happens . . . we're working on it." Ethel Merman in her biography, *Who Could Ask for Anything More?*, as told to Pete Martin, says that after the initial rehearsal session, someone asked Crouse when they were going to get the second act, to which he answered, "To tell the truth, we've got some revisions to make on the second act." Merman adds, "The truth was that they didn't even know what was to be in it."

Somehow, during the next few days, they were able to fill in the gaps in the first act and to write a second, except for the final scene, which they left a complete blank. Donald Oenslager had his sets ready for the first act and had made some sketches for the second but was stymied by the fact that nobody seemed able to tell him where the final scene was to take place. In bewilderment he appealed to Vinton, who in similar bewilderment told him to build an interior with an exterior feeling.

When the company started off for the Boston tryout, the final scene had yet to be set down on paper. It was during the train trip between New York and Boston, according to Ethel Merman, that "Crouse and Lindsay emerged from the men's room with a wad of paper in their hands and triumphantly announced that they had just written the last sheet. It was no gag," she claims. "They actually had just written it."

Boston tryouts are traditionally hectic and the nights and days during that of *Anything Goes* were frenzied for the two authors. There was endless note-taking at every rehearsal, followed by endless cutting and rewriting back in their Ritz-Carlton suite. Russel, with his remarkable self-renewing energy, kept going. Not Howard. He suddenly gave out, took to his bed and announced in all seriousness that he was dying. It was the first time that Buck had come up against his partner's hypochondria and for a time he was taken in. When Howard weakly asked him to send for his sister Rose, who lived in Boston, Russel called her in a panic. Rose was a no-nonsense person, like her mother, and she knew and loved her brother well. Over the telephone she sounded curiously unmoved by the news of his imminent demise and when she walked purposefully into the room, her opening remark was, "Howard, get out of bed!" Obediently he did.

The opening night had its usual crucial moments. The most spectacular was brought about by William Gaxton after his love scene on the moon-lit deck in which he sang "All

Through the Night" to Bettina Hall. For this he was impecca-
bly dressed in white tie and tails. After the song there followed a quick scene-cut to show the cabin he was sharing
with Victor Moore and to which he was supposed to be returning, elated over his romantic interlude on deck. Opening night, this short second scene completely slipped his
mind and, thinking that he had a costume change, he went to
his dressing room, where he divested himself of his trousers
only to hear his cue, at which he rushed back onstage in his
shorts, his trousers draped neatly over his arm, and spoke his
line to the astonished Moore: "What a night, what a dawn,
what a sunrise!" By some miracle and an oversight on the
part of the Watch and Ward Society, the moment got by in
Boston.

Anything Goes was an out-of-town hit, but even after the
opening the authors kept rewriting scenes, and Cole Porter,
who most of the time was back in New York, kept revising
sections of the score. At one point he telephoned Ethel Merman to give her extra verses for the "catalogue song," "You're
the Top" (that catchy and intricate collection of superlatives
in which Mahatma Gandhi rhymes with Napoleon brandy,
Arrow Collar with Coolidge dollar, O'Neill drama with
Whistler's mama, etc.). She took the new words down in
shorthand (La Merman had been a stenographer before someone discovered that "this doll from Astoria with a trumpet in
her throat" could "hold a true note as long as the Chase Manhattan Bank") and that night was letter-perfect in them.
Ethel Merman was always letter-perfect because she was a
real pro and Lindsay and Crouse adored her. Her analysis of
her own acting was simple and direct: "When I get a part, I
study it, then I do it. I go to rehearsals and listen to the direction. I make sure that I know what I'm doing on opening
night, and that I know the lyrics and the book backward and
forward." She never quibbled over songs. "I leave them the

○ ○

way they came out of the composer's head. If it's a good head, they'll be good songs without my editing them." The authors never ceased to delight in her instinctive timing; they said of her that she was the epitome of "doing what comes naturally."

Word had gotten around New York that the incoming musical was going to be a success. The opening night was heralded as "the greatest gala since the Depression" and tickets sold at the unheard-of price of twenty dollars apiece. Buck and Howard's reactions to that nerve-racking evening were to be standard behavior for them every time one of their plays had a première. Howard took himself off to the Players Club for a few drinks and a game of pool with his eye on the ball and his ear cocked for telephone calls from the theatre between the acts. Russel, utterly miserable, remained in the theatre. Far too unhappy to stay in any seat, he walked woefully up and down the space behind the back rows. Not so Cole Porter. Resplendent in full dress, he sat with fashionable friends down near the front, applauded enthusiastically and during the intermission waved happily at someone several rows behind him and called out, "Good, isn't it?" Russel's subsequent comment was that "Cole's opening-night behavior is as indecent as that of a bridegroom who has a good time at his own wedding."

Anything Goes was the musical hit of 1934 and ran for 420 performances. The two collaborators had worked well and amicably together and Howard suggested that they form a partnership. Buck wasn't sure. While his salary as press agent at the Theatre Guild could not have been more than $150 a week, it was a steady income. Moreover, he had lunched with Mark Hellinger, who, after congratulating him on his and Lindsay's success, said, "This happens to a guy once in a lifetime. This is the one. This is it." Russel's royalty check, because of Freedley's commitment to Bolton and

○ ○

Wodehouse, was a measly one half of one percent. Hellinger's balefully prophetic "This is the one" kept repeating itself in Russel's mind. "That's why," he confessed, "I hung on at the Guild."

Howard Lindsay went to work on a new play. This time his collaborator was that portrayer of tough Broadway-esque "guys and dolls," Damon Runyon. The play, *A Slight Case of Murder,* involved a former beer racketeer turned respectable brewer who rents a house in Saratoga for the racing season only to discover that his elegant abode also houses the bodies of four murdered hijackers who had tried to take off with a truck filled with bookmakers' money. The play, which was produced by Howard Lindsay himself, opened at the 48th Street Theatre, September 11, 1935. It failed to go down with the critics. Brooks Atkinson wrote, "Mr. Lindsay has directed with a ringmaster's whip. Everyone is on his toes and a good deal is outlandishly funny. But not enough to open the new theatre season with. We've had fresher, better plays from Howard Lindsay and we'll certainly have better, easier ones from Damon Runyon." *A Slight Case of Murder* ran for a scant sixty-nine performances.

Then in 1936 Lindsay and Crouse were back working together. Vinton Freedley was again going to produce a Cole Porter musical for Ethel Merman. Its title was *Red, Hot and Blue.* This time, in place of Victor Moore, her costar was that whiskey-voiced, irresistible vulgarian Jimmy Durante. In place of William Gaxton there was to be a newcomer named Bob Hope. Again Freedley had signed up Lindsay to direct the show and the team of Lindsay and Crouse to write the book. The collaborators immediately settled down to work; hardly had they got started when they ran into one of those stultifying mental logjams when all ideas and incentive stopped dead. It was a hot summer and air conditioning was unknown.   They were frustrated, hot and plainly stuck. They told their woes over the phone to Frank Sullivan, who suggested that they come right up to Saratoga, take rooms at that wonderful old antebellum hotel, the Grand Union, and write in the fresh peace and quiet of America's venerable spa. When they arrived there, Sullivan volunteered the further suggestion that they take a few of the new "energizing pills" he had discovered, which were helpful in getting a writer started.   They were called Benzedrine, he said, and were easily available at any pharmacy.

The authors compliantly took the pills, went spiritedly to work and in no time produced a first act which pleased them so much that they booked passage on a boat to Ireland.   After a few days at sea, they read over what they had written, tore it up and threw the scraps overboard.   Then they returned to New York and, without benefit of Benzedrine, came up with a book that was well suited for musical entertainment but would hardly live on in the annals of great American drama. George Eells gives a succinct résumé: "The low comedy plot concerns a rich widow (Merman) conducting a lottery run by an ex-convict (Durante) which she decides to throw to her lawyer (Hope) whom she loves, but who loves the memory of a girl (Polly Walters) who as a baby branded herself by sitting on a waffle-iron when he tried to kiss her.   The action, of course, finally brings the widow and the lawyer together."

Porter was ready with the score and some of the songs. The hit number, still a favorite, was "It's De-Lovely."   This had been inspired when Cole and his wife, Linda, on a round-the-world cruise, decided to rise early and watch the dawn as the ship sailed into Rio harbor.   Linda's words as she came out on deck were, "It's delightful!"   Cole following close behind exclaimed, "It's delicious!"   Then from over by the railing came the final words, "It's de-lovely!" from Monty Woolley, who had been up all night "lifting a few."   *Red, Hot*

○ ○

and Blue opened at the Alvin Theatre, October 29, 1936, to mixed notices and a public response which was not overwhelmingly enthusiastic. It managed to run for some five months. Merman, as was to be expected, came through with a performance of spirit and excellence. The fans of Jimmy Durante delighted in the zany bedlam of his preposterous acting. According to Ethel Merman, Jimmy was easy to work with. He learned his lines by having them read to him by "the well-known dramatic coach and Shakespearean student, Professor Eddie Jackson, of Clayton, Jackson and Durante. Eddie gave Jimmy his private version of Little Theatre technique; then Jimmy gave it his own individual touch." Bob Hope offered something of a problem. He had an uncontrollable urge to ad lib. It went so far that one evening, during a song with Ethel Merman, he took it into his head to lie flat on the floor at her feet. Merman, always the pro, was not amused. She complained in loud indignation to Freedley. I quote her words: " 'If that so-called comedian ever does that again,' I said, tight-lipped but ladylike, 'I'm going to plant a foot on his kisser and leave more of a curve in his nose than nature gave it.' "

Red, Hot and Blue was followed by another musical, *Hooray for What!* It was produced by the Shuberts and its great asset was that it brought back to Broadway Ed Wynn, who for six years had been reaping a fortune and squandering his art on the banalities of Texaco's "The Fire Chief" radio show. Lindsay and Crouse wrote the book. The plots of most musicals of the '30's hardly bear recounting. This one, based on an idea of E. Y. "Yip" Harburg, who also wrote the lyrics to Harold Arlen's music, concerns a horticulturist known, I'm afraid, as "Chuckles," who has invented a gas that exterminates fruit insects. It is capable, also, of exterminating people and the expected complications arise, involving foreign agents, delegates from the League of Nations and further baf-

○ ○

flements to bewilder the peaceable protagonist. The reviews were mainly congratulations on the return of Ed Wynn. Richard Watts rejoiced that "gone and happily forgotten are those unfortunate nights when the furious but feeble antics of the Fire Chief were demonstrating what terrible things the wanton wireless can do to a great comedian."

After the smash hit of *Anything Goes* and the more moderate successes of *Red, Hot and Blue* and *Hooray for What!* (which ran some 200 performances at the Winter Garden), Lindsay and Crouse were established as a team and it was inevitable that they should be summoned to Hollywood. The lure of that El Dorado had never tempted either of them. Lindsay claimed that the climate made him lethargic and that the pay was either too easy or not forthcoming, while Crouse dismissed it as a place where "they hold their religious services in a chapel called 'The Wee Kirk i' the Heather' because they couldn't think of anything cuter." Their contract was satisfactory — good pay, screen credits with their names appearing as the authors on any publicity — and what seemed to them the happiest aspect of the enterprise was that the story they were given to dramatize was to be made into a picture for W. C. Fields.

Fields was to play the millionaire owner of an ocean liner which, setting forth on its maiden voyage, was out to break the transatlantic speed record. It was an amusing story and they made of it an amusing script, which pleased them and seemed to please the front office; then, before any filming had started, there being no further need for their services, they returned to New York. When, ultimately, they saw the finished product, they were in for a series of shocks. Nothing remained of their original script except their two names as authors, a credit they would willingly have forfeited. The title had been changed to *The Big Broadcast of 1938;* it bore no relation to the plot. It seemed that W. C. Fields, who had always played a poor man, on finding himself cast as a rich man had walked off the set and refused to return until the Paramount "play doctors" changed the script. They solved the problem by writing in the equally starring role of the millionaire's twin brother, who was poor, to be played also by Fields. They prefaced the proposal with "We'll open with a double shot of the two of you in the shipping line's office, with the poor brother denouncing the rich brother. And there'll be a couple of other double shots of the two of you on shipboard." This was an alteration which was not reported to the original writers, but it satisfied Fields. The effect of the liner going ahead at full steam was done with a miniature model tossing proudly across the Paramount pool. Then some bright boy decided that one ocean liner was too tame. Why not have two? — one owned by the rich brother, the other by the poor (just how a poor man got to be the owner of a passenger ship was one of those mysteries buried in the archives of Hollywood). The result was an idiotic mishmash; in its review, *Variety* offered $10,000 to anyone who after seeing the picture could tell its story. In the "Phoenix Nest" of July 15, 1967, Lindsay wrote, "This picture has been run once on the late-night show. It might possibly be run again. I would advise you to see it, as I believe *Variety*'s offer still stands."

When the *New Yorker* began bringing out Clarence Day's "Life with Father" reminiscences about his Victorian boyhood in a conventional Manhattan brownstone, dominated by an irascible father, the Lindsays read each installment with interest. Actually it was Howard who read them aloud to Dorothy, whose eyes were bad at the time; and as he read, his interest turned into growing enthusiasm. He felt that here was rich material for a charming period comedy and he

○ ○

started making inquiries. He found out that Oscar Serlin, yet to make his name as an important manager-producer, had also realized the possibilities for a play to be made out of the Clarence Day stories and had already talked with the author's widow, who had given him a tentative option. Serlin, while out in California on a job for Paramount, turned over the idea to the screen writer Alan Scott who, similarly charmed with the stories, dashed off a picture script in which W. C. Fields would be cast as the explosive Father Day. Fields liked the script, the studio moguls were delighted with it but the Day family, who owned all the rights to Clarence's material, flatly turned it down. Serlin, however, managed to have another meeting with Mrs. Day, who finally agreed to let him try again to find the right playwright and, if an acceptable manuscript was the outcome, to think it over.

There was no written agreement; Serlin had only a verbal option, but it was enough to give him confidence to start things going once more. This time, to do the dramatization, he approached Howard Lindsay, who was all too eager and accepted the assignment without hesitation. At first he had every intention of working on the project by himself. Then he began thinking about Crouse. Up to that time, the two of them had been book writers for three musicals and he wondered if Crouse would be right for a straight play. Then he said to himself — and being Howard, in all probability he said it aloud — "Of course! Even if this is a straight play, Crouse is the one to write it with me."

Russel Crouse needed no persuasion. He too had read the Clarence Day installments with relish. Moreover, having written three books with American Victorian settings, he was an authority on the period and it was one which he loved. Gilbert Gabriel, the music and drama critic, said that "the heart beneath Crouse's modern blue flannel shirt always did and always will belong to Daddy's Era"; that he "relaxes in no chair but guaranteed Victorian. He rests his crested brow only upon sufficiently mildewed antimacassars." His acceptance of the idea for a *Life with Father* play was immediate and, without any written permission from Mrs. Day, he and Lindsay set to work.

Their collaborating pattern had started with *Red, Hot and Blue*. (*Anything Goes* had been too much of a frenziedly hasty job to result in any orderly form of approach.) *Hooray for What!* had solidified it and from that time on it never varied. Before putting a single word to paper, without so much as making a few notes, they'd meet for several hours a day and talk the project over — the plot, the situations, the characterizations, the opening and closing of each and every scene, just how the play must end. They'd talk for days, for weeks, if time allowed, for months. In the case of *Life with Father*, they talked for over two years — and just about daily. They talked walking down a street, they talked in taxis, over the phone; they talked at social gatherings, they talked on the decks of steamers. When the Lindsays and the Crouses went on a Scandinavian holiday together, they talked during strolls about Stockholm with such animation that they almost toppled into one of the canals, to the astonishment of the stolid Swedes. But mainly they talked in the sanctuary of their joint workroom, a study in the Lindsay house. Every afternoon and most evenings would be set aside for their meetings as both men hated mornings.

Dorothy, looking back on those sessions, says that through the closed door she'd hear a stream of shouts denoting approval or equally definite disagreement and every so often roars of laughter. Finally they had come to the momentous decision of knuckling down to the actual writing, and in this too the pattern never varied. Howard would stride about the room (Buck was to say of him that "Lindsay paces four thousand to five thousand miles per play," and Howard reported

○ ○

that "Crouse makes up at rehearsals pacing the aisles in nervous dejection") and as he strode, he'd try out snatches of the dialogue, usually at the top of his lungs. Occasionally there came a yelp from his collaborator, who would feel no hesitancy in saying, "That's the lousiest line I've ever heard," and suggesting an alternative, which his partner would dismiss with a loud "That stinks!" Neither ever took offense at the other's criticism, just as after a play was finished and produced, neither remembered which line was whose. After arguing a point, they'd finally settle on dialogue that was satisfactory to them both. Then Lindsay would continue his powerful recitative and Russel would bang it off on the battered typewriter. They were never self-conscious before each other. A secretary, they claimed, would have cramped their style. They proved this exactly once. It was during the hectic stages of their serious work in writing and re-writing the script of *Life with Father,* when they were also giving thought to some other plays for the future. Thinking that she might ease the additional burden of typing the dialogue, they engaged a young woman who proved to be both agreeable and highly efficient, but whose mere presence made them so uncomfortable, they realized from the start that they'd have to get rid of her. Neither having the heart to fire her, they gave her as a sort of consolation prize the part of one of the maids in *Life with Father.*

The verbal discussion of that play had taken the authors a little over two years. The actual writing took them just seventeen days. But a Lindsay and Crouse play when it was done was a finished work. Every line had been carefully thought out in advance, every bit of business planned and given in precise directions. During those two years and seventeen days they never once turned their thoughts to any other project although either could have found a dozen opportunities and Howard was even lured by Hollywood with a

○ ○

fabulously lucrative offer, which he resolutely turned down. Neither man had any income. They had created *Life with Father* purely on "spec."

The immediate problem was to obtain the rights from Mrs. Day and they made an appointment by telephone to meet at the home of George Parmly Day, her brother-in-law. Armed with the first act plus a detailed outline of the rest of the play, they journeyed to New Haven, where they were greeted with great formality by the widow, as well as Mr. Day, the treasurer of Yale University, and his wife. To Mrs. Clarence Day the memory of her husband and the tradition of the Day family were sacred, and it is no wonder that she looked with mistrust upon Lindsay and Crouse or any other playwright aspiring to dramatize her husband's boyhood as a satire on Victorian family life. The interview was very formal. After a brief exchange of introductory banalities, the Days aligned themselves on three uncompromising chairs; Russel made a hasty retreat into the adjoining hall, where he paced up and down in characteristic misery; Lindsay cleared his throat and started reading the first act in an attempt at his customary histrionics. The Days listened in silence and Howard's histrionics dwindled bit by bit into a routine and, finally, a lifeless reading. At the finish of the first act, he closed the manuscript, called out to his collaborator, "Come on, Buck, let's go," left the detailed outline of the rest of the play with the still silent Days and took the next train back to New York. In less than a week, to their utter astonishment as well as their utter delight, they received an official acceptance from the Days.

The rights were theirs and they were free to go ahead with the production. Their immediate concern now was to find the right players for the roles of Father and Mother Day. The Lunts were an obvious first choice. Alfred was enamored of the script and quite fancied himself playing that irascible yet

○ ○

fundamentally kind-hearted Victorian parent. He said to his wife, "I've been seducing you in the theatre for twenty years. Here's a chance to marry, settle down and have children. Don't you think it's about time?" Lynn was not at all sure. She said she couldn't possibly play eight performances a week worrying over getting him baptized. Lindsay and Crouse tried other stars. The role of Father was turned down by Walter Connolly, Roland Young, John Halliday and twice by Walter Huston. These turn-downs were not as discouraging to Lindsay as they might have been. From the very beginning he had secretly longed to play the part himself.

It was understood that Oscar Serlin would be the producer but they needed investors because Serlin at the time was barely solvent. Scripts were sent to potential "angels," among them Alfred Knopf, Cary Grant, Rowland Stebbins (a Wall Street financier), and Benny Goodman. None of them was interested in a play dealing with the joys and tribulations of a well-to-do red-headed couple, their four red-headed sons and a series of parlor maids who are constantly being fired, even though it was written with delicious humor and an authentically nostalgic feeling for New York of the 1880's. Robert Benchley expressed his reaction to the manuscript when he wrote to a friend who was a potential investor, "I could smell it when the postman came whistling along the lane. Don't put a dime in it."

As a slight anodyne to the hurt of these rejections, they got an offer to put on the play in Skowhegan, Maine, for a summer tryout. Ever since Howard and Dorothy had met at that theatre and played the young lovers in *Outward Bound,* they had longed to act together again. Oscar Serlin was all for Dorothy's playing the winsome if somewhat fluttery Vinnie, but he was dead set against Howard's playing Father. However, Serlin's was not the final word as he hadn't enough

money for even a summer tryout. Howard was determined
to act the part, but he too had no money. So the Lindsays
lost no time in raising it by mortgaging nearly everything
they owned — their house, the furniture, any possessions of
value. The cost of these mortgages plus extra loans from
banks mounted up to what was for them a terrifying amount.
Long after the immediate success of *Life with Father*, with its
promise of a long run, they continued to owe money and
were not even solvent until the play was well into its second
year at the Empire Theatre.

The summer tryout went well, if not spectacularly so. The
setting was makeshift, the costumes anything but the elegant
replicas of the 1880's seen in the finished production. As the
red-headed Father Day, Howard pasted on a red mustache,
half of which got dislodged on opening night. He subsequently grew his own "because I was afraid," he explained,
"a false one would blow off at one of my more gusty 'Oh
Gaahd!s.' Besides I found myself whistling around it or trying to talk over it."

The performances too were uneven, especially Lindsay's.
At first his characterization was violently pugnacious until
Dorothy gently advised him, "Howard, Father is not *bad*-tem-
pered, he's *hot*-tempered." At that he changed into a curious
manner of winning charm, to which Dorothy quickly put a
stop by saying tersely, "Howard, you're making love to the
ladies in the front row." By the end of the Skowhegan engagement, Howard Lindsay was well on his way to giving
one of the most memorable performances in the history of the
American theatre, deliciously funny, outrageous yet endearing, believable to the point where the audience is convinced,
as one newspaper account commented, that "Father Day has
every right, indeed every necessity to roar at housemaids,
snort at Democrats and howl his celebrated howl at the Deity
on High. His 'Oh Gaahd!s' seeming always to be addressed

○ ○

to an equal. The rest of his explosive protests bursting with the violence of a flying manhole cover." Lindsay, analyzing his own performance, said that "during most of the moments of Father's indignation, there should be almost uppermost his sense of incredulity that these things could be happening to him. It was very easy for me to lose this edge of astonishment and become exasperated. Lest I sound too damn noble, I wish to add that nothing helped me toward a conscientious performance so much as a conscious interest in the royalties."

During the long run of *Life with Father* (it ran on Broadway alone for seven and a half years and the Lindsays were to play the leads for five solid ones), Howard Lindsay became identified to the public even offstage as Father Day and without realizing it he must have identified with the part, for his bearing, his mannerisms became those of that self-assured autocrat. Crouse said he'd played the role so long, he really *was* Father Day. One good friend and fellow Player, the cartoonist Rollin Kirby, accused him of "suffering from an attack of galloping dignity." And once when he and Crouse, walking down a quiet side street, were suddenly confronted by an angrily snarling dog, Crouse stopped dead in his tracks, frozen with alarm, while Lindsay strode right up to the creature, stamped his foot in the Day manner and shouted, "SHUT UP!" at which the potential assailant turned in a manner less canine than sheepish and fled. Yet behind the austerely imperious manner, there was always the warm, the kindly man, who made himself available to everyone and could never say no to a hard-luck story. Russel Crouse in his article "Life with Lindsay" (*Stage,* November 1940) wrote that "there is a rumor that Raymond Massey just can't stop playing Abraham Lincoln — I am keeping a wary eye on Howard Lindsay who has played Father in *Life with Father* for so long, he is beginning to look like a walking daguerreotype. Mr. Lindsay is naturally of the Casper Milquetoast school and if he ever does

○ ○

let the character he is playing creep into his daily life, it is going to be an odd picture — something like a combination of Santa Claus and the Marquis de Sade."

All this was to take place after the play had been running for a number of months. It had initially to be got into proper shape for New York and that meant finding investors. Carly Wharton, the first Mrs. John Wharton, had read the script and was enthusiastic about it, as was Martin Gabel, who had seen the show in Skowhegan and was equally keen. Carly Wharton and Gabel were able to interest Howard Cullman in taking a share and they persuaded Jock Whitney to do the same. With the addition of a few further investors, they were able to meet the cost of production, which in those preinflation days was not much more than $25,000. As star and coauthor, Howard realized that he could not take on the additional responsibility of staging the production. A number of good directors were approached. It was a blow when each and every one of them turned down the offer. Dorothy Stickney felt the blow acutely. The story goes that Bretaigne Windust, that very polished, correct, Ivy League product of Princeton and the University Players, happened to be walking through Central Park when he saw a pretty lady sobbing on a bench. Going over, he discovered it was Dorothy, whom he knew well and who told him about the play and about their frustrations in trying to find the proper director, and asked if he would be available. Windust had barely heard her out when he jumped at the chance. He had excellent taste, a fine sense of showmanship and had already established himself at top level with his skillful staging of *Idiot's Delight*. He proved to be an ideal choice.

New York was preceded by a week's tryout in Baltimore, where the play went well but gave no indications that it was going to turn into what *Variety* might call a "Socko." Walking back to the hotel after the first performance, Howard said to Russel, "We've got a nice little comedy here. We might even get six months out of it."

On November 8, 1939, the most successful play in the history of the American stage opened at the Empire at Fortieth Street and Broadway. It was to run for 3224 performances, breaking *Tobacco Road's* record of 3182. (To be sure, they were both to be topped by *Fiddler on the Roof,* but that was a musical show.) The Empire was the perfect theatre for this period comedy. Entering the elegant "House of Frohman" and walking down the red-carpeted foyer, its walls hung with the portraits of the great Frohman stars, one had the same sense of glamorous tradition, gala and anticipation as one had when walking into the old Metropolitan Opera House, which at that time stood directly across the street.

Opening night was fraught with tension and minor mishaps which struck those concerned as major disasters. The curtain rose revealing the perfectly appointed breakfast–sitting room of the Days' brownstone townhouse, authentic in every Victorian detail except for a large price tag, which dangled from a Tiffany lamp. The first maid, on her arrival from the downstairs kitchen, dropped her tray laden with the breakfast dishes, which crashed all over the flowered carpet. Richard Sterling, playing the local minister who has come to ask Father for money for the new church edifice, suddenly drew a blank in the middle of his scene. Crouse said that when this happened he was, as usual, prowling miserably up and down at the back of the house. "When I realized that Sterling had blown," he said, "I hit the floor, but I found Serlin ahead of me." In addition to these misadventures, the child actor playing Harlan, the youngest of the sons, overjoyed by the warm reception they were receiving, at one point faced the audience and joined heartily in their laughter. Then at a later time he and Whitney, the other of the littlest

○ ○

boys, forgot their straw hats, ran back to their dressing room to get them and, returning, found that their scene was over and that Howard Lindsay had played it by himself. Telling about that night in a speech she made at the Cosmopolitan Club, Anna Crouse wound up saying, "I guess that's why *Life with Father* only ran eight years."

A reporter interviewing Dorothy Stickney in her dressing room one evening asked, "Don't you and Mr. Lindsay miss not having had any children?" Dorothy opened wide her large blue eyes, waved a hand in the direction of the stage and answered in astonishment, "Why no, because we have dozens of them!" She was referring, of course, to the boys who played the four Day sons. They were known to the rest of the company as "the redheads," although none of them had naturally red hair but had to have it dyed every two or three weeks; the hair first had to be bleached so that the dye would produce the authentic fiery shade. During the long Broadway run, there were twenty-eight of these young persons. Capable as each one was in his part, the day would come when his voice would begin to change or he'd grow too tall for his costume or the first hairs of a beard would suddenly sprout on his chin and he'd have to be replaced.

It is customary to think of child actors as hateful little showoffs. The management was fortunate in having nice boys for these roles, boys who were completely convincing as perfect little gentlemen. If a stage child is a brat, it turns out that one of his doting parents is to blame. Each prospective young Day had been carefully looked over and auditioned. Once when a replacement was needed for Harlan, who had suddenly grown too large for his breeches, or rather his kilts, a dreadful little youngster turned up accompanied by a dreadful and fatuous father. Dressed like Little Lord Fauntleroy and bursting with self-confidence, the child placed a toe on the footlights, bowed low and announced, "My name is

○ ○

Roy LeMay, God's gift to the entertainment world." "God's gift" did not get the part.

A little boy named Bobby did. He was taken into the company when he was seven. Lindsay took a special interest in Bobby because of the child's frankness and self-reliance. At his first rehearsal, he was asked, "Don't you think this is going to be fun?" Bobby's candid answer was, "No. I'd rather be playing in the park." However, he seemed to enjoy himself acting though he kept aloof from any cordial relation with the star. No matter how often Howard would try to engage him in conversation, Bobby's replies were always monosyllabic. Howard wrote: "I discovered that if I pretended that offstage Bobby didn't exist, Bobby would similarly agree that I didn't exist. There was no coolness between us. We didn't snub each other. Bobby was never ill-tempered or bad-mannered. He wanted to be ignored by me and he wanted the privilege of ignoring me. On that basis we got along famously. We continued to be invisible to each other for over two years."

After the first year, Bobby had grown enough to alternate his role of Harlan with that of Whitney, playing Harlan one week and Whitney a following one while a very young tot was being trained in the role of little Harlan. Lindsay wrote:

> The weeks he played Whitney, he played the part with great gusto, but the weeks he played Harlan, he was playing it with a sense of shame. He no longer enjoyed appearing in public wearing kilts and rebelling over eating his oatmeal. So we had to call a rehearsal for Bobby. The day of the rehearsal, someone told him to be careful to stand by for his cues . . . that the rehearsal had been called especially for him. "What!" cried Bobby. "Called especially for me? Don't they know I'm the one that doesn't *like* to rehearse?" Bobby grew up fast and had to be replaced. It had to be explained to him that it was not because he wasn't wanted.
>
> After his last performance, he came into my dressing room to

○ ○

say good-bye to me. Now that our association was over, he felt that he could recognize my existence and I think he was rather grateful to me for pretending that he didn't exist during his time in the company. He was sorry to go and I was sorry to see him go.

Some years later when Lindsay and Crouse were about to appear on the radio program "We the People," they encountered Bobby waiting at the studio stage door. Lindsay went on:

> He is now a young man of fourteen and we had a fine man-to-man talk. He seemed very glad to see me. He is planning to become an actor. I asked him if he were on the program with me and he said no, he had just come around there to get autographs. I never felt so flattered. I was reaching for my fountain pen when he added: "I'm just waiting here for Larry Parks." So we said good-bye to each other. At least I was no longer invisible.

In an interview Russel Crouse solved the child-actor problem. "We are going to buy a large farm," he told the reporter, "and raise our own actors. Our estimator estimates that with any luck at all we ought to be able to raise, when we get going good, at least three casts a year."

The "redhead" who did not have to be replaced was the young actor who played Clarence, the eldest of the Day boys. He was John Drew Devereaux, grandson of the adored matinee idol John Drew. He almost did not play it. Although he was a little older than the part called for, Devereaux was perfect in looks, in manner, in breeding. Moreover, he had played the part at Skowhegan but he was as yet unknown in New York. Due to the prevailing attitude that an incoming play must be presented with established Broadway actors, Montgomery Clift was considered for the part of Clarence. Clift proved disappointing. He was stiff, had no feeling for comedy and lacked the requisite endearing callowness of an adolescent youth. Howard was concerned. Driving home in a taxi with Dorothy and Ruth Hammond, who was to play Cousin Cora during the entire Broadway run, he remarked, "Remember how Jackie Devereaux played that scene at Skowhegan?" At that, Ruth chimed in enthusiastically, "Howard, why don't you hire Jackie and forget Clift?" It was a felicitous suggestion.

Devereaux made a nice hit on Broadway as Clarence, playing it for two years until he went into the army. At the finish of his last performance, Lindsay led him out before the audience and with tears in his eyes — for Howard Lindsay at heart was a sentimental man — made a speech expressing his pride in the young man's love of country and wishing him Godspeed and a safe return. Devereaux, who also had tears in his eyes, did have a safe return after a brilliant career overseas. Not only did he receive the Distinguished Service Cross, the Silver Star, the Bronze Star twice and the Purple Heart twice, his heroism at Bastogne was such that a hill was named after him. Devereaux Hill exists today.

There had been an earlier occasion when the star had led him out before the audience. That was during a Saturday matinee and Jackie up in his dressing room had become so absorbed listening over his radio to the Metropolitan Opera broadcast that he missed his cue for the end of the last act. All at once from the stage below there resounded Lindsay's loud "DAMN! DAMNATION!" immediately preceding his exit speech of "No, I'm not going to the office. I'm going to be baptized, damn it!" Realizing that there was his brief moment to follow, kneeling as a suppliant suitor before Mary Skinner, played by Teresa Wright, Devereaux shot down the two flights and onto the stage, to be faced by the curtain falling on an unfinished last act. There followed a stunned silence. No sound from the audience while the cast stood about as motionless as statues. Dorothy Stickney said noth-

○ ○

ing, but looked at him with pitying eyes. Lindsay fixed the culprit with a severe stare, pointed toward the audience and simply said, "No applause." He then ordered the stage manager to step out and announce that they would act the finale of the play over again. Devereaux was in agony. The curtain rose. Father repeated his last exit. Jackie rushed down the stage stairs with such haste he caught his heel on a step and was catapulted onto the set in a headlong reappearance, which was met with welcoming applause, and the curtain came down on the proper cue — the picture of him kneeling before Teresa Wright. After this there was an ovation. When it had subsided, the star led Devereaux, whose head was hanging, up to the footlights and said, "Ladies and gentlemen, I want you to meet the luckiest young actor in the country." That was his only reprimand. And it was characteristic of Lindsay's indulgence and kindness to youthful apprentices, especially those with talent and intelligence. He took a particular interest in John Drew Devereaux, who was well endowed with these assets, and there was a warm rapport between the two.

One evening when it was known that Mary Boland was to be in the audience, Lindsay summoned the cast to inform them that a well-known celebrity of the theatre would be sitting out front and that they must all give of their best, that Miss Boland had appeared many times in this very theatre as the leading lady for John Drew. And at that he gave Jackie Devereaux a knowing between-us-men wink, indicating that he knew all about the liaison between Mary Boland and his grandfather. The cast was duly impressed and gave a most polished performance. There came the scene when Father Day announces portentously to his eldest son, "Clarence, there are things about women I think you ought to know," indicates a low ottoman for the youth to sit on and places himself on a higher chair talking down to him, his knees

○ ○

somewhat apart.   During the course of this amusing yet
touching scene when Father skitters pompously around the
topic of the "facts of life" and ends by telling his son absolutely nothing, Devereaux realized that a small section of the
audience was beginning to titter.   Then suddenly he saw that
the fly of Lindsay's pants was not only open, but a portion of
his white shirt was sticking out quite visibly.   The star was
serenely unaware of his sartorial state.   Devereaux kept moving his position on the ottoman to form a sort of screen, but
his maneuvering was of no help.   At one point he managed
to whisper, "Your fly is open," but Howard took this as a
joke, smiled tolerantly and failed to look down.   Instead, he
rose and moved to the table at which he was to go over the
household accounts with Vinnie.   Halfway through this scene
of upbraiding his wife for her extravagance, he glanced down
at the pile of bills and instantly did a horrified double-take.
When eventually the moment came for his exit, he made it in
a curious crablike manner with his back to the audience.

The atmosphere backstage was that of a warm family.
There were sixteen in the cast and when any member had a
birthday, particularly one of the children, it was celebrated
with a cake in the person's dressing room while the entire
company sang "Happy Birthday."   At Christmas there was
always a party on stage with supper and drinks, a tree and
presents for everyone including the crew.

John Drew Devereaux has a vivid memory of nearly miss-
ing a Sunday night Actors' Fund benefit performance.   Driving down from Connecticut, he had allowed himself ample
time but as a result of heavy traffic and a bad accident on the
parkway, he had barely reached the outskirts of upper Manhattan by a quarter to eight.   And he found himself completely lost.   In desperation he parked his car, ran into a coffee shop and telephoned the theatre, telling them to get his
understudy ready.   A stranger overhearing his conversation

○ ○

offered to take him in his own car to the Empire Theatre. The man knew all the shortcuts and at eight-thirty Devereaux rushed through the stage door and bounded to his dressing room three steps at a time. There he found his understudy, who was streaking his hair with red; his only remark was "You son of a bitch!" Still in a panic and visibly shaking, Devereaux scrambled into his Clarence costume and rushed to his entrance position. Then his cue came, and from the top of the stage stairs he looked down on the familiar scene of the table set for breakfast where the family would gather: Mother, pretty and serene, sitting at one end where she can oversee the two smallest boys to make sure they finish their milk and oatmeal; Father lording it at the opposite end, about to help himself to a hot biscuit which Annie, the new maid, is apprehensively passing him. All at once he felt relaxed, where he belonged. He said later that it was like getting back from the army. Everything was right. Everything was familiar. The Day house, even this stage one, was home.

The stage doorman was a former actor, an old favorite named George Pierce. He was courteous to all visitors, but if he was wary about certain ones he'd keep them waiting with a polite "Just one moment, sir. I'll find out if he is free to see you." Often as not, having sized up the caller, he'd knock at the star's door and whisper discreetly, "I think it's a touch, Mr. Lindsay." Yet the person was always received and the Lindsay wallet was always open.

Kindness and generosity were instinctive to this man, as was tact. One Wednesday shortly before the Lindsays left the cast, word was sent back to Howard's dressing room that Mrs. Truman was coming to the matinee, which, as customary, was scheduled to start at two-thirty. Something unusual must have delayed that ordinarily punctual First Lady, for she didn't arrive by two-forty, nor had she by ten minutes to three. The audience was growing restless and Howard told the stage manager to ring up the curtain, but first he advised John Devereaux, "You know my line to you, 'Promptness is the first rule of good manners'? Well, I guess perhaps I'd better skip it this afternoon."

Lindsay had a dresser, a wonderful, elderly Negro named Merchant, who was not only devoted but who understood his employer's occasional vagaries, in particular his unpredictable bouts of hypochondria. Without warning, during a performance Howard would be seized with the feeling that he was coming down with something serious, if not fatal, and when the opportunity came, he'd stagger off the stage, sweating and seemingly wilting. Merchant, who always recognized these symptoms in advance, would be standing in the wings with a small glass of brandy on a tray. During the war, French brandy was hard to get, sometimes impossible, and he had to make do with some fiery Mexican variety. Whatever the brand, Howard would down it, make a quick recovery and, when it came time for his re-entrance, stride back onto the set as resolute and vigorous as ever.

And so *Life with Father* enjoyed its long and happy run of nearly eight years. An eminent psychiatrist came backstage claiming that it had great therapeutic value during this time of war. Servicemen or persons who had sons or close relatives in the armed forces came to see it, stayed to laugh, slowly unwound and for a time forgot their anxieties. Young people reveled in it because they saw in it their elders in a state of perpetual strife and uproar. Booth Tarkington, speaking from the point of view of an older generation, summed it up as "the promptings of memory." Howard Lindsay himself, modestly explaining its success, said, "It's such a purely American play that I feel it has a sort of subdued patriotic appeal. Also it's immaculately clean." Audiences were transported into a world of security, and at the end they didn't want to leave the theatre. The same people

○ ○

came to see it time and again, the sophisticates, the "home folks," the intelligentsia. Henry F. Pringle, in a *Saturday Evening Post* article, declared that *"Life with Father* is a civic habit." The list of eager theatre-goers included even the country's Chief Executive; a certain Sunday night during the play's early years was selected for a command performance in Washington to be followed by supper at the White House. The occasion was, of course, a great honor, but like all one-night stands, it was also a great scramble, the scenery, costumes and props having to be sent on ahead and the cast and crew coming down by train the following day. They were booked on a special express but heavy wartime travel and crowded schedules delayed them by nearly two hours. Howard and Dorothy were looking forward with keen anticipation to arrival at their hotel, a good bath and a reviving drink. They reached their hotel and achieved the bath, but the reviving drink was not forthcoming due to Washington's blue law that prohibited bars in the city from opening on Sunday. Backstage before the performance, the atmosphere was one of excitement mixed with high tension. Dorothy especially found herself in an extreme state of jitters, misplacing her hand props and frantically going over and over lines which she knew perfectly well. Just before the opening of the first act, standing in the wings waiting to make her entrance, and shaking visibly, she exclaimed with emotion and exceptional clarity, "I wouldn't do this again for the President of the United States!" Only the presence of the heavy front curtain muffled the remark before it could reach the ears of F.D.R., who was sitting in the front row.

Nerves eventually calmed down and the performance went swimmingly. It was followed by a delightful supper party at the White House, where the atmosphere was warm and gay. The Roosevelts were graciousness itself, the First Lady table-hopping in her easy, friendly manner, the President presid-

○ ○

ing at the head table and paying courtly attention to the two pretty women who flanked him on either side. One of these was Alison Smith. It was during her moments of flustered enjoyment that she made her remark about "the artichoke of the White House." Alison further distinguished herself when, during the first course, one of her large tortoiseshell hairpins loosened itself and fell into the soup.

There is a common misconception prevalent among the theatre-going public regarding performers in long-runs. "How can you," they will ask an actor or actress, "play the same part night after night?" They little realize that it's not the same part at all but differs at every performance according to the varying reactions of the ever-differing audiences. Howard Lindsay and Dorothy Stickney were well aware of this. Like all good artists, they were incapable of falling into any mechanical acting no matter how long they might have been playing a role. They were constantly aware of how each scene was going, how the rest of the cast was keeping up. One characteristic of a successful Lindsay and Crouse play was the vigilance of the authors. If certain moments were losing their spirit and, along with it, the attention of the audience, a rehearsal would be called and often as not lines rewritten or some different action worked out. They kept the freshness of an act going with the freshness of their minds, which were ever alert to new ideas. They were lucky in having Bretaigne Windust as their director for he shared their attitude. Night after night "Windy," as he was known to his friends, would slip into the Empire to watch a few scenes and take notes or go backstage with suggestions.

Lindsay and Crouse were by now an established team of considerable prestige. Their minds were brimming over with projects of which they actually had two in the works. Also, they realized that the time had come for them to set up

○ ○

a bona fide Lindsay and Crouse office; just where, they were undecided. There was available office space all over town, but they felt that someplace near the Empire Theatre would be more in order. What they ended up with was seldom in order but it was certainly near the Empire Theatre; in fact it was *in* it, on the third floor of the building — a former Frohman business office replete with heavy furniture, a worn carpet and a generous layer of dust. After a few months, Carl Fisher, their general manager at the time, had them moved to loftier quarters, literally perched with the pigeons on the top of the Empire. This too had served as Frohman business quarters. To reach it one went up in a creaky open-grilled elevator, although it was quicker to use the stairs. These quarters consisted of a reception foyer, behind which was a small room for a secretary and in front the official office of Lindsay and Crouse. This they arranged to their liking with two immense tables pulled into the center and parked squarely together so that, sitting at them, they were facing each other. Although there was a phone on each table, they were connected by a single wire and often incoming calls ended up in three-sided conversations. There was a small lavatory but no hot water, no mail chute and very little heat, but it suited the two men perfectly.

The day they moved in coincided with the arrival of the person who had been engaged to take charge of the office. She was Anna Erskine, daughter of the novelist and educator John Erskine. A bright, attractive young woman, she herself was a writer of short stories and magazine articles. She was also familiar with the theatre, having worked for both Joshua Logan and Dwight Deere Wiman. In fact, it was when she was production assistant for Logan that she had first met Russel Crouse. Logan was to direct and Wiman to produce a Rodgers and Hart musical, and at the Boston tryout they realized they were in trouble with the script. They sent an SOS

○ ○

to Crouse, who hurried up to Boston to see what he could do. There followed one of those all-night sessions in the Ritz. Miss Erskine, who was there to take notes, was impressed by Crouse's ability to put his finger on the weaknesses of the story as well as by his tact in making suggestions, and he, in turn, was impressed by the charm and intelligence of the pretty young woman. She remembers that "he was dear to the lowly working girl." When the session was over, he shook her hand and said, "I'll take you to lunch someday." "What I didn't know," she says, "was that he was always offering to take people to lunch, a meal he rarely ate as he never got up until noon."

Of the two projects on which Lindsay and Crouse were working, one was the possible production of a new play called *Arsenic and Old Lace* by Joseph Kesselring. When word of this prospect got about, Anna Erskine called Russel Crouse and asked if there was a job she could have with their coming show. Crouse informed her that she could not as someone else had already been hired. However, he again said that he'd take her out to lunch someday. Then, in the late summer of 1941, Miss Erskine was offered the job of secretary–production assistant and she went to work on Labor Day. The first thing she thought to do was to tidy up their rooftop quarters and turn them into ones resembling a businesslike office. "I tried to replace the heavy Shakespearean furniture and bric-a-brac we had inherited from former tenants with desks and contraptions of modern efficiency. It was no good. Lindsay didn't mind so much, but Crouse refused to come in for two weeks," she wrote in an article which came out in the Sunday theatre section of the *Herald Tribune*. She went on with her impressions of her two employers:

> They couldn't be more unlike. For instance Lindsay answers all his mail, including insurance and haberdashery advertisements. Crouse answers nothing, leaves everything on his desk

○ ○

except for precious odds and ends which he files in his pockets. This file includes addresses, grocery bills, jottings on future plays and sometimes even a check for $20,000 which he has been carrying around for five months.

Lindsay, being the more photographed, is easily identified by callers, so Crouse, tired of always having to say "And I'm Russel Crouse," has a carved name plate on his desk. It doesn't do a great deal of good, as it's always buried under old newspapers and the telephone directory.

Their tactics as producers are completely unorthodox. Lindsay has frightened many a timid actor by storming the outer office, grabbing the visitor by the hand and booming "My name's Lindsay. Glad to know you. What can I do for you?"

The actor probably never hoped to get inside, much less meet the producer. Sometimes the individual thus approached isn't even an actor; just a friend of mine or the man to fix the water cooler. This disappoints Lindsay as much as it confuses the caller.

It isn't only actors he takes by surprise. Many a young playwright twenty-four hours after his first brain child has been panned to kingdom come, receives a charming and encouraging letter from Lindsay, assuring him that the theatre needs playwrights and that he must try again.

The article was entitled "The Office of 'The Beamish Ones.'" They were given that name by Boris Karloff when he was appearing in their production of *Arsenic and Old Lace*. This absurdly gruesome yet gloriously funny comedy (it ran in New York for 1444 performances and in London for 1337, the longest in the British capital for any American play) came about when Joseph Kesselring sent the Lindsays a copy. He hoped that Dorothy would be interested in playing one of the dear, demented old sisters whose method of showing compassion to lonely, elderly men is to solace them with a drink of poisoned elderberry wine, then have them ceremoniously buried in the cellar. Howard handed his wife the script to read, saying he hadn't the time just then. Dorothy started

○ ○

reading it that evening, and as she did, she kept letting out little gasps and whoops of suppressed laughter, and ended up saying that nobody could possibly get away with a play on the subject of blithe madness and cheerful murder but that it was very, very funny.   Howard, his curiosity piqued, started to read and he too began emitting similar vocal noises.   The script, which was then called *Bodies in Our Cellar,* was uneven.   Some of it was in bad taste, as when one of the characters would open the cellar door and complain about the terrible smell.   But Lindsay saw the possibilities inherent in this insanely macabre farce and wired Russel, who was in California.   The wire read: "Shake your head, take a cup of coffee and read further.   Have just read a play about two charming old ladies who go around murdering old men. Very funny.   How would you like to be a producer?"   Russel wired back, "Buy it."   The two went to work as soon as they had made their agreement with Kesselring.   They all but rewrote everything, changing many of the situations and introducing some new characters.   But they were careful to give full credit at all times to Kesselring.

The play was ready in a few months.   Bretaigne Windust was engaged as director.   The dear old poisoners were beautifully played by Josephine Hull and Jean Adair.   John Alexander was engagingly mad as the brother who thinks he is Teddy Roosevelt and, under the delusion that the stairs are San Juan Hill, keeps rushing up them, shouting, "CHARGE!" He further busies himself digging the Panama Canal in the cellar.   It serves nicely for the disposal of his sisters' poison victims, each of whom he buries with full military honors. Then there is the dangerously insane brother with a record of homicides who has had his face lifted to resemble Boris Karloff.   It was a flash of inspiration that made them decide to have this sinister creature played by Karloff himself.   They had a hard time getting him to agree to do it.   Karloff was by nature a shy, gentle man and the prospect of appearing on a legitimate stage before a live audience filled him with panic. It took all of Buck Crouse's powers of quiet persuasion to do it and he had to go to Hollywood to pull it off. Before the Baltimore opening, he wrote for a local columnist, "I went to his house to sign him up with a pen in one hand and a contract in the other. But when he opened the door, I took one look at that face. I let out a scream that curdled milk for miles around and started running."

Further press stories stressed Boris Karloff's innate gentleness and shyness. Frank Sullivan, who as one of the investors was anxious to promote the show, kept sending in short items to the columns: "On Hallowe'en I suggested that it would be fun if I could take out Mr. Karloff, who was not rehearsing that night, and scare people with him. My request was denied on the grounds that he is scared of jack-o'-lanterns." Sullivan, feeling that occasionally he must assert his rights as a backer, sent the producers a wire saying, "Kindly replace Karloff with Hedy Lamarr."

Lindsay and Crouse didn't have to search for backers. There were plenty of people eager to invest. This time they decided to invite their special friends to participate with, in some cases, as little as $500. Richard Maney wrote that "the fortunate who invested in it profited to the tune of $18,000 for every $500. How do I know? I was one of the fortunates."

The tryout was in Baltimore. Marc Connelly, who went down to catch a performance, joined Crouse for a bite afterward. "When do you open, Buck?" he asked. "Tomorrow night" was the answer. "Too bad, too bad," said Marc. "If you could keep it out of town another two weeks, I think you'd have something." *Arsenic and Old Lace* ran in New York for over three years.

The opening was January 10, 1941, at the Fulton Theatre. Howard's wire to Josephine Hull was simply "Tonight, Jose-

○ ○

phine." The show was an overnight and overwhelming hit. The following morning there was frenzy in the box office because not enough tickets had been printed to supply the line-up, which stretched clear around the block. Within eleven days the first check went out to the backers and with it one of the characteristic letters Lindsay and Crouse wrote each month. The first one was written by them both:

> Dear Angel: Enclosed you will find our first statement. We think it is a charming document and hope that others more charming will follow. If there is anything in this about which you want to complain, we shall be glad to hear from you. Just address us care of the Dead Letter Office, Washington, D.C.

Further letters came each month, opening with "Dear Little Cherub" or "You Lucky Stiff" or "You Money-Mad People." One from Crouse went:

> Angel dear: Taking advantage of my absence from the city, Howard Lindsay, trying to show off recently, sent you a check . . . If Lindsay can give away money, I can give away more money, as proved by the enclosed check.
> Lindsay also enclosed a news bulletin with his letter. All right, if you want news I can give it to you. We have a Chicago company in rehearsal with Erich Von Stroheim in the lead. We wanted Al Capone, but couldn't afford to pay his back taxes. I might also add, to be on the safe side, we are holding two tickets at the Fulton Theatre every night in the name of Adolf Hitler. However, wait 'til he sits in them!
> You need not reply to this letter, but if it comes to our ears that you have any objections to the way this office is being operated, we will be glad to send you, free of charge, one bottle of Aunt Martha's elderberry wine.

The success of this first producing adventure was a source of astonishment to the producers themselves. When a reporter asked Crouse what had attracted them to such a macabre play, he shrugged it off with "We're both nuts. I don't want to take much credit on that score, because I'm not very

○ ○

nuts. Just a little bit. You'd hardly notice it. But that Lindsay, he's good and crazy!"

Arsenic and Old Lace soon enjoyed its long run in London and the rights were being sold for productions in European and South American countries. The backers received monthly news. "You've heard the good news from Buenos Aires, where we were terrificos! We are negotiating some South American bookings if we can find a guy who looks like Karloff and does the conga." Later, "Hold your breath for the opening in Sweden next month. Of course we'll be paid in *Krona* but remember the old saying 'Prosperity is just around the Krona.' " (It is not hard to realize that this last was written by Crouse.)

The following comes as a reminder that World War II was going on: "We hope to have companies in Berlin, Rome and Tokyo this time next year, all playing under the American flag."

One letter from Lindsay read:

Dear Limited Partner: You have been limited by Mr. Crouse long enough so I am sending along the enclosed check. This I hope will demonstrate to you that so far as the firm of Lindsay & Crouse goes, it is Lindsay who fights on the side of the angels.

Not to be outdone, the following month Crouse wrote:

Dear Angie-Wangie: You may breathe easier! Open-hearted Crouse, the backer's boy friend, has managed to get hold of the checkbook again, and if I can keep Lindsay out of the office for a few minutes, I'll see that you really get a check.

Another Lindsay letter went, "Dear Friend: Enclosed is a check for a good round figure. Hoping yours is the same." After three years they jointly wrote to their "angels," "Dear Stockholders: There is no reason why you should still be getting money from 'Arsenic and Old Lace' except that you happened to fall in with the two most honest guys since Abra-

○ ○

ham Lincoln." And toward the end of that long run, each investor received by way of a valedictory, "Sweetheart: Enclosed you will find a check for the amount of your original investment and 25% more. This is absurd." Not only were they the most honest of producers, they were generous to the point of lavishness. They once distributed little notes to the lesser members of the cast as well as to all stagehands saying, "Starting Saturday your salary will be increased 50%," and although Boris Karloff when he was first engaged turned down a chance to invest in the show, they set aside a block of shares in his name and let him purchase them after he had read the rave notices. They loved Karloff as a friend, but were constantly amused by his parsimony, and delighted in teasing him about it. Karloff's weekly salary was over $2000. One time the "Beamish Ones" arranged to have this sum delivered to him entirely in nickels. Another time they presented him with a new contract, limiting his salary to $25 a week plus any money tossed up onto the stage. Karloff took it all in good humor, and playing along with them he suddenly threatened to resign from the show, declaring it an outrage that he was forced to pay for his own make-up and forthwith demanding an immediate allowance for powder. A few nights later the management came into his dressing room bearing a large box done up like a Christmas present from Bergdorf Goodman. Karloff untied the ribbons, opened the box with justified caution and found that the contents consisted of tooth powder, foot powder, baking powder, roach powder, gun powder, Seidlitz powders and powdered eggs.

The next project Lindsay and Crouse had in mind was one about which they were cheerfully sanguine. Never did the times seem more propitious for a play dealing with routine life in a Maryland army camp being startlingly interrupted by the arrival of a burlesque company. And never did the authors experience a more immediate flop than they did with *Strip for Action*. It was an expensive flop, with a cast of forty-nine and many changes of sets, written less like a well-knit play than a series of vaudeville sketches. The critics found it funny enough but quite unimportant. The authors, who along with Oscar Serlin were also the producers, took this setback philosophically. Besides, they pointed out, look how much fun they'd had acquiring local color at the Gaiety Burlesque, the last of those houses of exuberantly vulgar entertainment soon to be banned by New York's City Fathers. In any case, there was much to keep them occupied — new ideas for future plays, in addition to negotiations for buying the Hudson Theatre. Much of Russel's time had necessarily been taken up by the illness of Alison, who, suffering cruelly from the brain tumor, had been moved back to their house and required full-time nursing. Running their rooftop office, Anna Erskine was efficiency itself. She says that the gentlemen were joys to work for. Crouse was always warm and friendly. Lindsay's brusque manner put her off somewhat and it took her a year to decide whether or not he was pleased with her work. Certainly he gave her plenty to do. Her duties included being there on Saturdays and holidays owing to the fact that Howard was appearing as Father downstairs. He'd dash into the office before the matinee, dictate a mass of letters and notes and expect to find it all typed and ready for his signature in his dressing room after the final curtain.

After Alison died in January of 1943 and Frank Sullivan made the abortive attempt to cure Buck of his depression by taking him to Hot Springs, where Sullivan himself went curiously to pieces, the Lindsays came to the rescue. They were about to have their annual vacation from their roles of Mother and Father Day. (Dorothy is quoted as saying, "I've just got to get out of this bustle!") Needing a change of scene, they took off for California and persuaded Crouse to come along with them. On that trip his spirits revived. He was with two people he loved and he found many good friends who had either moved to California to live or were out there working on film jobs. Friends meant everything to Buck. His thoughts must have turned to Anna Erskine back in New York, for in the spring she received her first personal letter from him. All it said was, "I dreamt about you last night. That will cost you $10." This first letter was followed shortly by a second, saying:

> Dear Miss E.
>
> This is the letter I promised you. It is a new
>
> kind of letter invented by me, designed for reading
>
> between the lines.
>
> > Love,
> >
> > Mr. C.
> >
> > (age 50½)

There was a full two-inch space between the lines. The first day of his return in May, he made good his promise to take her to lunch. It was hardly a tête-à-tête meeting; he brought along Herman Bernstein, the firm's general manager.

Both Buck and Anna happened to live on Forty-eighth Street and soon he began to take her home after work. Eventually he invited her to dinner and the theatre. Dinner was in the Oak Room of the Plaza Hotel, "where," he explained, "I make all my fifty-thousand-dollar deals." He continued taking her out more and more. He also began leaving her little notes, typed on her own machine. His typing was fast, two-fingered and full of errors. The first note left there, almost undecipherable, read, "Anna Erskine is a SweeTie Pie." Anna has it to this day. Clearly they were in love. Anna was sure that he was the husband for her. Russel was less sure;

○ ○

he was afraid of marriage. He kept reminding her that he was twenty-three years older than she.

After signing his name to some of the notes he was leaving in the office for her, he'd add, "Aged 52," then further add the exact number of months, weeks and even days as a baleful reminder of his seniority. Now and then the subject of marriage inevitably arose but he'd cut it short with some gloomy prophecy like "A tall, dark, handsome and younger man will come along and then you'll see! Mark my words." He was additionally uncertain as to how his partner would view such a marriage. That partner paid little attention to the romance until, possibly urged on by Dorothy, Howard thought that he ought to take steps to encourage it. During the summer of 1944, Howard and Buck went to California to work on the first draft of *State of the Union.* It was Howard's suggestion that they take Anna along, although when he and Buck were absorbed in the intricacies of plotting out a new play, they hardly needed a secretary. However, they paid her travel expenses, her salary and her quarters and keep at the Beverly Hills Hotel, which was all very posh. This generous and well-intentioned gesture did no good whatsoever. Russel, who stuck by his own strict code of morals, felt that as Anna was out there on salary it was unethical for him to pay court to her.

They returned to New York and the winter of 1944–45 was a miserable one for them both. Toward spring Anna began to get tough. She said she could no longer go on as they were and that he had to make up his mind. Anna modestly says, "I think the deciding factor was that he adored children, and had always wanted a family. For that he took the risk . . . On May thirty-first he proposed. I hardly let him finish the question." They were quietly married at St. Thomas' Chapel (now All Saints' Church) with only fourteen guests present — mostly family, plus the Lindsays and Frank Sullivan. Their

○ ○

honeymoon was at Niagara Falls from which Russel sent postcards to all his friends, saying, "Well, where would *you* spend your honeymoon?"

It was a joyous honeymoon. Buck bought a little hat embellished with the words "Niagara Falls" and wore it everywhere, even into the dining room. After a few days the thundering of the great flow of water began to tire their ears and he phoned down to the night clerk, saying, "The Falls are beautiful. Can you please turn them off now?" They received countless messages from the many friends who were overjoyed by the marriage. Edna Ferber wired: "It's the best news, dear Crouse and Anna, that I've heard in years. And now will you please, Mrs. Crouse, start to work on the matter of Crouse's shirts? He no longer needs their protective coloration." Frank Sullivan sent a startling request that they reserve the adjoining suite for Anna's father and his new wife, who would soon be arriving for *their* honeymoon. After returning to New York they moved into Russel's apartment on East Forty-eighth Street. Anna found there were five other occupants of the three-room quarters, namely, Crouse's cats. They went by the names of Peace on Earth, Good Will to Men, Gold and Frankincense (Myrrh had died some time earlier). Presiding over this pride of Nativity felines was a dowager cat named Miss Frothingham. She was a heritage from *Hold Your Horses,* having served as a live prop for one of Joe Cook's more labored gags, in which he called for a *pousse café* and was handed a large cocktail shaker from which he extracted a small black kitten. Miss Frothingham had to be fired from the show because of her growth and the inability of the chorus girls to stop giving her so much to eat that she grew too fat to be squeezed into the shaker. Miss Frothingham, along with the other cats, at first regarded Anna's presence as an intrusion. How she regarded them, she is tactful enough not to say. However, they soon made their own adjustments. Besides, the creatures were all elderly and one by one they expired naturally, in peace and dignity.

Not content to sit back and enjoy the royalties that were coming in from the various road companies of *Life with Father*, as well as those from *Arsenic and Old Lace*, which was still meeting with success in this country and in European and South American ones, the firm of Lindsay and Crouse kept busy with other ventures. In 1944 they had purchased the Hudson Theatre, along with Howard Cullman, Leland Hayward and Elliott Nugent. The first play they produced there was John Patrick's touching wartime seriocomedy, *The Hasty Heart*, about an embittered Scottish soldier doomed to die in a military hospital behind the lines on the Assam-Burma front. Staged by Bretaigne Windust and beautifully played by a good cast with Richard Basehart as the wounded Scotsman, it had a well-deserved success.

The only snag into which they ran was a technical one. The first-act curtain came down on the homesick young Scot playing his bagpipes in the hospital ward behind a screen and the American soldier, who hates bagpipes, saying disgustedly, "Bagpipes!" As Basehart hadn't the remotest notion how to squeeze a single note out of the instrument, a professional piper was engaged to sneak through a hole behind the screen and give out the proper sound effects. John Patrick recalls:

The first difficulty arose as to which union he should join — the Vaudeville Artists or the Musicians Union. A decision had to be made whether or not bagpipes comprised a musical instrument. The Musicians Union finally accepted him to avoid the wrath of Scotland. At one performance, however, due to a snow storm, he did not show up, all unknown to the actors. When the cue came and the piper had not appeared, Lindsay and Crouse crawled through the hole behind the screen and, holding their noses in

○ ○

simulation of a reed-like sound, began thumping their Adam's apples and giving forth plaintive squeaks in imitation of a bag-pipe. The actors looked at each other stunned. John Lund, who played the American, readily changed his reading from "Bag-pipes!" to an incredulous *"Bagpipes???"* The curtain fell and also the actors.

An act of kindness on the part of Howard Lindsay took place even before the opening of *The Hasty Heart*. An Eng-lish actor had been signed up for the role of the autocratic colonel in charge of the military hospital. He was a very good actor. He was also a very good friend of both Howard's and Buck's. He arrived for the first rehearsal, having come all the way from California, and it was obvious from the start that the man was completely wrong for the part. They tried him out on a second day of rehearsal with the same dis-couraging result. The unpleasant job of breaking the news had to be gone through. It was somewhat eased by the fact that the actor himself realized that he had been miscast. The situation was further eased by the firm of Lindsay and Crouse not only paying his way back to the Coast, but insisting that he accept a month's salary plus the gift of a small investment in the play.

The next year, 1945, Lindsay and Crouse achieved their most distinguished success. The idea for *State of the Union* was originally given to them by Helen Hayes, with whom they happened to be lunching one day. The conversation had drifted from a discussion of the country's postwar condi-tion into some speculation about the political campaigns which would be coming up in a year or two, and Helen sud-denly asked them if they had ever thought of writing a play about an honest and idealistic presidential nominee modeled on Wendell Willkie. They both jumped at the suggestion, and Miss Hayes, who had complete confidence in their writ-ing, agreed then and there to play whatever they came forth

○ ○

with. They had no contract with her, yet she went so far as to refuse other scripts that were submitted to her, saying that she was already tied up to do a Lindsay and Crouse play, which as a matter of fact had not yet been put down on paper. The reason for this was that the two authors had gotten themselves into another of those mental logjams of procrastination and were still in their discussion stage. Then one night Russel found himself at a party where a few guests were fooling with a Ouija board. Always intrigued with semioccult gadgets, when he got a chance to sit down before it he asked, "When will Lindsay and I start writing the new show?" The obliging little planchette sprang into instant action and spelled out the word "tonight." At that Russel dashed for his hat and coat, said good-bye to his hosts, hailed a cab, drove down to Lindsay's house and they wrote the first four pages.

It was finished in a short time, and while they were pleased with the result, they did not feel that *State of the Union* should be a Lindsay and Crouse production so they took it to Leland Hayward. That irrepressible maker of brilliant deals agreed at once and Paul Streger of MCA, the theatrical agency, who was in the room at the time, said, "You lucky son of a bitch!"

Helen Hayes failed to share Hayward's enthusiasm. When the script was sent to her, she turned it down. It was too political, she said. Her exact words were, "I could smell the cigar smoke coming from the back room." Her excuse was that she wanted to be with her children, but knowing that the flamboyant, fast-talking Leland Hayward was to be the producer, she begged them not to "let that Sherman tank get after me."

Hayward didn't even try. The play, a brilliant satire, was headed by Ralph Bellamy as a wealthy but honest and liberal "good guy" who is persuaded to run for President on the Republican ticket. Minor Watson was cast as his tough polit-

○ ○

ical boss, Myron McCormick as his even tougher campaign manager. His wife, the role Dorothy Stickney had so wanted, was played by Ruth Hussey, who up till then had been mainly a picture star, but proved to be lovely in the part. There was a lady newspaper publisher who is also the hero's mistress, well done by Kay Johnson. Beyond the excellent cast, Hayward put on a flawless production staged by Bretaigne Windust with elegant settings by Raymond Sovey. To add a further note of chic, the women were all dressed by Hattie Carnegie.

State of the Union was Lindsay and Crouse's one serious play, meant, as they explained, "to stir the conscience of the individual citizen" but to do so amusingly. It expressed their own convictions, which were close to those of Willkie and F.D.R. "We're what you call liberals," they said, "although we don't like the word very much. Our first concern," they went on, "is to say certain things and then to say them entertainingly. No one who writes for the theatre has the right to charge four-eighty for a noble message. The theatre is an emotional institution." They opened on the road, and although the play was witty and amusing, much of the press took it with serious admiration. In Detroit, it was hailed as "a call to the national soul of a people," and the review went on to say that "all members of Congress should be forced to see it again and again and again." And the Chicago *Daily News* went so far as to suggest that in 1948 one ticket should carry the words "Lindsay and Crouse for President."

One great asset the play had was the freshness and timeliness of its dialogue. This was because the authors rewrote lines every day to keep up with the latest developments in Washington. There were up-to-date references to current situations; well-known political figures were mentioned by name. One line in which Ralph Bellamy read aloud a newspaper headline was changed at nearly every performance. As

○ ○

the authors explained, "Congress can't move faster than Lindsay and Crouse." Lincoln Barnett, in his book *Writing on Life,* said of *State of the Union,* "When people ask if it is pro-Republican or pro-Democratic, the authors retort that it is pro-American. When asked if its hero is patterned on Wendell Willkie, Crouse usually replies, 'He's not Willkie. But he's certainly Crindsay — and maybe Louse.' "

During one performance in the tryout town of Pittsburgh, Crouse sat modestly in his usual seat at the back of the house, following every scene, studying the audience reaction to every line. A large lady sat next to him and kept eyeing him with glaring looks. After the final curtain, she rose and addressed him in tones of loud indignation: "I've been watching you," she said, "and you never laughed once during the entire show! You're the sort of person who gives Pittsburgh a bad reputation as a theatre town!"

State of the Union opened on November 15, 1945, at the Hudson Theatre and was an immediate hit with both public and press. It was hailed as "a literate and amusing comedy that renews one's wavering faith in the theatre," "a happy combination of wit and sense which makes playgoing the delight it should be," "a political satire which is as good-humored as it is pertinent," "never serious too long, never funny too long, it is, in short, a good mixture combining comedy, satire, wit and gaiety. *State of the Union* wins by a landslide."

It won not only the unanimous praise of the critics, but also the 1946 Pulitzer Prize. It was sold to Paramount with the unusual proviso that it must be released by the fall of '47. Feeling that amid all the comedy they really had something to say to the American public in this play, Lindsay and Crouse wanted to have it as widely shown as possible before the conventions of 1948. For the filming, they went out to Hollywood. One day when they happened to be having lunch in the commissary, Herman Bernstein telephoned from New York to tell them about the Pulitzer award. Howard took the call at the desk. He and Crouse were important people in the studio by then. Even picture folk knew of the success of *Life with Father,* so when he picked up the phone there was an understandable pause in the conversation at the nearby tables. Hiding his elation yet blushing with embarrassment, Howard said something like this: "Hello. Oh hello, Herman. How are you? Oh. Oh really! Well, that's good, isn't it? Yes, I'm glad. That will be fine, won't it?" Then, as he became increasingly aware that persons nearby were all eyes and ears, he ended abruptly, saying, "Thank you for calling, Herman. Is there anything new?" Turning to Crouse, who was standing impatiently at his elbow, he blurted out, "We've just won the Pulitzer Prize," and at that the entire commissary burst into applause.

When *Life with Father* was sold to Warner's in 1946, the Lindsays and the Crouses went out to California for the filming. Another person who went along was Mrs. Clarence Day, who, as chief executrix of her husband's material, had her own contract with Warner Brothers. During rehearsals of the original play she had been on hand every minute to make sure no sacrilege was committed in depicting the Day family. As she owned 50 percent of the rights, she usually had her way.

Mrs. Day's contract contained the proviso that she be present on every set during the screening, and she proved to be an exacting but helpful supervisor. There was an ingénue cast in the role of Mary Skinner, the part played in New York by Teresa Wright. She was dark-haired and quite beautiful, but retiring and extremely shy. Mrs. Day was distressed when she noticed (as she noticed everything) that this quiet young girl was burgeoning so in her bosom that her costume

○ ○

had to be let out three times. Her name was Elizabeth Taylor.

It was during this stay on the West Coast that Anna became pregnant. Talking about it now, she says, "In Hollywood there was nothing else to do."

Anna was elated. So was Russel. Worrier that he was, he also became prey to a thousand concerns of expectant fatherhood, making sure that his wife, who was young and certainly the picture of health, didn't overexert herself, that she obeyed all the doctor's orders, that she ate the proper food. One day when they were lunching with the Lindsays, Anna at the finish of the meal unobtrusively slipped a pill into her mouth and followed it with a sip of water. Lindsay watched the process longingly, then, prompted by his interest in every nostrum, said, "I'll take one of those if I may." Anna passed over the small box and after he had downed one of its contents quietly announced, "Howard, you've just swallowed a pill for the relief of morning sickness." Not in the least nonplussed, Lindsay merely bowed courteously and said, "It will probably do me a world of good."

Russel's joy was increased by the fact that he and Anna had bought a house on Sixty-first Street — a comfortable, spacious brownstone which required a certain amount of refurbishing. He studied all the model exhibits in the pages of *Good Housekeeping* and *McCall's* and, with the enthusiasm of a small boy in F. A. O. Schwarz, all but bought out Hammacher Schlemmer's department of gadgetry for the kitchen. Moving day found him in a whirl of activity. He arrived to discover Anna sitting in a comfortable chair, telling the workmen where to place the various pieces of furniture, and he strode about the premises with the pride of ownership. On inspecting Anna's room, he detected a faint smell of fresh paint. Remembering an old wives' superstition to the effect

○ ○

that if a pregnant woman were to remain too long in a newly painted room, she was in danger of miscarrying, he flew into one of his panics and persuaded Anna to spend that night at her mother's.

Buck continued to worry about further problems, most of them imaginary. One of his chief anxieties was the fear that this new involvement of marriage, the establishment of a home and family, might in some way disrupt his warm relationship with his partner. Herbert R. Mayes wrote of that affiliation, "I know of no personal relationship sweeter than that of Russel Crouse and Howard Lindsay," and John Mason Brown in his tribute after Crouse's death in 1966, said, "They were a union, one and inseparable. Their oath of allegiance was to a theatre in which craftsmanship was a source of pride, in which laughter and suspense were treasured goals, and humanity was human . . . More than being a fusion ticket, they were two theatre men whose typewriters beat as one." Not only their typewriters but their minds and hearts beat in the same rhythm. As Dorothy Lindsay in her own tribute to Buck put it, "They not only loved each other, they *liked* each other." They liked the same people, the same books, the same plays. Both men had a sense of humor. Lindsay's was more a sense of comedy, Crouse's a strong feeling for nonsense. Their agent for a time was Leland Hayward. One day when they were displeased at something he had done, or perhaps left undone, they had themselves photographed solemnly shaking hands outside the office of a rival agent and sent the result enlarged and framed to Hayward, to whom, needless to say, they remained loyal.

If they'd both been at the same party, one would call the other up afterward to discuss the evening. As Russel put it, "We've been together so much, we feel uncomfortable if we don't call each other up before going to sleep." They identified with one another and Dorothy swears she once heard

○ ○

her husband announce absent-mindedly over the phone, "Hello, Howard, this is Buck." But Crouse's concerns were groundless. His relationship with Lindsay continued to follow the same warm tenor of its ways and the two households were equally warm in their relationship. Herbert Mayes in a *Saturday Review* reminiscence (and fittingly the cover of that issue carries a reproduction of the Early American allegorical painting of happy animals called *The Peaceable Kingdom*) wrote: "If the word *dear* ever properly described a man, it described Buck Crouse. Evenings at his home and at the Lindsays were the most cheerful and *gemütlich*, and never were there more gracious hostesses than Dorothy Stickney and Anna Crouse." The two men once decided to have a moment of truth and each tell the other frankly what fault he found in his partner or what habit got on his nerves. After a period of serious thought, Howard told his partner that the only thing in which he could fault him was his violent manner of banging a taxi door after him when Howard dropped him at his street. Russel, after a similar period of thought, confessed to having his nerves shattered when Howard, seemingly apropos of nothing, would come out with a vehement Father Day "Oh GAWD!" making him think he had committed some unforgivable offense, only to find out his friend had suddenly remembered some kindness or obligation he should have met months, even years ago.

The Crouse baby was born on January 10, 1947 — a fine, healthy boy, and they named him Timothy. It was some weeks later that Anna found out what the proud father did that night. She says she never knew until the telephone bill arrived. "There were the people in Reykjavik, Iceland, whose number he couldn't get — but everyone else heard from him. He also sat down and wrote Timothy a four-page letter to be opened on his eighteenth birthday and he ordered a horoscope from Myra Kingsley. [Russel had a naïve belief

○ ○

in such things.] That horoscope is very comforting. It says that Tim's greatest prominence will be attained after he is sixty." Anna wrote that for an article called "Life with Timothy's Father," which appeared in the September 1947 issue of *Good Housekeeping*. Here are some other excerpts:

Ten minutes after Timothy Crouse was born and had yawned in his father's face, Father Crouse was his slave. As everyone who has seen "Life with Father" knows, the elder Day maintained discipline in his home. We maintain discipline too. Russel does exactly as Timothy tells him and Timothy can't even talk yet.

When Timothy first appeared, he looked so like his father, that if he'd had a typewriter in front of him, people would have thought it was Russel worrying over a second act. In the seven months since his birth, he has lost that harried expression, but the resemblance is still so great that Frank Sullivan has started a fund for plastic surgery.

Russel is not a typical father. True, he was found carrying a picture the day after Timothy was born and would show it to anyone who was so foolish as to give him the opportunity, but the picture turned out to be of an old peasant with a beard a yard long. When we really did have photographs of Tim, Russel was too shy to show them. If asked what Timothy looked like, he'd just point to his own face and say: "Me, as a Singer midget."

He has a theory that it is bad to talk baby talk to an infant. He seems to feel that whatever he says to Timothy will react on his subconscious mind, and that perhaps if he keeps the conversation on a high plane, Timothy's first word will be "Einstein" or "Dostoievsky." From the time the baby was ten days old, Russel could be found telling him the news of the day. You'd see him cuddling six and a half pounds of squirming pink and saying, "George Marshall has been appointed Secretary of State" . . . Whether it was the tone of his voice or the fact that Timothy liked to watch his father's mustache go up and down, he certainly remained quiet. There came a time, however, when Russel became overconfident and said to Timothy, "I don't see why your mother goes googly-googly-goo to you." Whereupon, Tim broke into his most winning smile and gurgled happily. Since then, Russel has been terribly torn between seeing that smile again and educating the subconscious.

Sixteen months after the birth of Timothy, Anna and Russel again became proud parents, this time of a daughter whom, in a flash of whimsical inspiration, they named Lindsay Ann Crouse. Russel was an adoring father, perhaps too adoring, for he was constantly worrying about the children, particularly Timothy, of whom he was sometimes overprotective. He rejoiced in family events like their birthdays, which he would share with them. Even before his marriage he enjoyed the same attitude with his friends. He was a great asset to the Christmas Eve party which the Lindsays gave every year although he sometimes failed to remember it before the celebration had gotten into full swing. Certain friends tell of one year when he suddenly remembered the occasion just as he was walking through Grand Central Station. Nothing daunted, he hurried into Doubleday's bookstore, bought out a goodly supply of their best sellers along with a pile of Christmas paper and ribbon, seated himself on a bench in the waiting room and managed to tie up the stock of gifts he was bringing each and every guest at the Lindsay party.

With his children he was gay and imaginative, always joining them in their games, which was not difficult for him to do as Russel Crouse always had a sense of youth. He liked to tell them fairy stories or nature tales, if they happened to be somewhere in the country (the advent of his children completely changed Crouse's former aversion to being outdoors). Along the way, he'd stop by some local store to buy them odd or amusing presents which caught his eye . . . a bag of pebble candy or a stuffed red snapper attached to a hoop. He was anxious to bring them up in what he considered the proper way. Not only did he try always to oversee their homework, he took pains with their religious upbringing.

ooo

All his life, Russel Crouse had been and remained a "believ-
ing man." Timothy and Lindsay Ann went with him regularly to church each week and attended Sunday School, and
every night he'd hear them say their prayers. There was one
evening when Lindsay Ann, still at a very youthful age,
lisped out, "Our Father, who art in heaven, *Howard* be thy
name." Before her mother could correct her, Russel with a
smile held up a restraining hand and said, "She's right. I
couldn't do anything without him." Looking back at her
childhood, Lindsay Ann recently told me that sometimes
she'd wake during the small hours of the night and find her
father kneeling beside her bed, his lips moving in prayer.
Russel's concern for his children may perhaps have been a
manifestation of his chronic impulse to worry.

He worried about them wherever they were, whether they
were crossing a New York street or whether one of them was
setting out in a boat at Annisquam on Cape Ann where the
Crouses went for the summer. Annisquam was Russel's particular worrying ground. Armed with powerful binoculars
and wearing a U.S. sailor's hat, he would settle on some
rocky promontory, train the binoculars on whichever child
was out on the water and follow every movement with anxious concern. Sometimes he'd venture so far onto the rocks,
any onlooker was more likely to be alarmed over his safety
than that of the child, who was managing quite well on its
own. After Russel's death, a local newspaper printed a
happy reminiscence of him:

> The big white house at 825 Washington Street remains a me-
> morial to one of the nicest guys imaginable.
> Crouse didn't drive a car, and when he walked to Shea's Vil-
> lage Market for his New York paper, he had a neighborly word
> for everyone . . .
> Some celebrities would scorn a small town dramatic enterprise.
> But Crouse encouraged a Cape Ann Festival of the Arts produc-

tion of "Life With Father," paid the royalty himself and twice went to the performance.

Crouse enjoyed being here where he and his family could unwind after a long winter season in New York. His wife Anna, daughter of John Erskine, entered into village life, annually heading up a children's toy and book booth at the Annisquam Sea Fair and helping to sponsor a parade for children on the Fourth of July morning.

Their son Timothy (then a student at Harvard) and teenage daughter Lindsay Ann took active part in the Annisquam Yacht Club events. One of the appealing recollections neighbors have of the famous playwright is his smile of happiness when Timmy did well in a sailboat race. Enhancing the appearance of bliss was a sailor's hat that Crouse liked to wear.

Russel entered into all local activities with the same enthusiasm his wife did. When he was elected to the Board of Governors of the Annisquam Yacht Club, he began his acceptance speech with, "I now pardon all political prisoners." When one of the members informed him one autumn that he was going to New Hampshire to shoot grouse, Crouse looked at him in terror, saying, "Shoot *what?*" The member repeated "grouse," at which Russel, looking vastly relieved, replied, "O.K. But I hope you don't make a typographical error!"

It was quite logical that Lindsay and Crouse should want to follow their period comedy about life with the head of the Day family with life under the more gentle tutelage of his endearing wife, so they wrote *Life with Mother*. And it is quite logical that, as in the case of many sequels, it fell flat. The production at the Empire was as elegantly authentic as the original had been. Guthrie McClintic's direction was flawless; the public welcomed the cast back like well-loved relatives. Brooks Atkinson said, "The Days are wonderful people and it is delightful to be at home with them again," and

○ ○

Howard Barnes said, a little more grudgingly, " 'Life with Mother' is no 'Life with Father' but it is a nice and amusing existence." Despite the welcomes, *Life with Mother* had only a brief run in the fall of 1948. Then, in 1950, the Lindsays decided that, instead of going to their old haunts in Europe for the summer, they'd spend a week or so in Colorado Springs.

Another person who had the same idea was Ethel Merman, who, after 1147 performances in *Annie Get Your Gun,* understandably needed a rest, so she went with her children for a vacation to the Broadmoor. Her arrival coincided with that of the Lindsays. One afternoon Howard was gazing out of their window, which afforded a fine view of Pike's Peak. At that moment it afforded a view of something else perhaps less majestic but in its way equally arresting: Miss Merman in a bright red bathing suit stretched out and sunning herself on the grass beside the swimming pool. He called Dorothy over. "Look," he said. "Do you want to see the most typically American young woman in the U.S.A.?" Then a sudden idea struck him. He walked to the telephone and called up his partner, who happened to be at his summer place in Annisquam. "Buck," he said, "you know that Perle Mesta has just been appointed Ambassador to Luxembourg. What would you think about a musical about a rich American hostess being appointed ambassador to some small European country and played by Ethel Merman?" What Buck thought was in the immediate and enthusiastic affirmative. Howard then strode back to the window and called down to the still recumbent Miss Merman, "Hey! We've got an idea for you!" But he didn't elaborate on the topic.

It was not until some months later when he and Russel had got their ideas working for *Call Me Madam* that they were able to meet with Miss Merman. In her memoirs she recalls that meeting: "I was to play a U.S. Ambassadress to a small

○ ○

mythical European country, and how the chargé d'affaires would try to tell me off, and how all the prime minister of that trick little country had to do to turn me into jelly was to look at me. I could visualize the whole thing for when Howard and Buck give you an idea of one of their story ideas, they practically act it out. Especially Howard. He prances up and down. He can't talk or think if he's sitting down."

For the music and lyrics, they approached Irving Berlin, whose initial remark was, "Who's Perle Mesta?" He soon found out and the songs and lyrics he subsequently composed were among his most memorable. One has only to think of "It's a Lovely Day Today," "The Hostess with the Mostest," and that immortal "double song," which starts out with "I hear music and there's no one there" and ends up with the equally familiar "You're not sick, you're just in love."

For the producer, they decided again on Leland Hayward, who had done so beautifully with *State of the Union*. They had faith and admiration for that extraordinary entrepreneur. Russel Crouse wrote about him for Sam Zolotow:

> What we have always been attracted by in Hayward is his faculty of being a little ahead of the game. To give an instance, he was probably the first to reach out for a distinguished fashion designer to do a feminine star's costumes. Ruth Hussey in "State of the Union" wore Hattie Carnegie gowns designed for her and the part and set a new standard. Mainbocher created a new Ethel Merman image in "Call Me Madam."
>
> Hayward has intelligence and taste. He goes after the best. If you think he's shooting too high he just says, "Why not try?" and usually gets what he wants . . . the best. He is a good co-ordinator, usually riding herd on the various factors in production, particularly in a musical, where there are many, with tact. And he has the best business manager in the business in Herman Bernstein. We know because he swiped him from us.
>
> He has faults, the principal one being that he is too generous,

being so eager to get the best that he pays too much for it on occasion. This can be tough on him and on a production. He can over-nag, but pleasantly. He can make a wrong judgment, as who can't? But with us there have been few such occasions. He's a right guy.

The personal relationship between Leland Hayward and the two playwrights was warm and affectionate, as one can gather from their letters and further correspondence. One letter from Russel, asking for the loan of a 16 millimeter print of *Mr. Roberts,* starts out, "Dear Pride of Erin," and goes on to assure him, "I will be your abject slave in my old age which is due to start in fifteen minutes," and ends up, "Fondly, Russel Crouse, Boy Playwright."

In those days, the sending of telegrams was an easy matter and Russel delighted in sending an occasional wire to Hayward. When the latter's production of *Anne of a Thousand Days* opened in Philadelphia and ran into a lot of trouble, Russel sent this sympathetic wire to Leland: "It only seems like a thousand days." And when, after a fabulously successful run of *The Sound of Music* in this country, that happy moneymaker was about to open in London preceded by a benefit performance for the Duchess of Kent's favorite charity, Crouse cabled Hayward: "Tonight royalty. Tomorrow royalties."

Hayward had an uncanny sense of the right touches for the right theatrical effect. One of his best ideas for *Call Me Madam* was that Russell Nype, an earnest young Harvard grad, who was cast as the juvenile lead, should add further seriousness to the role by playing it with a crew cut and wearing his glasses throughout the show. Nype's acting plus a beautiful singing voice made him one of the chief hits of the evening.

The opening was in New Haven and the first act was a wild success, but as Anna Crouse recalls, "There was something

○ ○

awfully wrong with the end of the show. Audiences left feeling not quite satisfied. Howard and Russel had a scene they loved — which they thought said something. Irving Berlin had a song he loved called "Free," which he thought said something. All during the New Haven tryout they rewrote and switched around and tried to salvage the scene and the song. Finally Leland said, 'Throw them both out.' He was absolutely right. From then on, the play was a solid hit."

They next played in Boston. The Sunday before, Ethel Merman, a devout High Church Episcopalian, wanted to take Communion, but her timing was wrong and rehearsals interfered. So the priest administered it to her privately in her dressing room. At the finish she thanked the kindly father and said, "I'd like to have you come to the theatre as my guest. You gave me a show and I'd like to give one for you."

Merman could be tough with her producers and authors. Lindsay and Crouse found it next to impossible to keep from making changes or additions in any text they wrote. Although they claimed that they made no changes after the Thursday of the second week's tryout, they made an attempt to sneak in a few during the last week in Boston, announcing brightly, "Tonight we've got a few little jokes." Merman in her memoirs writes, "I looked them in the eye with a congealed manner and said, 'Boys, as of right now I am Miss Birdseye of 1950. I am frozen. Not a new comma!' "

During the early months of the creation of the play they had written to Perle Mesta, or, to give her her due title, the United States Ambassador Extraordinary and Plenipotentiary to Luxembourg, asking if she had any objections to their using her as a model for the heroine of a musical about a wealthy American hostess who finds herself appointed ambassador to a small European Grand Duchy — to which the good-hearted Oklahoma millionairess not only assented with enthusiasm but, upon hearing that Howard and Dorothy

○ ○

were to be in Europe that summer, invited them to spend
some time as her guests at the American Embassy. It
sounded like a glamorous invitation but Howard balked at
the prospect. It was against his New England conscience, he
claimed, to accept the hospitality of someone about whom he
was going to write satirically. However, when they were in
Luxembourg they called daily at the Embassy and he was able
to study the way things were run, meet the ambassadorial
staff and establish a cordial relationship with the Ambassador. After she had returned to Washington while the show
was playing there, she attended a performance with Margaret
Truman and enjoyed it immensely, although Merman's ambassador was a far cry from Mrs. Mesta's, both as a hostess
and a diplomat. As Merman described her own performance,
"Under those wonderful gowns I was a kind of Tugboat
Annie gussied up by Mainbocher." The lady's comment to
the newsmen who waylaid her on her departure from the
theatre that evening was, "I only hope that someday I become
as great a diplomat as Ethel Merman is an actress . . ." and
that remark, wrote Ethel, "made her for me about six up on
Dean Acheson and Churchill as diplomats."

At one party of "notables" and the cast, Merman was late
in arriving because her son Bobby was running a high tem-
perature and she was waiting for the doctor, who was to tell
her that the boy had measles. When the star eventually did
get to the party she found Ambassador Mesta singing "Remember" to Berlin's accompaniment. Merman's comment in
a loud aside to Margaret Truman was, "If this Perle's going
into my racket, I'm going to ask your dad for a job in the dip-
lomatic service."

Call Me Madam was soon followed by a few plays which,
though pleasantly entertaining, were dismissed by critics and
public as not being up to Lindsay and Crouse standards. The
first of these, produced by Leland Hayward at the Morosco

○ ○

Theatre in the early autumn of 1951, was *Remains to Be Seen*, a comedy whodunit, directed by Bretaigne Windust and starring Jackie Cooper and Janis Paige. Also, featured in the second male lead was none other than Howard Lindsay, who proved to be excellent in the part. Acting had been Lindsay's first love in the theatre, and to be doing it once again was a happy change for him. He rehearsed with cheerful zest and none of the nervous qualms he always experienced when he was directing. As he explained this sudden sense of freedom, "Since I'm only an actor I don't have to think, and that's a relief." The cast was first-rate, the production in the best of taste, but *Remains to Be Seen* was far from being a hit. The audiences were unresponsive and the notices were what is known as "mixed," that word which damns with faint praise. In spite of its lukewarm reception, *Remains to Be Seen* had a moderately good run of 198 performances.

It was not the happiest run for the two authors, particularly for Russel Crouse. For all that man's angelic nature, there were times when he could become ill-tempered with a few people, and those people were directors, especially those who might rush to some tryout town where a show was in trouble and offer to make needed repairs in the way of staging or some changes of dialogue. When Joshua Logan arrived in New Haven and volunteered some recommendations about *Remains to Be Seen*, he and Crouse locked horns over a certain line that Logan disliked and wanted to replace with one of his own, which Crouse, upon hearing, instantly disliked. The ensuing argument was long and heated. Then Josh Logan wanted to go backstage and tell an actor he was wrong for the part, which Russel forbade him to do. There had been a similar blow-up between Russel Crouse and a director during the rehearsals for *Call Me Madam*. In this instance, the director was George Abbott, who blithely scrapped much of a scene written by Lindsay and Crouse and put in one of his own, a high-handed procedure which infuriated Crouse, who immediately went to the mat against Abbott.

The following season, that of 1952, the popular playwrights had nothing new in the way of a play fresh off the typewriter, but they got together to produce one by someone else. This was *One Bright Day,* written by Sigmund Miller, whose knowledge of the theatre and familiarity with the proper construction of a play had been gleaned from dedicated attendance at the meetings of the New Dramatists Committee. For once, Lindsay and Crouse were not of one mind about the advisability of going into this venture. Russel didn't like the script and had no hesitancy in telling his partner as much. Howard, equally stubborn, stuck to his opinion that *One Bright Day* was a good and actable play. On March 19, 1952, it was produced under their names at the Royal Theatre, received a poor reception from the audience and lamentably bad ones from the critics and closed after twenty-nine performances.

The failure of *One Bright Day* preceded by the tepid reception of *Remains to Be Seen* did not at all weaken the Lindsay and Crouse creative energy and by the autumn of 1953 they were ready with a new play, *The Prescott Proposals.* This was a drama about a woman who has been appointed the United States delegate to the U.N. and the complex situations which arise when the delegate from Czechoslovakia, who had been her lover years before in Prague, suddenly dies of a heart attack in her apartment just before she is to address the General Assembly on some important proposals aimed at bringing about disarmament agreements and international peace. Lindsay and Crouse hoped and felt that, as with *State of the Union, The Prescott Proposals* had something to say.

Leland Hayward immediately offered to produce it. He lost no time in signing up Katharine Cornell for the role of

Mary Prescott, the U.N. delegate. Howard Lindsay was obviously the choice for director, the sets were in the able hands of Donald Oenslager, and Hayward had again engaged Mainbocher, this time to create the clothes for Miss Cornell. The prospects seemed promising. The morning arrived for the first assemblage of the cast and crew and a run-through of the script. Russel had established the precedent of always telephoning Anna after a first reading of any of his and Lindsay's plays, "and," said Anna, "the sound of his voice is a pretty good indication of what the future of the play will be." In this case of *The Prescott Proposals* Russel did not call up his wife. He waited around silently listening as Lindsay ordered the stage manager to clear the stage and make the floor lines indicating the positions of doors, chairs, desks and sofas for an immediate position rehearsal. Katharine Cornell watched these proceedings with a look of amazement, and as she did, she turned pale. It was obvious to her that the Lindsay method of directing a first rehearsal differed from that of her late husband, Guthrie McClintic, by whom, up to that time, she had always been directed. McClintic believed in asking the cast to sit around a table with their scripts to familiarize themselves with the play as a whole and with their individual roles, repeating this read-through time after time until they all but knew the lines by heart. However, Lindsay, as was his practice, had already worked out every move, every action he expected from his actors. He had planned their entrances and their exits, where or when they should sit or stand. He had even planned the manner and tone in which their lines should be read, and this was a definite shock to Miss Cornell. Never during her long and distinguished career had a director had the temerity to correct her in the delivery of any of her lines, and now to be interrupted in the middle of a speech to be given a particular tone or emphasis upset her to the point where she became unsure of her own performance. One day, when unconsciously she went into a romantically dramatic pose characteristic of her acting and spoke her line in a throaty vibrato, Howard suddenly called out, "Kit! Stop acting like Katharine Cornell." At this, poor Kit burst into tears.

The Prescott Proposals opened on December 16, 1953, at the Broadhurst Theatre and was well if not wildly received. The critics wrote reviews which read more as if they were paying their respects to Katharine Cornell as well as to Lindsay and Crouse than giving way to any wreath-tossing. In fact, the play enjoyed what the French call *un succès d'estime*, which, to tell the truth, is not intoxicatingly enjoyable, but it's better than a flop. It lasted through 125 performances and by that time the industrious collaborators were busy finishing up the details for their next production, *The Great Sebastians*, a melodramatic comedy they had written for the Lunts.

This had been a happy task. Having Alfred Lunt and Lynn Fontanne as their models, these gifted writers had no difficulty in re-creating them in a pair of roles suited to their extraordinary talents, and in placing them in a variety of precarious situations with which they would be certain to cope. The authors named these characters Essie and Rudi Sebastian, internationally known as "the Great Sebastians," whose specialty is a mind-reading act so mystifyingly clever that it has been astonishing audiences the world over from Johannesburg to London. The setting for the play is Prague after the Communist takeover of Czechoslovakia and the time is specified as being a bare few hours after the death or, quite possibly, the murder of Jan Masaryk. The Sebastians are ordered to give a command performance at a reception in the home of a Red general. It has been discovered that they were close friends of Masaryk and had, in point of fact, had lunch with him that very day. This immediately arouses the suspi-

○ ○

cions of the authorities, who try to make Rudi, played by Alfred Lunt, sign a statement that Masaryk at lunch had admitted to having carried on a number of traitorous activities against the Party. Upon Rudi's refusal to sign the statement, the Great Sebastians are both arrested and handcuffed but manage to make a miraculous escape in the nick of curtain time.

This entertaining melodrama, presented by the authors and directed by Bretaigne Windust, opened at the ANTA Theatre on January 5, 1955, to a glowingly warm reception. The notices, overall, were excellent. John Chapman of the *Daily News* said, "It has been a long time since the Lunts have had a play good enough for them to be in and *Sebastians* is it . . . a charming, winsome comedy." Robert Comelan of the *Mirror* called it "great entertainment," and William Hawkins of the *World-Telegram and Sun* described the play as "funny and swift-blooming with the most expert craftsmanship imaginable." The only notice which contained a slightly sour note was written by John McClain in the *Journal-American*: "The play itself is a rather flimsy charade, but it gives the Lunts plenty to do . . . The play really ought to be better; but the Lunts couldn't be."

The two offerings of the team of Lindsay and Crouse after *The Great Sebastians* were anything but hits. The first of these was *Happy Hunting,* a musical starring Ethel Merman, for which they wrote the book, Harold Karr the music and Matt Dubey the lyrics. The direction was in the genial hands of Abe Burrows and the production was put on by Jo Mielziner. The show opened at the Majestic on December 6, 1956, and in spite of mixed notices, had a run of 412 performances.

After *Happy Hunting* came *Tall Story,* their comedy about college basketball, which was produced by Emmett Rogers and Robert Weiner and opened at the Belasco Theatre on

○ ○

January 29, 1959. This was a campus romp involving a gigantically tall basketball player and some shenanigans used to try to lure him into throwing the forthcoming game. It was directed by Herman Shumlin. After a run of only 108 performances, the play folded.

Years after *The Sound of Music* opened, a distinguished critic accused it of being overly sentimental, to which Oscar Hammerstein had his own reply: "Sentiment has never been unpopular except with a few sick persons who are made sicker by the sight of a child, a glimpse of a wedding or the thought of a happy home. *The Sound of Music* is based on the autobiography of Maria von Trapp. The plot is no invention of ours. No incidents were invented or dragged in to play on sentimental susceptibilities of the audience as some critics seem to feel." And Richard Rodgers added: "Most of us feel that nature can have attractive manifestations, that children aren't necessarily monsters, and that deep affection between two people is nothing to be ashamed of. I feel that rather strongly or obviously it would not be possible for me to write the music that goes with Oscar's words."

The Rodgers-Hammerstein collaboration was one which must have worked out as joyously as the Lindsay-Crouse one. In regard to it Rodgers said that it took him five to ten minutes to compose a melody for a lyric but that "when the lyrics are right, it's easier to write a tune than to bend over and tie your shoe laces."

Leland Hayward had seen dramatic possibilities in the story of Maria von Trapp and her family and he passed it on to Lindsay and Crouse, who lost no time in reading her book. They then wrote an outline for a play and that, due to the fact that Hayward had also signed up Rodgers and Hammerstein to furnish a score, turned into a libretto for an operetta. As Lindsay explained, "Although it's a true story, the setting being Austria seemed obviously one for operetta. We had to

○ ○

keep the story convincing and believable, not letting it get into the never-never land that operetta lives in." They managed to accomplish this aim and the book was as rewarding as the music and lyrics. Before production could be started there were a number of business details to settle. The original idea had come from Mary Martin, who was destined to star as the young postulant in the Austrian convent who becomes the governess for the von Trapp children, marries their father, the baron, and manages their escape from the Nazis into the safety of Switzerland. Mary Martin and her husband, Richard Halliday, had seen a German film about the von Trapp family, were intrigued by the story and were keen to get a stage play done on the subject. This meant obtaining a number of permissions, beginning with that of the German film company.

William Fitelson, the lawyer for Mary Martin as well as Leland Hayward, managed to get these clearances after six trips to Munich. He and the film representative made their negotiations speaking Yiddish. Baroness von Trapp gave her permission from her bed in an Innsbruck hospital, where she was recuperating from a case of malaria contracted in New Guinea. Then there were the seven von Trapp children, who were living all over the globe, and they too were successfully tracked down and *their* permissions given.

The further technicalities of production went swimmingly on their way. The director, Vincent J. Donehue, brought out the best in an exceptionally excellent cast of actors. Oliver Smith's sets, which ranged from the interior of an abbey to a luxurious *Schloss* in the Austrian Alps, were ideal settings for the colorfully authentic costumes, all designed by Lucinda Ballard — except those for Mary Martin, done by Mainbocher. It was apparent from the start that *The Sound of Music* was going to be a hit. The Lindsays and the Crouses attended the preview in a happy frame of mind. As they

○ ○

were being shown to their places, Howard announced, "Let's let Buck sit in an aisle seat and be miserable." Russel always considered Howard the senior member of the firm, and suffered terrible guilt if he had a better hotel room or better seats than Howard. But it would have been impossible for Crouse to have been miserable that evening or during the many subsequent performances they attended, either sitting with the audience, *or* standing backstage, watching this excellent cast — Mary Martin at her most enchanting, Theodore Bikel fine as the seagoing captain-baron, father of the seven children, whose unspoiled freshness when they burst into song was a relief from the average stage children. The other singers of whom the authors became especially fond were those who played the nuns, ladies with well-trained voices and such well-developed operatic proportions, Howard and Russel referred to them as "the bull-nuns." *The Sound of Music* was an instant hit, chalking up 1443 performances at the Lunt-Fontanne between November 1959 and June 1963, and had a similar success during the subsequent road company season, when it went on transcontinental tour. Then the following late spring the show was produced in England where it broke all long-run records at the Palace Theatre.

The movie version of *The Sound of Music* was as great a success as the play, perhaps even greater, as it proved to be one of the biggest moneymakers in the history of motion pictures, bigger even than *Gone With the Wind*. When informed of this, Lindsay remarked, "I never dreamt that in my last years I would have to cope with the greatest success of my career." Then, suddenly thinking of the taxes it entailed, he added, "I don't know whether to resent it or be delighted."

Much was made in the press about this cinematic triumph. The New York *Times Magazine* printed an article about it entitled, "Biggest Money-Making Picture of All Time — How

○ ○

Come?" This prompted Lindsay to write a reply to the *Times Magazine* which appeared in their letter column:

To the Editor:

Through long experience I have learned that a play in the theatre is one thing, and that a motion picture is something else. They are two different art forms.

The fantastic success of the picture of "The Sound of Music" must be credited to Robert Wise, producer and director, and scriptwriter Ernest Lehman. It was a success in the theatre but it could easily have been made into a failure as a motion picture. Joan Barthel's article "Biggest Money-Making Picture of All Time — How Come?" (Nov. 20) recalls to my mind a story about Maurice Barrymore, the father of all the Barrymores. Playing billiards one day at The Players, he made an extraordinarily successful shot. A profane onlooker exclaimed, "Holy God!" "No," murmured Barrymore, "no, not wholly God. I had a hand in it myself."

Much has been written of the success of "The Sound of Music" play and motion picture. Is it immodest of me to point out, because no one else *ever* does, that Russel Crouse and I had a hand in it?

Howard Lindsay

The person who was always ready to point out that the success of *The Sound of Music* was due not only to the Rodgers and Hammerstein score and lyrics but to the excellence of the Lindsay and Crouse book was Richard Rodgers. He worried that those two authors were not getting enough credit, and some years later he wrote in a letter to Dorothy that "what makes me happy about the way the show has been behaving through these years is that you and Anna are so pleased with it. It has been wonderful for all of us and you both must feel very proud of Howard and Buck. I am sure I have told you that my association with them was one of the happiest experiences of my theatrical life. It isn't exactly painful to know you either."

*

○ ○

It would be gratifying to be able to report that the fabulous team of Lindsay and Crouse wound up its career of success after success with a final hit in *Mr. President*. Although it was not publicly announced as such, this project was to be the last play they would write together. Everyone concerned with it hoped and prayed that it would be a triumph. The story was to be built around an honest and attractive President of the United States who, during the last four months of his second term in office, is on the verge of retiring to his Midwestern home town. With him in the White House would be his wife, young and still lovely, his daughter, lively and pursued by many beaux, and his son, a typically American college boy, but able, when a certain international crisis arises, to converse in Russian. While the script was as yet unwritten, they talked over the idea with Irving Berlin, who had contributed so much to the success of *Call Me Madam*. Berlin was enthusiastic and made them promise that he could compose the music and lyrics for the entire show. Leland Hayward's reaction was equally enthusiastic. Without a moment's hesitation, he agreed to produce *Mr. President*, hired Jo Mielziner to do the sets and costumes and signed up Robert Ryan as the Chief Executive and Nanette Fabray as his First Lady. He also engaged Joshua Logan as director.

Such a roster was a press agent's dream and Hayward's public relations department lost no time in giving out the news to the public at large. Never has there been such a brouhaha about a forthcoming production as there was for *Mr. President* even long before the tickets went on sale at the box office. All available dates for benefit performances were taken up by charities and other organizations. The advance sale broke all records; it came to $2,500,000, which both pleased the authors and at the same time frightened them for the simple reason that they had not finished writing the play.

Neither man was well. Howard's leukemia had already set

○ ○

in and most of the time he had to take to his bed, and Russel, who had just had an operation for a mesenteric thrombosis, was further recovering from the first of many heart attacks and should also have given up work on the play and, like Howard, have taken to his bed. Anna Crouse rushed to see Howard and begged him to postpone *Mr. President.* But Howard refused on the grounds of the advance ticket sales and the theatre benefits, including the opening night in Washington which had been taken by the Kennedy family for its foundation.

Finally the date for rehearsals came around. Of those agonizing days, Anna wrote:

> It was only the second time in the thirty years during which Lindsay and Crouse worked together that they let a script go into rehearsal which was not ready. The first time was "Anything Goes" — their first show. When they wrote that, they were young and healthy and could stay up all night and write, and then rehearse all day. With "Mr. President" they were both desperately ill and should never have tried to meet a deadline.

But they did, and, needless to say, the rehearsal period for them both was a trying one. Again Russel felt tension and resentment when it came to the director and no doubt Joshua Logan had similar feelings regarding Crouse. At one point Logan proposed a somewhat lengthy cut in the first act and the suggestion enraged Crouse. At another time, Josh wanted music under certain scenes pertaining to the ex–Vice-President's homecoming. Russel thought the idea preposterous in spite of Josh's claim that music under certain scenes in *South Pacific* had been effective. Josh persuaded Berlin to write the music. The result was not good and before an audience the scenes fell flat and were taken out.

Due to all the advance publicity concerning *Mr. President,* plus the rumor, originating God knows where but spreading like wildfire through theatre-going circles, that the play was

○ ○

on the subject of the Kennedys, the advance box-office finances continued to build ever up and up. Every newspaper
in Washington carried some item about the forthcoming
opening. The authors had their misgivings. Howard, who
realized the many weaknesses of the script, admitted his anxiety about attending the after-opening reception at the British
Embassy for fear he'd be run out of town. Russel, after they
had arrived in the capital, screwed up his courage and put in
a modest appearance at a mammoth press conference in one
of the big hotels. A large loud-mouthed lady reporter from
Dallas turned on him, asking indignantly, "Don't you know
this meeting is exclusively for members of the press?" Russel
smiled and quietly handed her his press card from the Kansas
City *Star*.

The Washington opening was like one of the gala Hollywood premières of the '30's, and the New York one, which
took place October 20, 1962, at the St. James Theatre, was
equally glittering. They were not, alas, indications of the future of the show, as the next day's papers testify. The New-
ark *Evening News* on its amusement page ran the headline:
PREMIERE IS FANCY BUT 'MR. PRESIDENT' NOT NEARLY AS GOOD.

The rest of the critics reflected what most of the public
felt — that this much-touted musical was a disappointing
run-of-the-mill affair. Walter Kerr began his review by saying, "It is always painful when a man you admire introduces
you to his awkward, charmless fiancée. What, you think,
does he see in her? 'Mr. President' is awash in people to admire . . . but there is nothing, alas, nothing, to win us over."

The next few days there were lines at the St. James box office. But they were composed not of eager ticket purchasers,
but of disgruntled ticket holders come to get their money
back. *Mr. President* lasted through 255 performances before
dying an unlamented death.

*

○ ○

Lindsay and Crouse seemed never to be without thoughts of another theatrical project, and they had a new outline working. But they were not to see it through.

It was just before the opening of *The Sound of Music* in London that Howard suffered the first attack of the disease that was to cause his death. Dorothy and Howard had a suite at the Mayfair Hotel. They were scheduled to see the last preview audience performance of the play that night. Howard seemed perfectly well in the morning and had a date to lunch with a friend. Dorothy went antique shopping in Brighton, planning to get back in plenty of time to dress for the performance.

When she returned, about four o'clock, she found Howard in bed with a terrifyingly high fever. She flew to the next room, shut the door and phoned Fleur Cowles, one of their close friends, then living in London. Fleur pulled wires and her doctor was there within half an hour. Within two hours Howard was in London Clinic under leading doctors' care. He had pneumonia and pleurisy. It was not until the next day that the doctors told Dorothy the terrible fact that he also had leukemia.

Dorothy's subsequent letters to Fleur show how grateful she was for her help during that crisis. In one, written after Howard's death, she explained:

> I lied to everyone — only the doctors and I knew the truth, and the greatest triumph of my life was that Howard never found out, never even suspected. When shingles appeared on his poor thin body, all he said was, "Well, thank God, I have something at last that the doctors have a name for."

The Lindsays were able to return to New York. Howard had what is known as a remission, when he seemed to be very well. So the following year they had a beautiful holiday in Switzerland together. After that, for the rest of his life, he was more or less a bedridden invalid.

Russel, emaciated and frail after an intestinal operation, was in and out of St. Luke's Hospital during the winter of 1966. After he had regained nineteen pounds, the doctors gave him permission to go with Anna to Puerto Rico for their daughter's spring vacation, and for a week there, Russel improved markedly. Then suddenly he came down with pneumonia and everything was a nightmare. Thanks to an eminent physician who was a good friend and who happened to be staying in the same hotel as the Crouses, they were able to book a flight and get Russel back to New York, where he was immediately rushed back to St. Luke's — his third stay in four years. He died there on April 3, 1966. It was Palm Sunday, perhaps a fitting day for this deeply religious man.

Howard had also been on a vacation. In spite of his leukemia, the doctors thought a few days in a warm climate would be beneficial. He and Dorothy were in Palm Beach when news of Russel's return to the hospital reached them. They tried to fly back to New York but there was an airline strike and no train reservation until Sunday. The news of Russel's death reached them just as they were boarding their train. The trip was ghastly for both of them. Howard kept getting off at every station which might carry any New York papers. He stayed up all night and at Washington he again got off, to send a wire to the New York *Times* correcting some mistake of which it had been guilty in its obituary of Russel.

On the occasion of the Russel Crouse Memorial held by the Dramatists Guild in the Broadhurst Theatre on May 27, 1966, John Mason Brown said about him:

> Buck taught me many things. I learned from him that gentleness can be strong; that wit can sparkle without malice; that a hungry curiosity about life does not involve prying; that a successful man can be helpful; and that in a good man goodness is an interior virtue that shines from within. Buck could worry and

○ ○

was wise enough to do so, but he was never drowned by life. He doted with reason on his family, and as a father was just the opposite of Clarence Day. He was tender with his friends . . . indeed in every way he was a comfortable person . . . fun to be with, fine with the sudden jest, and delightful in summoning memories. He knew everyone, having such friends as Eugene O'Neill and Frank Sullivan. He knew about almost everything too. He collected life as a blue serge suit picks up lint.

Years and years ago when William Archer died, George Bernard Shaw, in an uncharacteristic moment of emotion, wrote, "When he went, he took a piece of me with him." I understand this. When Buck died, he took a piece of me with him.

The shortest and perhaps the most touching words were spoken by Dorothy Stickney. After reading, and reading it beautifully, Russel's favorite passage of the Bible, the Fourteenth Chapter of the Gospel according to John, she went on to explain that her husband was too ill to be present but that he had tried to write a proper message and gave up, "because, as he said, 'Buck isn't here to help me.' "

A few days before the Lindsays' last Christmas together, the Mother Superior from the convent next door to their house asked if some of the nuns could come in and sing carols for Mr. Lindsay, who, they had heard, was ill. They assembled in the Lindsays' parlor and Howard listened from his bed as their voices rose to him from the floor below. Dorothy wrote to Fleur:

Fleur, I must tell you of the most eerie and precious and wonderful thing that has happened to me for a long time. I had a Christmas present from Howard! I was alone in the house wrapping presents, feeling desolate and longing for some sort of contact with him. I had gotten out a box of unused cards and labels from last year and among them I suddenly found a card from Howard that had once been on a present he gave me. In his handwriting it read: "To my wife, the law of kindness was on her tongue — from her completely honest husband, Howard."

I must explain that this was a quote from our favorite epitaph on the tombstone of my Grandmother and Grandfather Stickney. Howard and I found it in a little overgrown country cemetery in Vermont when we were out exploring one day. The inscription read: "John Stickney — Born   — Died   ; a completely honest man," and below it, "Elizabeth Stickney, his wife, the law of kindness was on her tongue."   Howard and I joked about it and agreed that if Grandfather was a completely honest man, it was a darn good thing that Grandmother had the law of kindness on her tongue.

One of the last of these letters to Fleur went:

He was entirely aware right up to the end. I was sitting by his bed holding his hand when he looked at me with very clear eyes and said, "I have traveled a wonderful road with a wonderful companion, and I've enjoyed every foot of the way." A few minutes later, he was dead.

I planned every step of the memorial service the way Howard would have approved — and also to forestall the kind of memorial he would not have liked. I did it in order to give the vast number of people who loved him a chance to say farewell. Four of his friends spoke — one for the New Dramatists, one for the Dramatists Play Service, one for the Dramatists Guild, and one for the Players. I selected and edited the Psalms that were read and the minister spoke them clearly and with conviction. None of it was dreary. Howard loved "The Battle Hymn of the Republic" which we had printed for everyone to sing, and everyone did, and it ended with a lift.

The service for Howard was held on February 15, 1968. Among all the eloquent and moving tributes, I quote from the concluding one, by Dennis King, who had followed Howard Lindsay as President of the Players:

We were dining together one night at the club and, as usual, the conversation turned to the theatre. And I said, "Howard, it's a staggering thought, but between us we've given over a hundred years of service to the theatre. I know what it's given me; what's it given you?" He paused. "What's it given me? Great excitement. It's been my education. Where else could I have traveled so far? I have been in the streets of Corinth when Jason and Medea hurled harsh words at each other. I was at Aulis when the Greek fleet sailed for Troy. I was at Mycenae when Orestes returned to kill his mother Clytemnestra. I've been in the forest of Arden. I have been on the ramparts of Elsinore, and I have been in the drawing-room of Lord and Lady Windermere in London. Where else could I have traveled so far?"

Envoi

In 1958 a special Tony Award was given to the two most successful and best-loved playwrights of the country in recognition not only of their contributions to the American theatre but of their long and untroubled partnership, which had endured for over thirty years. Stuart W. Little of the *Herald Tribune* staff talked with them both about this extraordinary record. "I looked it up the other day," said Lindsay. "I thought the Goncourt Brothers in France might have gone on longer, but it seems they were listed as *brothers* long after one of them had died." And Crouse, to get in his bit added, "We're the longest collaboration since Sodom and Gomorrah, but for different reasons." But Lindsay and Crouse were not brothers. They were friends, men whose friendship meant everything that was warm and joyous and creative in their lives, outside of their marriages — though these, too, were a happy part of their friendship.

Neither man had the individual ego that demanded sole credit for creative work. They enjoyed writing together. There

○ ○

were good days when the work went well and they were exhilarated. There were frustrating days when no idea seemed forthcoming. Then, at least, they had companionship. There have been, to be sure, other collaborations beginning with Beaumont and Fletcher, but that Elizabethan partnership was troubled by frequent disputes and the interruptions of being called upon to fulfill occasional duties at Court. As Bennett Cerf pointed out in his "Cerfboard Column" in *This Week,* "Beaumont and Fletcher could tolerate each other for only six years. Kaufman and Hart parted professionally after ten. Gilbert stuck it out with Sullivan for twenty stormy ones, and there were long periods when they weren't even on speaking terms." Lindsay and Crouse, on the contrary, spoke every day and spoke long and volubly. They spoke about whatever play they were writing, they spoke about situations and characters that might be useful for future shows. They talked about where they had been the previous evening and whom they had seen, they talked about the morning news, about the political situation, and they talked with animation and amusement, whether over the telephone or in their study in the Lindsay house where the sound of their laughter carried to every floor.

One can't help wondering if other collaborators in other occupations so relish their work together. Have the tycoons of finance met to discuss their big deals with a similar sense of amusement? Has Mr. Merrill rushed with haste to start an animated discussion with Mr. Lynch? And the famous partners of merchandise come to mind. Did Mr. Fortnum and Mr. Mason celebrate with a bottle of port the success of their latest raspberry preserve? When Lindsay and Crouse worked, they did it because they liked to work and chiefly because they liked to work together.

Once, for some charity event, Howard and Russel were asked to paint a picture, the subject to be of their choosing. Painting was not one of their talents, and the result would have made a

○ ○

child of four blush with shame. It was clear, however, what the picture represented. There was a box office and a line of people standing in front of it — so many people that the painting ran off the page. Underneath was printed THE MOST BEAUTIFUL SIGHT IN THE WORLD. It was a sight Lindsay and Crouse saw more than most.

INDEX

○ ○

○ ○

○ ○

○ ○